No Wealth for Levinia

1837-1912

Levinia Perry came to the mining town of Mountain City, Colorado Territory, from Cornwall, England, to marry Hugh Champion. This story chronicles the difficult lives of Levinia, Hugh and their ten children.

Amy Hoskin Hill

Adaptation, Foreword, Afterword, Addendum and Notes

by **Dennis Mayfield**

Great great grandson of Levinia and Hugh Champion

Copyright 2012 by the authors of this book
Amy Hoskin Hill and Dennis Mayfield.

The book authors retain sole copyright to their contributions to this book.
All rights reserved.
Third Edition 2017.

Published 2013.
Printed in the United States of America.

This book was published by BookCrafters,
http://bookcrafters.net
bookcrafterscolorado@gmail.com

Levinia@casamayfield.com

All photos, unless otherwise noted, are from
Dennis Mayfield's family collection.

ISBN 978-1-937862-30-5
Library of Congress Number 2012953245

About the Author

Amy Hoskin Hill was born in Central City, Colorado, on January 5, 1891. Her parents were Lillie Champion Hoskin and Jack Hoskin. Lillie was the 5th child of Hugh and Levinia Champion, the subjects of this story.

Amy Hoskin Hill died in San Rafael, California, on August 8, 1984, at the age of 93. She attended Denver University and Colorado State Teachers College. During her long career, she taught school in Colorado for fifteen years, was appointed by President Calvin Coolidge as the first postmistress in Arapahoe, Colorado, in 1927, and again by President Herbert Hoover in 1931. She and her husband, T.H. "Harry" Hill, operated hotels and resorts in Colorado and California.

Mrs. Hill moved with the family in 1954 to Stinson Beach, California, where the family operated Sea Downs Resort. After taking up writing, at the late age of 70, she managed to publish three books: *Murder on the Mountain*, a murder mystery; *Thoughts Expressed*, a book of poetry and poetic prose uncovering her thoughts during a lifetime of hardships and contentment; and *Hindsights*, a collection of early Colorado family history and stories written in collaboration with her husband, Harry Hill.

This book, *No Wealth for Levinia*, a biography of her grandmother, Levinia Perry Champion, remained unpublished at the time of her death in 1984.

Foreword

My grandmother, Amy Hoskin Hill, the author of this book died in 1984. Following her death, her unpublished manuscript, No Wealth for Levinia, and all her research was packed away. If it were not for my interest in learning about my Cornish ancestors, who came to Colorado in 1863, the story my grandmother tells of the hardships of her grandmother, Levinia Perry Champion, may have been lost forever.

One day I remembered my grandmother's manuscript. When I opened that box and began to read, all the family names and dates I had collected suddenly came alive. I was so overwhelmed with the extent to which she had gone to ensure the accuracy of the material she had collected, that the idea to have her work published was born. I felt it important, not only for her descendants to gain understanding of our family, but also for those interested in learning of the hardships of this pioneer family in the mining area that became Central City, Colorado.

The story begins with Levinia's arrival in Mountain City, Colorado Territory, from Cornwall, England on September 26, 1863, to join Hugh Champion. Hugh was a Cornish hard-rock miner, who had promised to send for Levinia and had arranged for them to be married the day she arrived. Levinia spent her entire married life in Central City, Colorado.

Life was not easy for Levinia and Hugh. At the time of Hugh's death at age 48, four of their ten children had died. For the 26 years of her life following Hugh's death, Levinia was forced to take in boarders and laundry to support herself and her family. By the time Levinia died at age 75, two more children had died. Hugh, Levinia and many of their children and grandchildren are buried in Central City.

The manuscript was researched and written over a ten-year period beginning in the 1960s. It is based upon observations of the author and stories told her by her mother, Lillie Champion Hoskin, Hugh and Levinia's fifth child. I have supplemented the original manuscript to create this book.

A review of this manuscript in 2004 by James J. Prochaska, P.E., then

Executive Director of the Gilpin Historical Society and Museums in Central City, Colorado, noted several instances where dates, names, locations or descriptions might be different if this were written based upon current knowledge. I have added End Notes to selected passages in the chapters, as a result of Mr. Prochaska's review. However, they do not distract from the understanding of life in the early territorial and statehood days of Colorado.

The Afterword was added to supplement the original Epilogue. It adds information not known to the author at the time of her death. The information includes the disposition of many of Levinia's personal belongings. The most significant being the family striking clock and the family Bible. The Bible was returned to me by a perfect stranger ninety-nine years after Levinia's death.

Also included is the birth, death and burial information for Hugh and Levinia and their children and family born to their descendants.

Because of the Cornish tradition of naming children after siblings who have died, I have added (I) and (II) following their names where that has occurred.

Dennis Mayfield
November 2012

Acknowledgements

The first, and most important acknowledgement, must go to my grandmother and author, Amy Hoskin Hill, for her desire to tell the story of her grandparents' lives. I also acknowledge her for placing a spark in my young mind so that I might someday become interested in genealogy, open that box containing her unpublished manuscript and make her dream of seeing her work published a reality!

Acknowledgement goes to James J. Prochaska, P.E., who read and re-read the manuscript and provided clarifications, that have become End Notes to certain passages. His review, comments and encouragement resulted in the publishing of this biography. He was, at the time of his review, the Executive Director of the Gilpin Historical Society and Museums in Central City.

Acknowledgement also goes to friend and neighbor Brenda Neal. Brenda, a retired English teacher, worked tirelessly to ensure consistency of punctuation without changing the author's writing style.

Grateful appreciation goes to my wife, Gay, who proofed the output of the electronic scanning of my grandmother's original typewritten manuscript.

Dennis Mayfield
November 2012

Table of Contents

1. Arrival on September 26, 1863..1
2. Reflection..5
3. Wedding...13
4. New Home...18
5. Cornish Meals..20
6. Conditions in Camp..24
7. Gold Bubble Burst, Planned Move to Mexico, Flood...............27
8. First Child Born..33
9. A Death, A Birth, A New House..36
10. Richest Square Mile on Earth, A Birth................................41
11. Cycle of Life and Death..47
12. Bobtail Tunnel...53
13. Another Birth, Progress and Prosperity.............................56
14. Fire and Miners' Strike...60
15. Move to Caribou..67
16. A Difficult Birth in a Snowstorm..72
17. Fire in Central City..78
18. Grasshopper Plague, A Child Nearly Dies, Another Birth.........85
19. Cycle of Life and Death Continues....................................92
20. Opera House Opening, Colorado Central Railroad Completed...99
21. Hugh's Mysterious Disappearance, A Crippled Daughter.......104
22. Hugh Returns, A Birth, A Death.......................................108
23. The Tenth Child Born, Hugh Becomes a Citizen, Changes to the Opera House..113
24. Hugh Has Silicosis, Another Flood...................................118
25. Hugh's Death on New Year's Day, January 1, 1886.............130
26. Mining Improvements, Family Makes Plans for Life Without Hugh........134
27. Improvements in Central City, Difficulties with Albert.........138
28. Marriage of Daughter Lillie to Samuel John Hoskin, Birth of a Granddaughter, Amy Hoskin..144
29. Marriage of a Son, Levinia is Unhappy.............................150

30. Gold Mining Boom, A Daughter's Death..160
31. The New Generation's Cycle of Life and Death..166
32. Mine Disaster, A Daughter Witnesses Murder..173
33. The Hoskin Family Moves A Very Long Day's Ride Away, A
    Granddaugher's Death..181
34. A Daughter Marries and Divorces, More Grandchildren........................186
35. A Daughter Marries and Moves to California, A Son's Death..................191
36. Levinia Shares Keepsakes with Granddaughter Amy, The
    Champion Name is Hopefully Preserved...196
37. Levinia Leads Granddaughter Amy on Nostalgic Tour of Central City.....205
38. Levinia Sees Herself Through a Photograph..213
39. Levinia's Death on Easter Sunday, 1912..215
40. Levinia's Burial Next to Hugh, Twenty-six Years After His Death............218
Epilogue by Amy Hoskin Hill..220
Afterword and Addendum by Dennis Mayfield..229
Bibliography..237
About Dennis Mayfield..239

Chapter 1

Arrival on September 26, 1863

On September 26, 1863, the first Overland Stage from the East brought Levinia Perry to Denver City, Territory of Colorado, on the Platte River. At that time, Denver City was a sprawling village of motley buildings, among which were a few new and more modern erections that showed substantial growth.

Levinia was on her way to Central City, a gold camp on Gregory Gulch in the Rocky Mountains, to marry Hugh Champion, a hard-rock miner.

Central City. Photo Courtesy of History Colorado (Scan #20004773)

The young Cornish woman was slender, fair-haired and blue-eyed, measured five feet and nine inches in her bare feet and weighed 115 pounds. Responsibility made her look older than her twenty-five years. The oldest of six children, she had helped raise three brothers, John, Sam and George, and two sisters, Margaret and Marjory. At the same time, she worked in a sewing room under an accomplished seamstress, to learn to make the special handmade dresses some of the ladies in the vicinity preferred and could afford. Upon the death of her widowed mother, Levinia assumed full care and responsibility for the family, but she didn't lose a single moment's time in her apprenticeship at the sewing room. Finally, through diligence, perseverance, a genuine love for her work and favorable circumstances, she became full owner and manager of two sewing rooms in which several women worked. Some of them were fully trained, some were apprentices. Among those trained were her sisters, in whose capable hands she left her business when she departed for America to join Hugh Champion, her childhood sweetheart.

Levinia had two reasons for making that arrangement with her sisters. First, was the rent she would receive monthly for the establishment. That sum, small though it was, she figured would help with expenses in the unknown surroundings she anticipated in America. She liked being more or less independent and having something on hand if she needed it. Her second reason was her inherited Cornish caution to have something to fall back on if present plans didn't work out. She told herself that if life in the new land proved impossible, if Hugh and she were to return home, they would have a going business to tide them over until Hugh found a good connection in their home vicinity. Then she could stay at home, keep house and raise the family Hugh and she wanted.

As she got out of the stagecoach at Denver City, she was tired. The tedious voyage across the Atlantic by steamship, the trip by train to the Missouri River and the long ride across the plains in the cumbersome Concord Stage, swung on thick straps instead of springs, had wearied her. She walked in the cool bracing air to clear her head, dizzied by the rocking, swaying and lurching of the heavy coach and to relieve her body stiffened by the long-held sitting position. She was happily aware that she was about to begin the last lap of her journey to join Hugh.

She thought, "This is September 26, 1863, the most important day in my entire life! It is my wedding day!"

Eager to get started on her way, she turned to the stage stop to ask how soon the Mountain Stage would leave. But a bearded, middle-aged man wearing a jaunty cap, heavy clothing and laced boots stopped her.

Arrival on September 26, 1863

"'Ee be Levinia Perry, Ma'am," he announced in an assured voice.

Astonished by the mention of her name by an absolute stranger so many miles from where she was known, she stood speechless.

The man smiled broadly and explained that he was Tom Lakin and drove the Mountain Stage when the regular drivers were off duty.

"Hugh Champion tole me t' look fer 'ee, Ma'am, as 'ees bin lookin' fer 'ee fer days. We couldn't calculate just whin 'eed get 'ere. Hugh's bin 'opin' 'eed come on my stage today, Ma'am. 'Ee be waitin' at the church property up the Gulch a ways, 'ith t' parson to tie th' weddin' knot, Ma'am."

He motioned to the stage and four horses in front of the stage stop.

"I be startin' up the mountains soon now, Ma'am. Th' stage is ready 'n all the passengers 'cept 'ee' re inside." Her pulse quickened in anticipation and she walked with him to the stage, a smaller vehicle than the Overland Concord.

Reluctant to get inside and assume the same position she'd held for so long, and to inhale the smoke most male passengers caused with their pipe, cigar or cigarette, she asked Tom Lakin if she could ride with him on the driver's seat.

He eyed her with critical surprise. "Tain't at all regular, Ma'am," he began.

She broke in earnestly, "I'd like to see the country we go through and I'm wondering if you'll tell me about Hugh and the camp I'm to live in."

"Wa'al, for a short time, just whin we're on the gentle slopes, Ma'am. 'Tis too dang risky fer 'ee t' ride up there whin we're goin' over th' very rough part of th' trip, Ma'am. I be 'avin' me 'ands full'ith t' 'orses 'n th' stage t' 'ave a scared female hangin' on t' me fer safety, Ma 'am. Ee'll git inside's soon's I tell'ee," he said firmly.

"I will. And thank you, Mr. Lakin," she said. With his help she climbed to the seat beside him still wearing her coat and gloves. He tucked a blanket around her knees, yelled an urgent command to his team and they left Denver City.

As the stage went steadily on, the horses labored more and more as the grade became steeper and steeper. Lakin told her Hugh Champion was healthy and hardy, was do'ing well at his job and was planning a home for her.

She asked him to tell her about that home, but with importance in his voice, he said, "If'n I tell 'ee, it'll spoil Hugh's surprise," and he switched to the subject of the discovery of gold in Gregory Gulch. "About 30,000 crazed men rushed there expectin' t' find gold 'n become rich,"[1] he said, then added ruefully, "only a very few found any gold. I was one of that first bunches of

---

[1] Based upon the 1860 Census, the population of the Gregory Gulch area (Gilpin County) was 4,973. Its population in the 1870 census was 5,493.

mad men 'n I sure didn't git rich. I've bin lucky t' work at different jobs 'n t' drive th' stage now 'n then."

Because he used so many Cornish expressions, she asked if he came from Cornwall.

He laughed heartily and said he was from the state of Ohio, but had been with Cornish miners in and around the gold camps so long he knew he talked a lot like the "Cousin Jacks."

"Cousin Jacks?" she repeated.

He explained that many a new Cornish arrival who got a job in the mines, asked his employer if he would hire his cousin, Jack, if he came over from the homeland and asked for work.

"So folks've taken't' callin' every man from Cornwall a 'Cousin Jack' 'n' each woman from there a "Cousin Jenny." Then he added, '"Ee's a Cousin Jenny, Ma'am."

Levinia smiled in amused agreement and asked specific questions about what was ahead of her. But Lakin's answers were so vague she decided she'd better wait and see for herself, to accept whatever she found in that unknown world and never to question Hugh's wishes or plans in any way, whatsoever.

That resolute decision came from a very bitter experience Hugh and she had shared two years before, when Hugh left for America. As she relived the anxiety, the hopelessness and the helplessness that followed that occasion, her spirits lowered and her heart became heavy.

Chapter 2

Reflection

As she went back over that last evening with Hugh, she fingered the ring she wore; the "keeper" he had placed there two years before when she promised to marry him. She remembered his exact words:

"Will 'ee marry me whin we kin see our way clear t' 'avin' th' family we want?"

Before she could give her ready answer, he went on, emphasizing each word.

"Will 'ee marry me whin I kin keep 'ee as 'ee deserves, whin 'ee can stay 'ome an' not 'ave 'ee's business t' share 'ee's mind?"

She understood. Her success in her sewing rooms had put her on a higher financial level than his as a laborer. He couldn't earn as much as she was making. And they were faced with the stark fact that their country was going through a period of hard times. Tin mining had slowed down. Employment was hard to find and to keep. Nevertheless, she gave him her promise to marry him and he put his "keeper" on her finger.

Soon after their engagement, Hugh was laid off. Though he was a good and a willing worker and had different kinds of skills, mining, building with lumber and stone, and was an able member of a fishing fleet, he couldn't find a job of any kind. But their love kept them optimistic. They hoped things would work out, that times would get better, that Hugh would get started on something that would improve the situation and make it possible for them to marry. In an effort to lighten Hugh's spirits and solve their problem at least for a time, she suggested to him that they marry, rent a cottage and, until he was earning again, they live on what she took in at her sewing rooms. She went on to explain that she figured that whatever money her shop brought in was his as well as hers.

As soon as she made the proposal, she realized that Hugh didn't approve. Though he wasn't exactly angry, he spoke decisively, "Vinia, 'ee, be sure I won't live off of a woman, not even 'ee that I love bettern' my own self. My wife won't work outside er 'ome. I be th' bread earner. We won't marry till I kin 'old me 'ead up."

He took her in his arms and kissed her. "I love 'ee Vinia. 'Ee'll wait 'ith me?" he asked. She clung to him and promised she would. So day after day they waited, hoping, wanting each other.

She remembered one evening so vividly, so regretfully, she was waiting for Hugh in the small yard of the cottage in Pen Pall, Hayle, Cornwall, that had been in her family for generations. Hugh's home was some two and one half blocks from it. It was customary for Hugh to come see her after she closed her shop for the day. As she waited, she wondered if he had been successful that day in finding employment. If he hadn't, she hoped she could find words of encouragement.

It was a warm, balmy evening, the countryside was beautiful in its spring colors. The climbing roses on the stone fences were profuse. There were full-blown blossoms and tiny buds among the dark green leaves.

Into that peaceful setting Hugh came, his step jaunty, his walk purposeful, his eyes aglow with love and something more. Hugh, at twenty-three, was stalwart, barrel-chested, darkhaired and brown-eyed.

She ran to meet him, arms out-stretched, lips ready for his kisses, her heart beating wildly with hope that he'd found a way for them to marry.

In his arms she heard him tell her that he'd learned that young Cornish miners were wanted in America to dig the gold out of the mountains in Colorado Territory.

"I be leavin' fer the gold camp, Mountain City, soon's I kin get passage money together," he announced. Then, before he could get her reaction, he rushed on, "I be makin' guid there, Vinia. I kin do th' minin'n timberin' and I kin work 'n stone fer walls. I be makin' guld pay. A man 'as t' try when 'ee can, Vinia," he added firmly.

Before she could find her voice, after hearing the cruel blow that he was leaving, Hugh tried with gentle words to reassure her.

"I be savin' wut I can t' send fer 'ee. I be sendin' fer 'ee as soon's I 'ave boat fare for 'ee. 'Ee'll cum t' me 'n marry me, an 'ee'll 'ave children as we've talked."

Gently Levinia suggested that they marry before he left. "Naw! I not be tyin' 'ee dawn at way! Woman, can't 'ee see waat I 'ave t' git dun first, before we marry?"

"But I love 'ee, Hugh," she began in explanation. But he cried out that he thought she was the one woman who would understand that he was trying to do the best he could for her, for himself and for the future they'd planned.

When she didn't tell him that she did understand, and before she could convince herself that she knew she shouldn't go with him and become a burden in the questionable step he was taking, he told her sharply that he was glad he found out in time that he'd been altogether wrong about her.

"'Ee's not willin' t' do wat I know is best fer me 'n fer 'ee! 'Ee wants 'ees owan way!"

Mutely, pleadingly, she held up her hand with his "keeper" on it. Hugh swore. 'Trow it away! It doan mean anythin'! Hit be hall hover, 'tween us!" he declared hotly. He thrust aside the other hand she held out toward him and swung about, leaving her hurt, disappointed and thoroughly angry, the "keeper" clasped to her wildly beating heart.

Next morning, after a night of tearful thinking, she made up her mind to seek Hugh, and ask him to overlook her disagreement with his wishes. She would tell him she loved him more than he'd ever known, and promise to stay at home and wait for him to send for her.

When she went to his home early next morning to talk to him, she found that, after talking to his widowed mother, his two brothers and his sister that he was off for America. He'd left on the midnight boat.

She questioned them and she learned that they'd pooled all their savings for his passage and that he'd promised to write when he had something to tell them. But he hadn't mentioned her name or one word about the quarrel he'd had with her.

Now, two years later, as she rode toward him on the Mountain Stage, she relived the long anxious months when she hadn't heard from Hugh directly, only through his mother, who told her she had had no message from him for her. They were cut off, as though they had never even known each other!

To Levinia, it was very evident that stubborn Hugh still had his changed opinion of her, that he was through with her forever. She worried about the entire situation, wondered what she could do about it.

Finally, unable to bear the fact that their engagement was indeed broken, that Hugh no longer loved her, she made the first desperate attempt at reconciliation by writing him at the address given his family: Mountain City, Colorado Territory, U.S.A. She told him casually about the activities of the community he had left, but not one word about their quarrel. She'd begun to think he wasn't going to write to her but at long last he answered her last letter.

After that, they exchanged letters. In spite of the long time they took for the ocean passage, the uncertainty of the stages over the plains, and the high price of getting mail into the gold camps from the lowlands, the letters brought about a real reconciliation. And finally, Hugh's question came, "Be 'ee free t' marry? Caan 'ee cum 'ere 'n marry me, Vinia? I love 'ee 'n want 'ee," he added at the bottom of the letter.

Her loving willing answer was dispatched at once and in due time, the money for her passage by steerage, her fare for the train and stage to the West and many instructions about the trip, reached her. But the most important words Hugh wrote were of his love for her and his impatience to see her.

She lost no time in making plans to leave for the new world. She arranged with her sisters to run her sewing shop until she could decide what to do with it. She told her brothers she would write as soon as possible and tell them whether or not America offered as much as Hugh's enthusiasm seemed to indicate. But, judging from the fact that Hugh had sent only enough money for her to sail by steerage, instead of by better passage, she felt that he wasn't making the large sums he'd hoped for when he left.

She thought of adding enough of her own money to enable her to cross by higher class than steerage but decided against it. Hugh wouldn't like that. His pride would be hurt by it. She couldn't afford to do anything that would influence his opinion of her. That one instance of going against his wishes had taught her such a sad lesson that she was determined to be exactly what he expected and to do everything he asked of her.

She packed two satchels. In one she put the wedding dress she'd made of hand-woven material, the undergarments that went with it, and shoes she thought would be appropriate for the occasion she had hoped and prayed for, for so long. In that satchel, too, were recipes for Cornish dishes and a few small keepsakes from her parents' home cottage. In the other satchel she packed the clothing and articles she figured she'd need on the long trip ahead of her.

Then she bade farewell to her relatives and friends and to Hugh's, and departed for America, leaving behind her all the stress of business and every shred of responsibility.

Seated on the high seat of the stage that was taking her to Hugh, she realized, that though they had climbed steadily into the higher elevations where the air was getting colder, she was impatient at the progress they were making. The miles fell behind them so slowly and she was almost provoked when Lakin stopped the tired horses at a station at the top of a long grade, to change teams and eat the lunch prepared for the passengers. She was so eager to get on her way that she couldn't eat and begrudged the time she felt they wasted by stopping. Poised as she was on the verge of an entirely new life, she waited impatiently to get on her way again.

When they were ready to start, Lakin told her she had to ride inside from then on.

"I'm not takin' the responsibility of 'avin t' look out fer 'ee," he declared flatly, and turned to one of the two passengers.

"This is Rufus Smith. 'Ee's a merchant in Central City. 'Ee'll tell 'ee somethin' about The Gulch," he added quickly. Then he climbed to his seat and they were off.

Rufus Smith was tall and very friendly. He placed her at a window so that she could see as much as possible. She watched with interest as the fresh horses covered steeper and steeper hillsides and went slowly and cautiously down the grades that almost stopped her heart in fear, as the coach lurched above and around dangerous heights. She was grateful that the driver had ordered her inside.

The stage stopped above a steep slope. Tom Lakin got down and began to work on its rear wheels. The merchant explained to her that he was "rough-locking" the back wheels by putting lengths of wood between the spokes of the wheels to keep them from turning so as to slow down the progress of the vehicle. This precaution, he said, kept the stage from running into the horses as they went down the steep slope and helped hold it from going over the sides of the road into the deep gully or ravine below.

When Levinia shuddered, he explained that this route into the mountains through Golden Gate Canyon, along Tucker Creek, and up Eight Mile Canyon was a much better route than the one a Dr. Casto and his party had taken to join John Gregory at the spot where he had found gold a few days before. Casto's route, he told her, was over Guy Hill, Dory Hill and Silver Hill with a mule-drawn cart loaded with supplies. Two men with axes cleared the trail ahead and two others held the cart back on the steep inclines by ropes fastened to its axle. This method kept the cart from going over into bottomless depths below the trail.

"The Casto route was used for two months as 30,000 pioneer prospectors poured into Gregory Gulch," Rufus Smith said. "But the route we are on joins the first route farther on and is the main stage route and commercial road to Central City." Levinia silently questioned the term, road. Surely the rough trail they were following couldn't be called a road! (This route was used until the Peak-to-Peak Highway was built in 1939).

Her companion went on to tell her that after following the course of streams around Denver City, John Gregory found the source of the gold in a ravine that ran west. The spot was named Gregory Point and Gregory Digging after him. Later it became Mountain City and later still became a part of Central City.

No Wealth for Levinia

The stranger's recital reminded Levinia that Hugh had written her that same information about the gold camp where he was. He had sent her a clipping from the Denver City Rocky Mountain News of May 28, 1859, in which W. N. Byers, editor and founder of the newspaper and a prospector himself, had announced: *The first vein of gold-bearing ore quartz was found by John Gregory in Gregory Gulch, May 9, 1859.*

The talkative storekeeper told her that Mountain City was a gold camp between Black Hawk and Central City and that a fourth camp, Nevadaville, was a short distance beyond. He said the county of Gilpin, named after the Territorial Governor, was only 15 miles by 12 miles and was created in November of 1861, which, she informed him, was the year Hugh Champion came to America.

Another bit of history mentioned by Rufus Smith was that recruits from the gold camps had gone to fight on the side of the North, the Union States, in a war that had broken out over slavery in the South. That same war was still going on, he said.

Boastfully, the merchant reported that a Masonic Temple, the first in Colorado Territory and in the vast expanse between the Missouri River and the Pacific Coast, had been erected at Mountain City a few days after the discovery of gold. It was about 20 feet square, he said, built of logs, chinked and plastered with mud inside and out.

Enthusiastically, he gave the exact information about the Masonic Temple. Book A, page 59, of the records of the Gregory Mining District, now a part of Gilpin County, gives the following entry: *"On June 12, 1859, a committee of three brethren presented a block of ground on which to erect a Masonic Temple."*

His interest in the locality was very evident as he went on to tell her about the school, with 116 pupils enrolled, that was held in Central City and that Washington Hall had been built there for a Town Hall and Court House. Then he explained that an Episcopal Church and a Catholic Church, as well as a Methodist Church, were already organized.

The local newspaper gave these facts about the Methodist Church, Rufus Smith quoted the clipping.

St. James Methodist Church is the oldest Protestant Church organized and the oldest building extant in Colorado. It was organized July 10, 1859 by two missionaries, Reverend W. H. Goode and Reverend Jacob Adiscanse. Reverend George W. Fisher, a wagon maker and lay preacher, was the first resident pastor. Services are now held in the home of Clara Brown, a former slave.

From the Central City Register Call of July 10, 1859, one hundred years after the organization, is the following observation about the Methodist Church in Central City: *For a century, services have been held without Interruption.*

Levinia quoted from a newspaper clipping Hugh had sent her about the middle gold camp, Central City, built at the widest spot to be found along Gregory Gulch. *The Register Call building in Central City was put up in 1861 for an additional office, and printing machinery for the Daily Miners' Register was set up. Later, a third story was added to it by the Masonic Orders for a Lodge Room.*[2]

Rufus Smith nodded in affirmation and told her the early prospectors' laws (put into effect soon after the discovery of gold, to be carried out in the operation of mining) were used as models by mining organizations ever since, which was proof of their value.

Levinia felt added interest in the land Hugh had chosen and asked her to share. Her heart seemed to sing in her anticipation of living here.

The stage left the wooded country through which they had traveled and came to bare bleak ugly mutilated slopes covered with tree stumps and pitted with, what Smith told her were, "Prospect holes" dug out by prospectors hunting gold. When she exclaimed at the devastation, he explained that the trees had been cut for the building of sluice boxes, cabins, stores and roads in the gold camps.

Before long the stage came to rude cabins perched on the side hills of what, he said, was Gregory Gulch.

It was one mile wide by four miles long and a narrow stretch of road ran through the four camps. Some two miles, over the hills from Nevadaville, was another camp. It was named Russell Gulch and ran parallel to Gregory Gulch. These five camps were known as "The Little Kingdom of Gilpin,"[3] Smith told her, with an air of importance.

Abruptly, the stage left the rough country and descended into Black Hawk which she was told, was the center of milling and trading.

After a stop there to deliver express, they went on up the slope to Mountain City. There Lakin left the mail at the post office, a rude building, just above the great gaping opening pointed out to her in the mountains to the left.

"That is where John Gregory found the gold," Smith reported with a sweeping motion that included the many mine structures on the hills surrounding the spot where the hillside lay open.

She turned as he pointed next to the sides of the narrow Gulch. On each side she saw buildings that looked as though perched on rickety stilts that seemed to hang to the slopes, ready to collapse at any minute. Her spirits

---

2 One of the oldest buildings in the city, construction began in May 1864. The Daily Miner's Register moved into the building in November 1864. The third floor, completed in December 1864, was built specifically for use as a Masonic Lodge.
3 Author Lynn Perrigo, refers to the "Little Kingdom of Gilpin", in his publication "Little Kingdom," but he suggests it was called this much earlier. No other specific reference can be found.

sank then, as the stage proceeded slowly uphill from the Mountain City post office, which Smith explained served the entire Gulch. She saw cabins that were partly hidden where the hillside had been cut out to make room for them. There were cabins and store buildings in the other spaces of The Gulch and there was mining activity everywhere. She saw great plumes of smoke reaching skyward from the numerous shaft houses that dotted the hills, and she heard the persistent hammering on buildings going up everywhere there was a space, while the mills' steady monotonous thumping told another story.

Tom Lakin's voice interrupted her awed realization of the great activity around her and aroused her expectation to see Hugh. "Hugh's awaitin' fee at Central City, up the hill a ways, Ma'am, where the new Methodist Church will be built some day soon," he informed her and motioned to the grade ahead.

As the stage climbed, Levinia wondered where one camp ended and another began, for there were continuous rows of rude cabins, stores and tents at almost every foot along the narrow Gulch and signs of mining were everywhere. And in between these were wrecks of broken sluice boxes, rotting water wheels, and parts of broken machinery rusting in the sunshine.

Naturally neat and orderly, her lips tightened in disgust.

A little further on, she saw more cabins but she thought these were more substantially built. They were in a group in a wider space at the side of the stream and the mines were farther back from what she thought was a settlement.

She was right. Rufus Smith announced, "This is Mountain City."

The stage stopped at the Wells Fargo Express Office,[4] where a group of people waited. From the driver's seat Tom Lakin let out a triumphant yell, "I got 'er this trip, Hugh!"

In front of the group she saw a man dressed in trousers that were tucked into heavy laced boots. A heavy jacket swung back from over wide shoulders, showing a white shirt. He wore a full beard and a slouch hat. He looked absolutely wonderful! It was Hugh!

He threw his hat into the air and leaped toward the stage, calling loudly, "Vinia! Vinia!"

---

4 The Wells Fargo office site was originally occupied by a log structure build in 1860 and operated as a saloon. In 1868, the hurdy gurdy was gone and an express company and bank located there. The current building was constructed in November 1874. Wells Fargo occupied the first floor. A year later, the Casino saloon opened for business.

Chapter 3

Wedding

Somehow, the stage door opened. Levinia never knew whether she, the storekeeper or Hugh swung it wide, but suddenly she was outside in Hugh's arms. His embrace threatened to crack her ribs. His bearded lips covered her face from brow to chin and continued to her throat. Too overcome with happiness to even try to speak, she clung to him.

She didn't know her storekeeper friend had left. She didn't notice that Tom Lakin had driven on up the hill. No one, nothing mattered! She was with Hugh!

She was brought back to the present by a lusty shout in which she distinguished her own name and Hugh's. Looking over his shoulder as she stood in his arms, she saw that Hugh and she were surrounded by a group of many rough-looking men dressed as Hugh, except for the white shirt.

She looked quickly into Hugh's face. His confident smile somewhat dispelled her fear and her rapt scrutiny showed the thick dark hair that curled around his head, just as she remembered. She spoke into his ear, "Hugh, dear Hugh, I love you so very much!"

Another cry from the group made her stare in growing apprehension. "Them's our friends, Vinia," Hugh told her enthusiastically and turned her around to face them, laughing as he did so. They surged closer. She clung to him as he spoke to them.

"This 'eres my Vinia. She's come from Cornwall t' marry me, t' be wife t' me," he announced proudly. Then he kissed her soundly, threw his head back, squared his shoulders and laughed happily while he stood with an arm around her.

A roar came from the group that she realized was becoming larger. On the fringe she could see a few women, a fact that surprised her greatly. She was unable to understand why any of those people were there, nor why they shouted. She couldn't tell whether their cries were of approval or of displeasure.

Partly in fear, partly in perplexity and wondering why Hugh seemed so pleased by their boisterous demonstration, she trembled.

She thought them very queer friends. She'd never heard of such a gathering when a girl and a man met after a long period. It almost provoked her to have them there. She wanted no one but Hugh!

Hugh spoke in subdued excitement, telling her the preacher was waiting to marry them. Quick to respond, she told him she had brought a new dress to wear at their wedding.

Hugh squeezed her and tried to explain that he'd made some plans so that their wedding would be as much like a Cornish ceremony as he could. But he looked so uncertain that she quickly assured him she'd be pleased with whatever plans he'd made.

The next few minutes were filled with unexpected activity she found hard to follow. With her as a passive figure, Hugh's plans began to unfold. First, a small dark very striking and poised woman, a year or two younger than Levinia, came from the group. Hugh introduced her as Maude Whitesley. She smiled up at him and patted his arm so possessively that Levinia felt jealousy creep into her happiness. The stranger's critical dark eyes swept over her and in a flash Levinia could visualize herself as Maude Whitesley saw her: disheveled, rumpled and weary. She wished she could have met the beautiful, well-groomed Maude under circumstances in which she was at her best, instead of her worst.

For the first time in her life, she felt unimportant, even insignificant. She was unable to utter a word, but t was quite evident that Maude didn't expect her to, for she took her by the arm, and with Hugh following with the two satchels that contained all of her belongings, hurried her to a cabin close by.

At the cabin door, Hugh set the satchels down, took a key from his pocket, unlocked the door and put the key back into his pocket. Then he picked up the satchels and, without hesitating, carried them inside and through a second door into another room. From his manner and evident familiarity with the cabin, Levinia readily assumed it was his own. Her quick glance around the first room showed expensive furnishings she hadn't expected to find in a gold camp, certainly not in Hugh's cabin.

When he rejoined them and stood somewhat disconcerted before them, Maude Whitesley laughed in amusement and playfully shoved him out by placing both her hands on his back. She said, "For Heaven's sake Hugh, get out of my house so that I can try to make your bride more presentable."

"So," Levinia thought, "this isn't Hugh's cabin. It is this woman's home!" Quickly she remembered the key Hugh had and concluded that he'd been there before, perhaps many times, for he certainly knew his way around in it. It was evident to her that he had thought she would get ready in the other room, so he had carried the satchels there.

For an instant, she stood uncertainly, then, with coolness she didn't feel, said, "I'll go get my wedding dress," and went quickly into the second room. Without actually looking at the dainty, feminine furnishings there, she brought both satchels out, dropped them with an impatience she seldom felt, opened the smaller one and took out the precious, special dress she'd made, so happily, for her wedding. She shook it tenderly, then, more vigorously, pulled it here and patted it there, but the wrinkles were so deep from pressure in the satchel, they wouldn't come out. It took Maude Whitesley's sudden offer to apply a hot iron from her stove to smooth them out.

While Maude used the iron, Levinia washed as best she could at a basin in one corner of the room. Then she donned the under things that went with the dress Maude handed her. When she had it on, her companion looked her over so critically that she squirmed inwardly. The dress had a long sweeping skirt and tight basque, made in Cornish style out of Cornish hand-woven material. This dress she'd worked on so lovingly was very simple when compared with Maude's beautiful gown of fine material.

Levinia met Maude's amused glance squarely and with spirit, asked, "Well?" Maude shrugged with unconcern and then said, "Hugh was right when he described you to me." But she didn't repeat what he had said. Instead, she turned to the door. "Hugh must be wondering what is taking you so long," she announced impatiently.

Levinia followed her from the cabin. Just outside a tall, handsome man, in a long-tailed coat and striped trousers, stepped forward.

Maude said lightly, "Mack Bedford is your escort to your wedding," and hurried away.

Levinia threw a quick glance back to the spot where she'd met Hugh. He wasn't there and the group had dispersed. There was no one in sight.

In dismay, she looked at the stranger. Mack Bedford was very distinguished looking. He had a heavy, blond mustache. His thick light hair had a decided wave. His blue eyes smiled as he bowed and offered her his arm.

"Hugh asked me to bring his bride to him and the minister," he told her, and added, "I am very happy, indeed, to oblige Hugh in any way I can."

He drew her along a path to the right, over a rising piece of ground. At its crest, he stopped and motioned ahead. In the clearing she could see rude benches upon which sat quite a group, waiting in silence, in almost solemn anticipation, she thought. They cast interested glances over their shoulders as she and Mack Bedford came up behind them.

Suddenly, there came a melodious harmonizing of several voices in the familiar Cornish wedding music, filling the air with tones that lifted Levinia's heart and spirits and brought tears of understanding. She thought how carefully Hugh had planned, how well he understood how she would react to the music of their homeland. As Mack Bedford and Levinia walked down the opening between the benches, she saw in the space ahead a sober Hugh. A pleasant-faced man stood at the right, while a young man, she took for the minister, waited in front. Just as they reached them, two men arose from the group on the left front and their voices, a clear tenor and a mellow baritone, were lifted in the Cornish wedding song.

As the familiar music swelled, Levinia was almost transported back to Cornwall and to the little stone church Hugh and she attended. She was happy, touched and gratified that Mark Bedford and those others had helped Hugh when he asked them. Dear, friendly Hugh! He hadn't changed. He was still far more gregarious than most Cornish and much more trusting than his countrymen usually were. In fact, she concluded lovingly, Hugh never sees a stranger, everyone is his friend!

Hugh drew her with him to stand in front of the minister, Maude Whitesley and Hugh's attendant.

Levinia forgot everything except the fact that she was marrying Hugh Champion. When he slipped the gold ring next to the "keeper," her happiness seemed fully complete. As the setting sun's last rays fell upon them, then slipped out of sight behind the towering mountains, she thought it spread a benediction over the service.

Afterward, she met the Reverend B. T. Vincent, who was to help her in her early struggles and in her grief in the new land. Reverend Vincent was not the resident pastor but he became that official the next year. At the time of the Champion marriage, he was publishing a small religious paper for juveniles. It was called "The Casket" and remained in print for several years.

She met Jim Mitchell, Hugh's Cornish attendant, who was also his mining partner and who became her staunch friend from then on. Sing Lee, a Chinese laundryman, who wore his black hair in a long queue, Hugh explained, had talked him into wearing a white shirt for the wedding. Hugh laughed and added that Sing Lee had furnished several white shirts because they hadn't known exactly when she would arrive. So, Hugh told her he had put on a clean white shirt after work for several days before he met the stage, hoping she would be on it. In a low voice, no one else could hear,

Hugh said he'd bet that Sing Lee had removed those laundered shirts from the bundle he had ready for the biggest man in the camps, a mine owner in Black Hawk. Sing Lee grinned widely and didn't deny it.

Hugh presented others, men of different nationalities as well as Cornish, and the few women who were eager to speak to her and to feel the wedding dress. They told her it was very beautiful and suited her well. Levinia was relieved after Maude had silently ridiculed the dress.

She learned that Mack Bedford was a gambler in Central City and that Hugh had asked him to escort her because he was handsome and had "fancy clothes." Maude had been chosen because she knew exactly what to do, was pretty and her good "duds" looked fine on her. Maude was a widow. Her husband had died of exposure after he'd been thrown out of a gambling house for cheating at cards. She was living in the cabin he built and furnished with funds he received from his family in Boston as payment for staying away from them. Maude was to receive a certain sum from them every month, as long as she didn't marry again or return to Boston. That sum allowed her to live fairly well in the cabin and provided her with well-chosen clothes that made quite a showing in the mining camps.

It was late afternoon when Hugh announced to the group that he'd arranged for drinks for them at a certain saloon in town. They weren't long in leaving, and the women also left, telling Levinia they'd see her again soon.

Hand in hand, Hugh and Levinia went to Maude's cabin. Maude was there and met them with pleasant words. She picked up some of Levinia's garments and seemed to disapprove when Levinia said she was going to wear her wedding dress. But she smiled at Hugh and patted his arm playfully as she spoke directly to him.

"Your new bride will need a woman to confide in and to keep her company in this man's world. As you very well know, Hugh, I am always ready to offer a shoulder for the lonely to cry on."

Hugh didn't seem to understand the insinuations Maude put into her words. Levinia felt he was only concerned with the possibility that she would be homesick and would find things different and strange in the new land. He put an arm around her as though to protect her.

Levinia thanked Maude with exaggerated warmth, while she made up her mind that the assured, patronizing widow would be the very last person she'd come to for any reason whatsoever!

Outside the cabin, she heard wagon wheels and a horse snorting.

Chapter 4

New Home

Jim Mitchell was there with a livery team and a spring wagon to take them to Nevadaville, where Hugh and he worked. Hugh had a cabin ready there as the first Champion home.

Jim was tall and quite slender, when compared with Hugh's big body. He was a year younger than Hugh and looked to him for leadership. He backed Hugh, in most instances, but sometimes his judgment was better than Hugh's. Thinking himself right, he held his own against Hugh, flatly expressed his opinion and stood by his words. Jim was slower, steadier, less impulsive and assertive, but both were more or less moody, had surges of happiness and gloom that influenced their behavior momentarily.

Hugh helped Levinia into the wagon and got in beside her. Jim put the satchels in the back and climbed in at her other side. They bid Maude a cheery goodbye and Jim drove up the half-mile grade to the fourth gold camp in Gregory Gulch. Levinia asked where Jim lived and was told that he'd "batched" with Hugh in the Nevadaville cabin until Hugh began to prepare it for her coming. Then he'd moved in with another Cornishman in camp.

She snuggled close to Hugh and he held her in a strong arm as the team climbed. Before she really expected it, they stopped at a cabin whose outline she could see against the sky, and quite close by she could make out a building Hugh told her was the California mine where he and Jim worked. He explained that the word "Nevada" meant snowy, so he guessed their home could be called "White House," and they laughed together. He helped her down and took her to the door, then told her to wait. He went in and lit a lamp, just inside, then he returned to carry her over the threshold, calling out the Cornish welcome home. She didn't realize that Jim dropped her satchels and drove off to take the rig back to the livery, for Hugh closed the door behind them and took her in his arms. It was the moment for which they had waited. After two years, they were together again.

Later, he lit the kindling and wood he'd laid in the stove earlier in the day and drew up the chairs he'd made out of tree stumps, into which he'd fashioned backs from willow branches. He placed them close to the spreading warmth of the fire.

But Levinia couldn't sit. She had to look around her new home. Hugh followed her about, talking fast, telling her what he'd done to try to make her feel at home. She saw where he had chinked the spaces between the logs with mud mixed with straw and dried grass, even bits of leaves and twigs, to make the cabin warmer and keep out the wind and snow.

He'd made the table of rough pine and rubbed the top down until it was beautifully smooth. He explained that he'd made a bargain with a mining official who had brought some possessions with him from the East, when he'd come to Central City on mining business. When he'd finished the assignment, he sold some of the things he decided not to ship back.

There was a pad-mattress that was, Hugh assured her, much much better than the straw ticks found in the cabins in the camps and in the so-called hotels. There were pillows and blankets and a yellow bedspread, which Hugh called a throw, on the homemade bed in the corner.

Levinia examined the dishes and the few cooking utensils and pots Hugh had purchased from the same official. She decided that one of the pots, which had a close-fitting cover, could be used to brew their tea. Another, slightly larger, "Would do to boil the plum puddings," she announced happily. She was well pleased when she saw the washtub. This, she declared, would have a double duty for laundry and as a bathtub.

But it was the stove, with its small oven, that pleased her most. She told Hugh she'd worried about baking the Cornish "pasties" and saffron cake. This stove, she decided, was the most important article they had, for it solved the baking problem as well as heating the cabin. She was as proud of it, as she would have been of the finest range in the world.

She was making verbal plans to scour the floor next morning with wood ashes, when Hugh kissed her and thanked her for accepting the few things he'd been able to gather together for their use.

She clung to him in understanding and told him it was all so much better than she'd expected and had hoped for in the new country. She had she declared, all that life could give her. A few minutes later held in Hugh's arms, she met his passion with hers, one as strong and demanding as his.

Chapter 5

Cornish Meals

In the days that followed, while Hugh was at work, Levinia made trips down the long slope from Nevadaville to Central City, Mountain City and Black Hawk. Sometimes she went merely to walk, finding the country fascinating and the people interesting. Sometimes she went to make a few purchases of the staples she needed and could afford, from the meager expensive supplies she found in the crude stores. As she expressed it to Hugh, she found things too "dear" to buy. She found the best bargains in the store of her stage friend, Rufus Smith, but even his prices were too high.

But she had to have the makings for the "pasties," the Cornish meat pies with beef or veal, or both, potatoes, onions and turnips (rutabagas preferred). Cut-up, raw meat and diced vegetables were placed a little to one side of the center of a circle of rolled-out pastry dough. Next, the smaller half of the circle was flipped over to meet the edge of the larger half and fastened with a twist, peculiar to Cornish cooks, which sealed the edges securely. Then the plump half-pie was placed in a flat pan, a slit was made in the top for the steam to escape, and it was baked until the meat and vegetables were cooked.

Pasties, one of the main meal dishes of the Cornish, were sometimes served at home, but their chief use was to provide a full meal for the hardworking miners, who carried them in their lunch pails.

These dinner buckets, or Cornish "nose bags," were of two kinds in the mining camps of that time. One was kidneys" was carried by the miner over his shoulder by a strap, fastened at each end.

The other type of dinner pail, the one used most, had three compartments: the lower part was for the Cornishman's tea, the center section, about four or five inches deep, contained the main course of his meal, and above was a

20

shallow pan, some two or three inches deep, to carry pie or cake. Sometimes a cup rode upside down on a projection from the cover, but most of the early-day dinner pails didn't have this feature.

It has been said that Cornishmen didn't eat their main meal first, then the dessert, with tea taken during the courses. Instead, many Cornish began at the top of the pail. They ate the dessert first, then the body of the meal, and finished the lunch, which they called "croust," with the tea in the bottom of the bucket.

Another Cornish main dish was "hoggan," unleavened bread-like dough with salt pork in the center. This was sometimes sent in the lunch pail. So was "likky," an onion pie, baked in a dish lined and covered with pastry. When the boiling onions were almost done, a hole was made in the top crust, and the contents of a whole egg were poured into the steaming pie and baked a while longer.

Tripe was another Cornish meat dish. Fried until browned and served with fresh-baked bread, it was considered a great delicacy.

Kidney pie was an old standby with the Cornish people. Beef or mutton kidneys were boiled until tender, then the broth was thickened and a crust of dough was made for the top and baked.

Mutton was cooked with vegetables into a stew, and veal was boiled with onions and parsley into a delicious dish the Cornish called "Irish" or "Island Boil," because it resembled the well-known Irish stew.

Levinia found that in order to have parsley at hand for flavoring the meat dishes, the Cornish women who had been in camp awhile, kept the herb growing in their homes, wrapping it very carefully on winter nights to keep it from freezing. She was given some by women who had a supply until she could start some for herself.

She also obtained a "starter" for her bread from them. For this "starter," a cupful of the bread "sponge" was put into a container and sugar was added to keep it "alive" and "working" until the next time bread was needed. The night before baking day, the "starter" was added to the water in which potatoes had been boiled. Very often mashed potatoes were put into the liquid. Sugar was added, then enough flour to make a somewhat thick paste, which was the "sponge" for the next day's baking. This sponge was kept as warm as possible during the night. In cold weather, it was placed inside thick coverings of paper and heavy woolen material to keep it "working." (Freezing would ruin its leveling power; chilling could delay its efficiency.)

The next morning, the sponge was mixed with flour and salt was added. The dough was kneaded thoroughly and well and set out to rise in a warm place in the kitchen. When it had doubled or more in size, it was made into loaves by cutting or pinching off the desired amount of dough. This was kneaded again between the hands and placed into greased pans. When "light" enough, gauged by its height in the pan or judged by lifting the pan with its loaf, it was baked about an hour in the oven. The Cornish women could determine the correct heat by holding their hands inside the oven for an instant.

Chicken pie, the favorite Cornish Sunday dinner, was made by boiling a fat chicken, shipped in from Kansas or other near-by states, in enough water to more than cover it. When the bones could be removed from the meat, the broth was thickened. A rich pastry crust was laid over the top and slits were made in it, through which the creamy bubbles of the gravy oozed.

For breakfast on Sunday, the Cornish had codfish. Salted and dried and flattened on the coast, it was brought into camp, layered in boxes, and sold by the pound. On Saturday evening, the fish was set to soak in cold water to freshen it. Sunday morning it was taken out of the brine, put into fresh water and boiled until tender and flaky, and then served with butter or other shortening.

Split pea soup required the peas to be yellow, rather than green. It was made with soup bones, those of cured meat preferred, and onions and turnips. When served, it had tiny pie dough dumplings floating on top. Broad beans (limas) were cooked with smoked meats.

The Cornish had a cake they called saffron cake. It was made somewhat like their bread, but was sweeter, and contained shortening, lemon peel, and currants, which were imported from Greece. It took more sponge than bread because of the other ingredients and the dough was softer than bread dough and kneaded less. It was colored and flavored by saffron (also imported), and steeped in boiling water. If available, eggs were added, but Levinia found that eggs and milk were very scarce staples.

In spite of that, she became a good cook, careful and frugal and able to substitute when she didn't have, or couldn't get, what she needed.

One of her abilities was the use of suet (beef fat) as shortening for frying and in place of lard as well as for making pastries, plum pudding, dumplings and "soup balls." She didn't render the suet by frying it down and using it as lard. She cut it into tiny pieces and worked it into the dough, to melt as it cooked or baked.

She made several varieties of pies from the fruits she could obtain. Dried-apple pie was flavored with nutmeg, which was sold in its original form of football-shaped nuts and had to be grated before being used. Hugh made her a grater by driving a nail into a piece of tin, then drawing the nail out and making other holes with it. She scraped the nutmeg over these holes to get it grated into flakes for her baking.

Then there was prune pie. She boiled the dried fruit and removed the pits, often cracking them and adding the inner nuts to the prunes before making the pie. Sometimes she saved the small pits and used them as a confection.

Dates, when she could get them, were shipped in a mass or block of some twenty or thirty pounds. With a big knife or a heavy, two-or-three pronged fork, the grocer cut or tore off enough dates to satisfy the weight the customer requested. The dates were cooked, the pits were removed and the fruit cooled, before being put into the lower piecrust. Date pie was very, very rich and delicious.

Currants made good pies, too, but they were so dirty when purchased in the store that they were a chore to use. They had so many stems and leaves mixed with them that they had to be picked over, washed and cooked, then usually thickened and mixed with lemon.

Raisins were also shipped in bulk. Levinia used them with dried apples and lemon for pies and for a raisin pudding the Cornish called "figgy obben."

Missing the eggs, fresh milk, poultry and mutton she had had from her own back yard in Cornwall, Levinia resolved that, as soon as she could manage, she would have a cow and some chickens. Not even Hugh's aversion to having them changed her mind. She told him she would take full charge of them. She declared she'd be glad to have something more to do and it would prove to be a great help in maintaining their home, as well as supplying the scarce articles.

Because of the 8,500 feet in elevation, Levinia experienced some difficulty going up the hill from the lower camps to her cabin. Gradually, as time went on, she became more used to the climb and it didn't tax her lungs as much as she trudged along, often carrying groceries, which she termed "stores."

In her letters to Cornwall, she described the country and said she and Hugh were well and happy and hopeful of the future. But Hugh admonished her not to build up his mother's hopes about coming to America to join them.

"'Ee's better hoff at 'ome, where 'ee knows 'ow t' live, than 'ere hin this rough country," he said firmly, and she agreed. So her messages didn't contain the elation she felt over coming to the new land. She told herself there was time enough to tell her brothers and Hugh's that there was work here and a chance to grow with the new country. "When we are on our feet and can help them, we'll tell them they should come," she thought.

Chapter 6

Conditions in Camp

Levinia Champion, custom-bound "Cousin Jenny," found things in the mining camps so very different from what she considered adequate. Here she saw and heard much that strained her strict sense of morals and convention. But that, she thought hopefully, was being balanced pretty well by the fact that there was actual religious, civic and cultural progress being made in the young community.

Among the residents of the camps, she saw people from various foreign countries and from all walks of life. Some were dressed in full or partial costumes of their own lands. Others, wore all sorts of clothing, from the roughest garb of the prospector to the flashy attire of the gambler. The business and professional men, the promoters, heads of mines, mills and businesses, wore the conventional clothes of the section of America from which they had come. She saw several Negroes, too, in the vicinity, brought there by their southern masters. There were a few Mexicans, with sombreros and all, and quite a few Chinese, who laundered the garments brought to them.

In some respects, the camps were even worse than she thought possible. Soberly, sadly, regretfully, she saw the whole situation in its true perspective: the poor, almost impossible living conditions, the obvious filth of clothing, skin and surroundings, the contaminated streams, the garbage and refuse, tossed about carelessly, the exposed human excrement. She saw the flies and other insects that form a real threat to health, while medical care and medicines were so scarce, one hardly knew there were any.

She realized the great peril, too, in the falling rocks and timbers in the mineshafts. And in the danger of premature and belated explosions in the hand-drilled holes made by miners in the mines to blast out the ore for the

Conditions in Camp

many mills in Black Hawk and other close vicinities, as well as for the many arastas scattered about to crush the ore.

Levinia was very much interested in the arastas. Each was a circular basin or vat with a stone bottom, with a post placed upright in the center bearing two arms, to which were chained heavy stones. These were revolved around the posts and did the grinding. Quicksilver was placed in the bottom of the vat, and the ore with water was fed into the enclosure and was pulverized. The gold in the ore adhered to the quicksilver, forming what Hugh explained, was an amalgam, which was heated in the same manner as in the stamp mills.

Her fear grew, too, around the great possibility of fire in the unguarded camps and in the forests back of them. All in all, Central City, and her sister camps, gave almost negative conditions for people to settle. But Hugh's staunch belief in the new world, which offered an individual the freedom that Cornwall couldn't, made her steel her heart and mind against all the obstacles that made living and progress difficult. Besides, she could see for herself that the people were aware of the present drawbacks in their surroundings and were preparing to do something to improve them. She was determined to join their forces and help, as Hugh did, and urged her to do.

The Champions looked forward with infinite faith to the future of the mining camps. They worked together and with others, who were striving to make new homes in the strange land that promised so much yet required the utmost of human courage, determination and endurance, added to a resigned acceptance of God's will.

Hugh and Levinia didn't live in Nevadaville very long. Before winter set in in earnest, Hugh and Jim were offered a much better job in a mine in the lower part of Central City, still called Mountain City because the post office, which served the entire district, was there. (Because Mountain City had been incorporated before Central City proper, the Post Office wasn't changed at Central City, to the spot where Laurence and Main Streets unite, until October 1869, six years later. After that change, the residents of Mountain City had to walk up the hill to get their mail.)

The young Champions moved their possessions to a cabin, quite close to where John Gregory found the "lode" gold four years before, and made it into a home.

They were very happy. Everyone and everything was going well. Better and more permanent buildings were going up. Law and order prevailed. The community was growing.

A report from Guy House on long, steep Guy Hill, on the Denver City gold camp route, said: *157 loads of hay, 165 loads of freight and supplies, drawn by*

1,282 oxen and 224 mules and horses passed by this summer going to the gold camps. It is estimated there are 40,000 people in Gilpin County this fall.

All in all, the year 1863 showed good times, for mining reached its first peak, then almost two million dollars, in The Gulch!

By the end of that year, most of the important mines had been sold to Eastern companies, whose main interest was the quotation of the stock on Wall Street Exchanges and not the gold mining in the distant gold camps of Colorado. Because of this reckless buying and selling on the Stock Market, there was a six-month's period when Gregory Gulch really was "The Richest Square Mile On Earth," and though the weather that winter was the worst that region had ever known, the district rejoiced.

During the second week of 1864, Levinia knew she was pregnant. The young couple was very happy that their long-planned for family was on its way. They talked and talked about the coming child. They both knew it would be a son, and that his name would be William John Champion!

They went even further than naming their first child. The second and third would be girls named Lillie and Edith. In case either were a boy, his name would be Albert.

Their hearts were light. They were in good health. Hugh had a good job. Their cabin was comfortable. They had friends, who shared their belief in the future of the country. They were to have their first child in September.

Then suddenly without any explanation to Levinia, who had made special efforts to be friends with her, Maude Whitesley, the beautiful young widow, left town on the stage. With her was a mining engineer, Edgar Thrombly, whom rumor said, she would marry in Denver.

When the stage left Central City that day, Levinia was in the vicinity to pick up supplies and was surprised when she received a note, delivered by a boy, telling her Maude had sold her cabin and wanted the Champions to have what it contained. That evening, Hugh and Levinia hurried there and found dishes, pans, blankets, throw rugs and two tubs. One tub was larger than the one they had, so would be better for Hugh to bathe in, while the other was an enamel one which Levinia said she would save to bathe the baby.

Chapter 7

Gold Bubble Burst, Planned Move to Mexico, Flood

The happiness and the good fortune in The Gulch didn't last. On April 18, 1864, the gold bubble burst! The stock market broke suddenly. All Western stock collapsed without any other explanation than mere speculation. In August of the previous year, Pat Casey, the individual owner of mines and mills in the county, had sold his entire holdings through negotiations on Wall Street, which started wild New York speculation on Gilpin County properties.

The entire Gulch was thrown into confusion. No one knew what to do or what to expect. The panic in the East, and the uncertainty of the future in Gregory Gulch mining, hit the gold mines and the miners with full force. It struck Hugh Champion with a velocity that floored him completely. He didn't know where to turn.

In his consternation, he listened to a promoter who had mining interests in Mexico. This man promised him a good job with advantages, and full transportation for him and Levinia, if he would go back with him when he had filled his quota of miners for his enterprise. He explained that the couple could live in a town that offered much better living conditions and a warmer climate by far, than the bleak winters in Gilpin County and food was much cheaper there.

When Hugh presented the picture of the move to Levinia, she wanted to turn the proposition down flat. But instead she sat quietly. She felt she couldn't face such a drastic move at that time, even if she'd been inclined to go on such a "long-shot" adventure, for her child was due in September.

But she saw that Hugh was impressed by the good offer that the Mexican mining company was making for experienced miners, with transportation for them thrown in. For the first time since she had joined him in Central City, he was discouraged by the right-about-face mining had taken, and she realized that he was studying the odds of staying where he was and the chance offered him. She wished he weren't so impulsive about "seeking greener pastures" as she termed his restlessness. She wished Hugh would talk it over with her and consider her side. While she waited for the decision she felt sure he would make, she prayed that he would allow her to give her opinion in the matter.

Finally, he informed her he was going to Mexico. The promoter gave the specific date he would send the stage to the border and from there south to the Mexican town where they would live.

As before when he had revealed his plans to leave, he was gentle but firm. This time, however, he was willing to listen to what she thought about the move and was ready to persuade her to agree. He was willing to take her with him this time. In fact, he told her he never would leave her behind again.

When she told him frankly, that she was afraid to set out on such a journey in her condition, with no assurance that she would have medical aid, when and if she should need it, Hugh smiled and kissed her. He reminded her that Mother Nature took extreme care when a child was on its way and if the mother-to-be was strong and well, as she was, he was positive that all would go well.

He explained that he was as concerned as she was about the baby coming, so he had asked the promoter all sorts of questions. He told him that long before it was time for the child to arrive, they would be well settled in the town where there was an excellent American doctor, who came there to work for the large mining company that furnished schools, churches and stores for their employees.

So Levinia saw that Hugh's mind was made up. She gave no other argument against their going, but Jim Mitchell spoke out very strongly against it, not only turning down the chance to join them, but saying Hugh was a fool for pulling up stakes.

Levinia understood why Hugh wanted Jim along, for no Cornishman ever worked alone on a mining job. If, for any reason, he wasn't able to go to work, his partner was told and he made arrangements to work with someone else, or stayed at home until the absent partner was on the job once more. It was a Cornish superstition. They always worked in pairs and were quite dependent upon each other during working hours. So it was natural for Hugh to want Jim with him on the new job. But Jim refused to go. He said he preferred to stay and wait for things to straighten themselves out.

Hugh was greatly disappointed, but dogged. They made preparations. Levinia got together the few possessions she wanted to take. Then they sought the promoter and asked him if it would be possible for her to take an extra box of things for her baby, showing him the tiny garments she'd made for the expected little stranger. The man, an educated American from New England, was interested and offered to pay the excess baggage rate on the extra articles she thought she should take. This promise and a first-hand acquaintance with Hugh's future employer, made her feel a bit better about going, but her heart was heavy and her mind refused to accept the move as a good one. Then, with her usual determination to have something on which to fall back if it became necessary to return to the gold camps, she persuaded Hugh to agree to have Jim move into their cabin and look after their things, which he did.

When the time came to leave, Jim kissed Levinia soberly and shook Hugh's hand as though he was saying goodbye forever. It was Jim's manner that made Levinia's heart even heavier that day, May 19, 1864, as the stage that carried them and other Cornish miners, swung through Black Hawk and began the climb over Dory and Guy Hills. She dreaded the trip over the mountains. She remembered when she'd been over the route before, the precarious grades above deep canyons, the steep climbs over narrow and gutted "roads," where an inch to the side would mean the tipping of the coach into wooded gullies, that route which must be taken to reach Denver City, where they were to change to a stage going southward toward the border into Mexico.

When they reached the grade above Golden City[5] at the mouth of the canyon, they could see great expanses of water spread over the lowlands below them, in which houses and other buildings were isolated.

They didn't know that early that morning a twenty-foot wall of water, caused by three days of heavy rain and cloud bursts, had raced down Cherry Creek in West Denver City. It spread out over a wide section of neighboring land, carrying death and destruction with it and undermined many of the buildings and businesses along its bank!

Nor could they know that the mad waters of the Platte River were rushing to meet those of Cherry Creek, bringing even more devastation!

They learned more about the flood later from a personal account of Susan R. Ashley, who had been in it.

At about 2:00 this morning of May 19, a soldier from Camp West, West of Denver City, called from in front of our house, a wall of water 20 feet high is pouring down Cherry Creek and is spreading here! Cherry Creek had been a dry sand bed for years. The Rocky Mountain News Office, the Methodist Church, a boarding house, and other buildings were built on its banks.

---

5 The settlement at the mouth of Golden Gate Canyon was Golden Gate, not Golden City. Denver City was named for Kansas Governor James Denver. When Denver City, Highlands and Auraria were united in the spring of 1860, the name was officially changed to Denver.

These toppled into the rushing water as it undermined them, and sheep, hogs, cattle and chickens were washed away. Soldiers saved many lives by their warning and help. The water came up to Perry Street, showing us that water from the Platte River would be upon us! We rushed to save our personal effects. We moved everything but the kitchen stove to the second story. For three days and nights the water rose and fell. Our cellar was filled with water, but the house was still dry, the flood didn't cross our doorsill. At one stage of the terror, I saw a kite land, after several trials, on the west side of the creek. To this a note was attached with instructions to draw in the string. A rope was fastened to it with a basket containing reports from absentees and notes of inquiry. Before night of that day, a ropewalk united the two parts of the town and the more venturesome of the absentees joined their families. The City Hall, the safe and all the records were swept away and the city much destroyed in that section. When the water subsided, many buildings were moved from West to East Denver, and from then on, East Denver was the residential part of the city.

(A full account of Mrs. Ashley's experiences of the Cherry Creek Flood may be found in the Colorado Magazine, Volume XIV, March 1937, under "Reminiscences of Early Colorado.")

The Champion's first real knowledge of the flood was when the stage was stopped that afternoon at West Denver by bedraggled soldiers from Camp West, who had been on duty the night before when the floodwater hit the town.

Standing at the road barrier in the mud and wearing rubber boots and oiled slickers, the tired soldiers engaged in no small talk and no conversation beyond the mere necessity. They turned the stage back without ceremony; ordered the driver to go away from the edge of town. There he was to rest his teams for a short while, then drive back up the grade to a ranch house near the road, where he was to ask for shelter overnight for his passengers. Early the next morning, he was to take the stage and its passengers and luggage back to where he had picked them up! There would be no travel into the towns below the foothills for several days, at least.

The promoter tried to explain to the soldiers where he and his charges were headed and asked to be allowed to stay somewhere near until they could continue their journey. But the soldier said firmly that he had to do as he was ordered: send them back to their starting place and have them wait until they were notified that they could go through Denver City, on their way south.

When Hugh tried to put into his own words his feelings about going on later, the soldier in command lost his patience and told him he was damn foolish to want to take a pregnant woman into the dangerous zone, expecting her to go on a long journey after the water subsided, to the extent that emergency passage be attempted, at least a week, and maybe longer.

So discouraged, yet thankful they hadn't reached Denver City a day earlier, to stay all night there on the first lap of their trip, thus themselves becoming victims of the flood, they went back as ordered. They stayed with the family at the specified ranch over night, but Hugh and Levinia slept little, whispering together about what faced them.

Next morning, after breakfast was served them by the sympathizing rancher and his wife, the promoter and Hugh had a talk that became quite heated at times. Hugh, who was superstitious as all Cornish are, declared that being stopped by the flood was a sign that he wasn't to go on to Mexico. He was taking his wife back to Central City for good!

Hugh's firm decision influenced the other miners, and they also said the Mexico proposition was off.

The promoter refused to pay their fares back to the gold camp, so they counted their money and found that each man had enough to get himself back to Central City, but Hugh didn't have the money for Levinia's fare.

At once, from a pocket hidden in her inner bodice, Levinia produced English money she'd brought from Cornwall, and paid her own fare.

Though pleased that this difficulty had been overcome, Hugh seemed irked by the fact that she had withheld from him the knowledge that she had money of her own, hidden away. His pride had been brought to the front once more, and it took quite a bit of straight talking later for Levinia to show him that she'd been saving the money for just such a tight spot as they'd been in that day, and that his pride had been saved by her having the money with her and ready. She reminded him that it would have been much worse if he had had to ask the stage driver for credit, and to borrow money from Jim to repay him when she got home. Finally, Hugh saw that she was right. He kissed her gently, and with quite good grace, she thought when she remembered that the Cornish found it hard to acknowledge a wrong or to admit a mistake.

In her innermost heart, she was relieved that they weren't going to Mexico, but she didn't talk about it to Hugh. She merely said she agreed with him that it wasn't meant that they leave Central City. Hugh nodded and held her close. Then he announced that he had an idea in mind about how the Cornish miners could help bring about a new era for Gilpin County mining.

As soon as they arrived at their cabin and saw Jim, who was very pleased at their return, Hugh told him what he had thought out. Jim accepted the idea of trying to introduce Cornish ways of handling a situation, like the one that confronted the gold miners since the panic.

This was the system called "tribute pitch," which was the leasing of a mine or a part of a mine, by two, three or four men, who banded together to work the holding on shares with its owner. Usually, the miners stood all the expense and, if profits were made from the work, a percentage agreed upon was made to the mine owner. Sometimes, the company or the owner of the mine shared the expenses so that the contract-lease might give the stockholders a larger share of the profits.

The "tribute pitch" system, which the Cornish called "tutwork," was presented to the owners of the closed mines by Hugh, Jim and other Cornishmen who were called in to sell the idea. Some of the owners accepted the chance to reopen the mines and put the new plan into practice.

This gave the "tributes" a living, though there was a great deal of back-breaking work involved. Sometimes, and in many instances, it was necessary for the miners to walk long distances to the mines where "tributing" was welcome. They worked long, ten-hour shifts, in cold and wet drifts; running the risk of cave-ins and the break-through of water from idle mines close by or above, and labored in bad air, by flickering candlelight.

All this change worried Levinia a great deal, but her real concern lay with the methods Hugh and his fellow miners had adopted when they had taken up the "tutworks" or leasing in the mines. She was well aware that the men went down into the shaft at the start of a shift and each one had two or three extra candles thrust into a "jumper" pocket or in the leg of his copper-toed boot.[6] In the other boot-leg and in his pocket, explosives for the day's blasting operations were carried, while in his hand, with his dinner pail or "Tea Bucket," he held the required length of fuse tightly coiled.

All in all, though, many mines remained closed and idle, and others were abused by the mismanagement of untrained superintendents, sent out by equally ignorant owners. Hugh and other Cornish men made out all right during the period from 1864 to 1869, when mining got on its feet again, as they had hoped and expected.

Specifically, the miners felt that the reopening would come about when new capital arrived from the East and a new type of shrewd and earnest mining manager would take over and develop methods to recover the full mineral contents of the various ores, putting honest mining back in The Gulch.

In the meantime, much of interest had taken place in the vicinity. Perhaps the event that pleased Levinia most was the start of building the walls of the Methodist church on the lot purchased by the Church organization in 1861. She rejoiced when the Methodists incorporated Colorado Seminary, which was to become the University of Denver, and finally, Denver University.

---

6 A child's copper-toed shoe is in the Gilpin Historical Museum Collection

Chapter 8

First Child Born

The most important event of all to Hugh and Levinia Champion was the birth of fair-haired, blue-eyed William John on September 23, 1864! He weighed eight pounds and eight ounces and was long in body. His parents were very proud. To them, the world looked bright, though there were some clouds of territorial trouble in the offing.

Little William John was christened by Reverend B.T. Vincent, the minister who had married the Champions. He was a frequent visitor at their cabin and on each occasion he held a prayer meeting with Levinia and her neighbors, whom she called in when he came. Levinia was religious. From the very first day in her new home in America, she had read the Bible and held prayer every evening. Though Hugh didn't hold her deep faith, he joined her in this ritual.

Early in the year 1865, there were rumors that the Civil War between the States was almost over. This news brought prayers of thanksgiving and hopes that, with the closing of hostilities, times would be better in the nation and in the gold camps.

On April 15, 1865, word was received by telegram that President Abraham Lincoln had been assassinated. The next day, a black-bordered newspaper announced his murder by a man named Ford, in a theater. The terrible news linked the miners with the rest of the nation mourning Lincoln's passing.

For a short time, there was a feeling of helplessness in the camps. Then on May 26, came the wonderful news that the war was over! General Lee of the South had surrendered to the North! This good news raised the spirits of everyone and a celebration was planned for July 4, the first time Hugh and Levinia realized that date meant so much to America. From then on, they held a new sense of responsibility to the land of their choice and Independence Day became very important to them.

That same month of May, Reverend Vincent staged a benefit at the Montana Theater for the St. James Library. The entertainment, put on by the residents of the mining towns, was a great success. There were vocal solos and quartets, a band, instrumental solos, songs by the Sabbath School children and group singing in which the beautiful melodious harmonizing of Cornish voices was displayed to a very pleased and appreciative audience.

From that time on, the people of the community realized there was talent among them and an effort was made to develop their various abilities. Qualified individuals gave time and directions to form singing groups and church choruses, which became well known and advertised.

In addition to such church entertainments, as followed that opening, the community saw performances by professional actors who came from Denver City to put on skits and plays. In fact, Central City and her sister-towns were on the Golden Circuit, a route followed by the well-known actors.

The Champions didn't attend these performances often even though they, like all the Cornish, loved drama very much, for they felt that they ought not to spend their scant money for mere entertainment. Besides, they were saving every penny they could to buy a house. Now that they had a family, they were determined to have a home of their very own. So they added to the very modest sum Levinia still had from her Cornwall savings and the small amount she received each month from her sisters as rent for sewing rooms back home. Hugh's wages took care of most of their expenses, although sometimes Levinia spent some of her own money to make it go around. But she was very careful not to humiliate her proud husband by telling him she did this.

With the home in mind, they agreed that the only money they would spend, after paying expenses, would be for the church in which they were very much interested. In addition to the church donations, Hugh spent long hours digging out the ground for the foundation of the church building, and Levinia helped the other women raise funds, in every way they could, for the church.

Suddenly, Hugh stopped working on the church. He gave as his reason his opinion that the excavation should be deeper and the mortar for its foundation was not of the correct mixture for the weight that would be put upon it. So he would have nothing more to do with it, but others went on with the work Hugh was positive would be useless.

July 4th that year was a great day in and around Central City. The streets were crowded. The saloons were filled. Fights took place. There were picnics and contests at the gardens of the Brewery up Eureka Street, just above the town. There was boating on the lake that had been formed from the surplus water brought in by a ditch, a distance of twelve miles, dug by the Fall River Water Company from Fall River, to supply water for the mines. When not needed, the extra water was stored in a depression in Lake Gulch Community, over the hill south of Central City. Crowds gathered there at a pavilion called the Lake House to go boating, to watch the boats or to sit and eat and drink. Everyone seemed happy and hopeful in his own way. The inhabitants of The Gulch were care-free and happy as they celebrated Independence Day.

Chapter 9

A Death, A Birth, A New House

Within a few days after the celebration, little William John, a very strong child up to that time, had trouble breathing. He developed a high fever and died suddenly on August 11, 1865, at the age of ten months and eighteen days.

The death of the little boy was hard to take. It was a terrible blow to his parents. After helping them lay the small body to rest under a beautiful tree in the church lot, Reverend Vincent gave them sympathetic understanding and reminded them that, since Levinia was three-months pregnant, another child would be theirs to help fill the vacant spot in their lives. All that helped, but nothing really softened the loss of their precious little one.

As though the baby's death was the beginning of more trouble, many mines and mills shut down until by fall, The Gulch was relatively quiet. Hopelessness and dark clouds crept over the Territory, Central City and the other gold camps. First, the farmers on the plains below were pestered by grasshoppers which ate the crops and left the fields as bare as the ground itself in some areas.

The Denver Rocky Mountain News, October 9, 1865, bore the item that seemed to sum up the damage: It is generally conceded that but for the grasshopper plague the plains would have produced its own supply of breadstuffs, vegetables and food for stock. They have destroyed the crop totally in many places and injured it in all.

The mining camps suffered by this great loss, for the plains supplied most of their needs.

Another shortage in supplies was caused by the Indians, who burned the supply trains that came across the plains from the East, thereby cutting off all that was available for the mining section. The Platte River Route was ravished

A Death, A Birth, A New House

and destroyed for two hundred and fifty miles; even communication was cut off at intervals. Levinia remembered one time when all communication with the mountains was stopped for two months.

In an effort to arouse a force to combat this destruction by the Indians, Territorial Governor Evans issued the proclamation.

"Patriotic Citizens, I appeal to you for defense of your homes and families against the merciless savages. Any man who kills a hostile Indian is a patriot; but there are Indians who are friendly and to kill one of these will involve us in greater difficulty. It is important, therefore, to fight only the hostiles, and no one has been or will be restrained from this."

There was a great response to the call. The gold camps sent a company, known as the Mountain Men, to join twelve hundred volunteers from the plains. In due time, the Indians were thrust back and order was restored.

But hard times prevailed. Many gave up in their helplessness. Though Hugh and Levinia felt the pinch severely, they kept up their spirits. Hugh was working at "tutwork," making only enough that winter to keep them in food without going into the savings, designated as house money. They made their clothing do, though Levinia found it necessary to put patch upon patch on the clothes Hugh wore at the mine. She racked her brain to make up recipes using only supplies she could get until the supply trains could travel again and the plains would produce once more. They some way got along and thanked God that they did.

During the first part of that winter, which was a long and hard one, they lightened their grief over losing little William John by planning for their coming child. They talked about the house they wanted so badly in that part of Central City, which had been Mountain City, before merging with the larger camp. The conclusion to settle there, which was to them still Mountain City, was influenced by the facts that property was cheaper there than in Central City proper, and more Cornish lived there. Besides, the two largest producing mining properties, the Gregory and the Bobtail, in which Hugh hoped to work again when mining came back to its own and times became better, were situated between Black Hawk and Central City, very close to the latter.

So they looked and looked for a house there, hoping to find one they could afford to buy and move into in time for the expected baby to be born in their own home.

But Lillie, a plump dark-haired darling, was born January 25, 1866, in the rented cabin. From that moment the little one occupied the greater part of their hearts and plans.

Shortly after Lillie's birth, Hugh found a man who wanted to sell his home and would take the amount they had saved. Negotiations were made and on

Good Friday, March 26, (a good omen, they figured) the Champions moved into their new home on Miner Street, a short street in between, and running parallel to, Lawrence and Gregory Streets, both of which ran from Black Hawk to Central City. The warranty deed recorded in Book 28, page 624 at the Court House, and signed by Hal Sayre, Notary Public, at 9:30 a.m. on March 26, 1866, gave the following description of the property.

"One certain building lot with the house thereon bounded on the north by an alley; on the south by California Street and on the west by N. P. Simpson's Tailor Shop. Said lot being twenty (20) feet front by eighty (80) feet deep. Situated in Mountain City, Gilpin County, and Territory of Colorado."

The indenture naming Benjamin T. Ewing, as the party of the first part, and Hugh Champion as the party of the second part, states that the sum of the transaction was nine hundred ($900.00) dollars.

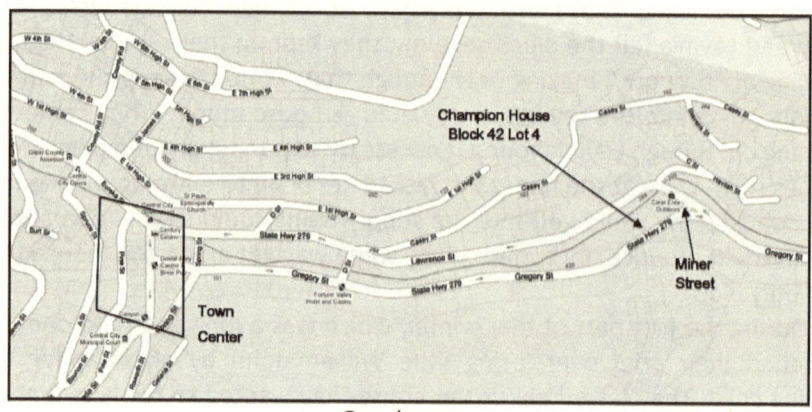

Google map.

Hugh found the lot some seven (7) feet narrower at the back than at the front and had it resurveyed. Later in a City Plat of the street, a drawing showed the lot as odd-shaped. (This plat may be seen on the wall of the Court House in Central City, Colorado, and a Mayor's Deed 1878, on page 236, book 62, shows the corrected lines as 32 feet front and 25 feet back of the 80-foot lot.)

The house had five rooms, three downstairs and two on the second floor of the story and a half building. There were seven steps up from the street and a square porch which led to the kitchen door, and a narrow porch led left to the front door that opened into a room they called the parlor. Behind the parlor there was a small bedroom.

The kitchen was a long and narrow room running along the side of the entire length of the house. There were four doors in this room: the door to the street beyond the square porch, the backdoor to the yard, the door to the parlor and a high-up short door in the back left corner of the kitchen that opened onto a landing. From the landing one turned almost abruptly to the left to ascend the dark, quite narrow, almost hidden stairs to the upstairs room which included a large square bedroom over the parlor and a small one above the downstairs bedroom.

At first sight of that landing and the stairs leading up from it and around the corner, Levinia laughed heartily, but it soon became a problem to her. For when she opened the high door in the corner of the kitchen, the landing thus exposed had no stairs in sight, and could be seen only by looking around the corner. The landing was some four feet from the kitchen floor, and there was no way to get onto it unless she put one knee up onto the landing, pulled the rest of her body onto it, then stood up before she could turn left and go up the stairs to the floor above.

As she descended, she had to stand on the landing, open the door, and slide off the landing, those four feet to the kitchen floor, or scoot forward to land cautiously on her feet in the kitchen.

Hugh built her steps that were fastened together, so that she could place her feet below the landing when she wanted to go upstairs, but most of the time she found them in the way and just one more piece of furniture in her narrow kitchen. So she set them aside, more and more, as she became quite adept in scooting onto the landing without help and getting off it when she came downstairs.

She told Hugh, since the three first floor rooms gave her enough space for the stove, bed, table and chairs, lamps and small rugs, they'd had in the cabin, she didn't go upstairs often anyway. So the portable steps were taken to the cellar that was dug out beneath the house, and stored there.

The Champions were very proud of the appearance of the buff-colored exterior of their home, of the white picket fence across its front, and the well-proportioned windows. However, they admitted there were too few windows, one in each room, except the parlor, which boasted two facing the street.

Hugh's expressed regret that they had little furniture and that it was, on the whole, homemade. Levinia replied that one has to have something to look forward to having, to hope for and to work toward. So, for the moment, even though Hugh fretted because they couldn't afford any furniture they termed "store-bought," they were willing to do what they could to make the home more livable.

Hugh built shelves in the kitchen for the dishes, and all the pans that would hang, were hung behind the stove. The others were placed on shelves he put into the space beneath the chimney.

In the parlor there was another chimney support. In this space, behind the small stove Hugh had obtained second-hand, he put more shelves.

No Wealth for Levinia

Having no other furniture for the parlor was their greatest problem. But Hugh made a wide bench, upon which Levinia laid a large canvas envelope she'd stuffed with chicken and goose feathers she had saved from the fowls she'd been able to buy since she had come to Central City, and duck feathers obtained from birds Hugh and the neighbors had shot on the lakes around the towns. These she had washed and then dried in the sun to make them fresh, sweet and fluffy. The stuffed canvas was then covered with the yellow "throw" Hugh had had when she came, making a pretty and quite nice couch for the parlor.

Next, she braided brightly-colored rags into large oval rugs for the floor and made curtains from flour sacks she'd soaked in kerosene to remove the printing, and bleached in soaked wood ashes, then dyed to bright colors. When the curtains were made, she trimmed them with neat and carefully placed "featherstitching." She was glad she had only the two windows, as flour sacks were hard to get, because most of the flour was shipped in barrels.

Somewhere, Hugh found three chairs that needed repairing. He made them sturdy again, and dickered for a large chair that had a broken rocker. He fashioned a new rocker and put it on, then carried it inside to the parlor and motioned to Levinia, who stood in the kitchen watching him, the baby in her arms.

He put her into the rocking chair. It began to rock in rhythm as her body moved. Hugh, sat on the couch and began to hum a Cornish lullaby. Levinia joined in, her soprano blending in beautifully with his baritone. The child relaxed and went to sleep on its mother's breast. Her parents smiled happily at each other. Their happiness was complete.

Chapter 10

Richest Square Mile on Earth, A Birth

That year mining dropped abruptly from the two million dollar mark, in ore value Gregory Gulch had produced, to only three quarters of a million. Consequently, many people left the vicinity to seek other jobs or other mining activities. Great pessimism prevailed in the community. There was much talk of pulling out from the gold camps, unless something developed to hold them.

But those who were determined to stay were doggedly optimistic.
Although the Catholic Chapel had burned down, the cornerstone for a new Saint Patrick's Catholic Church (renamed St. Mary's of the Assumption in 1894) was laid and a Congregational Church was built. That building (the Congregational Church) was used until 1901, when the present Clark Grammar School was built to take its place.

The fact that there were only 27,901 people in the county was very disappointing. It was, however, apparent that some Eastern capital was coming into the gold camps to try out new methods for extracting all the valuable metals in the ores. When things looked so glum, that encouraged those who had hung on to look forward to better times.

It was N. P. Hill's first Colorado smelter that brought about much of the renewed mining hopes. In 1867, Hill, a smelting specialist and professor of chemistry at Brown University, came to Black Hawk and put up the smelter with Eastern capital, making it a contributing factor in establishing Gilpin County mining on a firm basis.

Hugh told Levinia that Hill had been sent out on several trips by Eastern capitalists to formulate a method for treating difficult ores. He had taken samples of Gilpin County ores to Frieburg, Germany and had shipped seventy tons of the ores to Swansea, Wales. It was his studies that brought success for Colorado mining.

Hugh explained to her that the technique invented by Hill was a reverberatory process using copper as a collecting base for the precious metals and he described the process to her. The ores that were high in sulphur were roasted in out-door heaps, while other ores were crushed and roasted in furnaces. The roasted ores, properly mixed, were smelted in reverberatory furnaces (the roof reflecting the material treated), producing a copper "matte," which they shipped to Swansea, Wales, for refining.

Later, Hugh told her that when a Cornishman named Richard Pearce became connected with Mr. Hill's company, he introduced what Hugh said was the Zirvogal process for refining silver, and developed his own secret process for refining gold. From that time on, the refined silver and gold were shipped directly to the United States Mint, and the copper was either shipped as an oxide, or melted into bars without sending any of it to Swansea.

Hugh bragged that this company was the only smelting company in the area that ever produced refined metals. The others were the blast furnace type, where the metals were collected into lead bullion and shipped to refineries in the East, or elsewhere.

From the time the Hill smelter was put into operation, with one calcinating furnace, the vicinity took on new life and Levinia took an added active interest in what was going on around Central City. She was greatly concerned with the growth of the town in the four years she'd been there. Her love of walking brought her close to the changes as she went about with Baby Lillie in her arms.

Mostly, she walked uphill to Central City proper, going across Miner Street, on which her house stood, to Lawrence Street which branched out about a mile above into two streets in Central City, Main Street to the left, Eureka Street to the right. To cross either of these three streets, at the junction, one stepped on quite large boulders that had been sunk into the ground at short intervals to serve as stepping stones, to keep the walker out of the mud in wet seasons and in showers, and out of the dust in the streets, at other times.

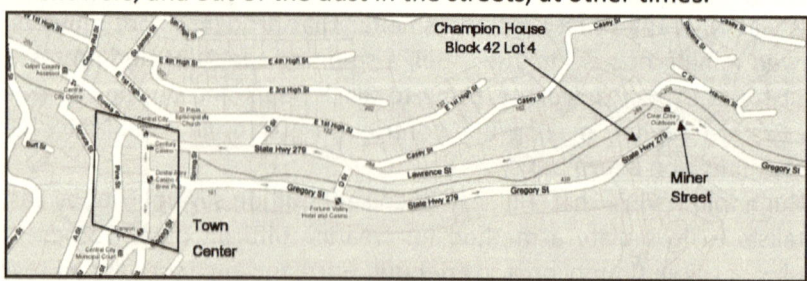

Google map.

At first, Levinia had found these stones a real challenge. It required true balance to stay on them and move forward, a feat those who imbibed too freely found impossible. But she found it easier with practice and could step from one to the other and cross the streets without slipping off once.

Most of the stores were on Main Street. There was also a rooming house, termed a hotel, a bakery and the post office, which faced both Main and Gregory Streets. Gregory Street ran from Gregory Point, a short distance from the Champion house, through the old town of Mountain City and along the left side of Gregory Gulch to Central City, entering at the foot of Main Street. Here it branched out to form Nevada Street, leading to Nevadaville to the right, and Spring Street to the left, which went over the hill to Russell Gulch, where Green Russell had found gold just after John Gregory had located his first find at Gregory Point.

The Methodist Church lot was on Eureka Street, with only the foundation walls called "The Ruins," because work had ceased there, as well as Washington Hall, Register Building, Wells Fargo Express Office, the bank, the Presbyterian Church, the Concert Hall and the Montana Theatre.

On Lawrence Street were the Congregational and Episcopal Churches, Lawrence Hall, a restaurant, and the Powder Company's brick building.

But the part of Central City where she lived had gone forward, too. Here in The Gulch, surrounded by hills, on which were numerous mines, lay the camp which was still termed Mountain City. In it were several mills, and many, as Levinia classed them, cabins, houses and residences. It had two hotels, the Iowa House and the St. Louis House, and two boarding houses, Mrs. Daly's and Mrs. Trevarthal's. There were two grocery stores, W. Bennalack's (sometimes misspelled as Bennaloch) Grocery, and the one on the ground floor of the Hadley Cabin, a two-story structure built in 1859, by a Major Hadley. The second story of this building had a stage and crude benches; the first theatre in the Rocky Mountains was known as Hadley's Hall. Besides being the place where traveling actors put on their performances, the building was used for other gatherings. At one interval, the Catholics used it to hold their services. At another time, a German school was held there.

In addition to these buildings, the old gold camp Mountain City, had a post office, a general store run by H. J. Kruse, a saloon owned by Tom Parsons and Simpson's Tailor Shop.

The short street, known as Miner, had only four lots with buildings at that time: the saloon, Mrs. Trevarthal's Boarding House, the tailor shop and the Champion home. Below was open space that was soon filled with homes, the Andrews' house next to the Champion's, then the Parsons and Edwards' homes.

All in all, Levinia considered that Central City had progressed such a long way that it was becoming a permanent city, while its lower extremities, Mountain City, and Black Hawk just beyond, were more than holding their own in growth and mining.

That year, 1867, Levinia got Hugh to take the first decisive step in adopting the United States as his own country, by making a Declaration of Intention to become a citizen.

(This Certificate of Intention, made on the twelfth of August, 1867, before Horace H. Atkins, Clerk of the District Court in the County of Gilpin, and Territory of Colorado, when Hugh Champion was twenty-nine years of age, was treasured by Levinia.)

In 1869, the game of baseball was introduced in Denver and spread to the mining towns. Central City soon had a team called "The Central City Stars."

Hugh became much interested in the new game and watched the practice and the exhibition games, even going to other towns in a wagon with friends, to see his hometown team play ball.

In spite of the steep slopes and the fact that there seemed no space large enough for a baseball diamond, there actually were two in the vicinity. One was on Bobtail Hill, between Black Hawk and Central City, where there was quite a large flat area. The other was above Nevadaville on the mesa.

Much later, a diamond was formed below the railroad depot at the junction between Spring Street and Nevada Street in Central City. This spot was afterwards covered by the tailings from the Chain-O-Mines Mine.

Hugh took part in the single-jack contests in rock drilling, which the Cornish called "oney," because only one man participated.

He used a hammer that weighed five pounds in these contests. Five pounds was the maximum weight allowed in such a contest, the normal weight being four pounds, a fact that made Levinia proud of her strong husband.

The man used both hands in a single-jack performance, whether in everyday procedure or in contest. One hand was to keep the steel drill turning in the moistened hole in the block of granite, the other to drive the drill in with the hammer. Because of his strength and skill, Hugh did it very well.

He and Jim Mitchell entered as a two-man team in the double-jack or "twoys," or "shillalee," as the Cornish termed this type of sport. In this, the men took turns keeping the steel drill focused along an agreed upon line on the granite block, turning it slightly between strokes of the hammer, to keep it from sticking fast in the constantly moistened hole, and swinging the heavy hammer, while a third man changed drills between hammer strokes, without a lost motion or stroke.

Hugh's team worked up a record of driving a series of twenty-two half inch holes in the granite, in only ten minutes, only a half inch short of the best record made in a double-jack contest.

Hugh also wrestled and due to his physique and dogged persistence, was very successful, though at times he said the referee or "stickler," in the match favored the wrong man. In these matches the contestants wore trousers and loose sack-like blouses made of canvas, which Levinia found out, needed repairing after each match.

Levinia, Hugh and Jim took part in the winter sport called "The Snow Slide," riding in a bob-sled down the two-mile course from Nevadaville to Black Hawk, a drop of five hundred feet in that distance. They skated at a rink in Black Hawk and in the basement of the Tappan Hardware store in Central City.

In summer, they enjoyed dancing at the Brewery Gardens, in Eureka Gulch above the city. Sometimes, they rented a rig from the livery and drove to the lake in Lake Gulch above Spring Gulch and over the hill from Central City, to picnic and watch the boats on the artificial lake. But Levinia refused to ride on the clumsy excursion boat, so Hugh didn't either. It was enough for them to sit on a bench with Baby Lillie and watch the others.

They loved music, as all Cornish do, and there was quite a lot of it in town to satisfy their longing: band music, choirs, group singing at entertainments and in the homes, where "sings" were held. And at Christmas time there was carol singing, when the Cornish groups went from house to house and from mine to mine singing carols, which they called "curls," of old Cornwall.

The Cornish called the treble clef the "air" of the song. Alto was the "second," tenor was the "counter" and the bass was "base," the lowest tone.

Hugh and Levinia, and their Methodist friends, were much concerned over the delayed church building. They were glad when in 1867, Reverend O. H. Adams from Illinois Conference brought about a renewed interest in it by making his congregation, which met in rented rooms, homes, theatres, but mostly in Washington Hall, a proposition.

He told them that if they would raise money to put up the walls and the roof of the church building, he would raise money in the East to finish it.

The people were eager to see this done, so the money was pledged and Reverend Adams went east to get the funds he had promised. Upon examination by the contractor, it was found that the foundation walls already put up and then abandoned, were unfit for two reasons: the excavation wasn't deep enough and poor mortar had been used for the walls, which proved that Hugh had been right when he had given up working on the church.

So the walls, "The Ruins," had to be torn out, making it much more expensive than had been estimated. More contributions were made and

Reverend Adams went east for more money. Work went on under a contract with N. H. Root, who said the building would be a pattern for people in the future to follow.

That summer came the second plague of grasshoppers. They took everything green, everything they could eat. The plants, Levinia was so proud of on her porch, were devoured. Even the washing on the clothesline in her back yard was ruined or destroyed totally. This was an additional loss, for that morning she had washed all the baby things Lillie had outgrown and had hung them out to dry and whiten in the sun, in preparation for the child she was expecting. Her second daughter, Edith, was born in their own home on November 24, 1867. The child was fair and blue-eyed like her mother and contrasted with the dark-haired, dark-eyed Lillie, making their parents very proud of their beauty and thankful for the blessing God had bestowed upon them.

Through the successful processing of the difficult ores, the improvement in stamp-milling and consolidation, the vicinity began to thrive again and The Gulch was once more being spoken of as "The Richest Square Mile on Earth."

Chapter 11

Cycle of Life and Death

Hugh was doing very well. He had a good-paying job in the mines close to home, and did some rock work on the side, in the true Cornish way, building dry rock walls and retaining and supporting structures. Much of this Cornish rock building was coming into use around Central City. Structures ranged from fences to buildings, giving a look of firm permanence and actual durability to individual properties and company buildings alike. Much of this stonework was put up in front of houses, being built on the hills, to keep the houses from slipping and to form front yards.

Space for buildings was scarce. The hills had to be utilized when the town spread out and streets had to be built on stretches dug out of the hillsides and reinforced for stabilization, as the need arose. There were five High Streets on Bates Hill, First High, Second High,[7] and Third High and so on. Some buildings were put on the level of a street and a flight of steps inside led to the second story or the third, as the case might be. The door of the top floor opened out on a back yard cut out in the hill, or on the street above. Some of these buildings had kitchens on the top floor. Owners did their laundry there and hung the clothes to dry in the yard above.

Rooming houses on Main Street had their offices on the first floor, and guests were taken up a long flight of stairs to the rooms on the second floor. To the surprise of these guests the next morning, they could step from the corridor door onto the street above, among the sheets and other articles hung there to dry.

The Champion house was built some ten feet above Miner Street and had steps going up to it. It was all open beneath the house, and made a good

---

[7] Although there are several references to Second High Street, no maps have been found that shows its location.

place to store the wood when it was brought in and unloaded at the back of the long lot. Hugh cut the wood to burn in the kitchen stove and the parlor heater into stove lengths. There was a trap door, with steps to get the fuel from down below without going outside, in the kitchen close to the stove, a wonderful arrangement in the severe winters.

From the back of the house, through the kitchen door, there were some twenty steps leading down to the quite large back yard, where the out-house, called the "back house" or "privy" stood. About a hundred feet below the bottom of the lot, Gregory Creek[8] ran toward Black Hawk. Beyond the creek was Lawrence Street, the thoroughfare through the towns.

To the left and back of the Champion lot, but across the alley that lay between it and the creek, was the Elliot Mine. To the right and down a few rods was the Rule barn, where horses and mules that pulled some of the quartz wagons, were kept.

At the right of the house, so close that not even a child could get between, was the Tailor Shop. Beyond it was Mrs. Trevarthal's boarding house, a large frame building built up from the street in front and even with the Champion house and the Tailor Shop. In back it had a long series of wooden steps and landings that led to the yard below, with its out-house and wood shed, then to the alley beyond.

Next to the boarding house and toward Central City proper, was an alley, then a small building used as a workshop, then Tom Parsons' saloon, a large building with a space beyond. Across from the saloon and in front, was another space called "the square," from which Miner and Gregory Streets, and Packard Gulch opened. On the other side of the square was Bennalack's Grocery, which had living rooms above. Beyond, as one went toward Central City, were the homes of Champion friends, then the Buell Mine. From that mine, a narrow path ran along the narrow street (Lawrence) to the center of Central City.

When better times came, Hugh put up a high board fence around the lot behind their house. He erected a shed that was to be used as a barn for the cow Levinia had announced she intended to have, as soon as she could get one, and for the chickens she had already bargained for with the stage driver. He promised to buy them in the plains below and see that they were hauled over the mountains to her.

In the meantime, Levinia learned all she could about what happened around town and in the outside world, developing a keen interest in all that went on in the country of which she was trying to become a part. She read the local paper, The Register Call, the Denver papers, though they were days

---

8 No newspaper references can be found to Gregory Creek.

old before they reached her, and the Eastern papers some of her friends and neighbors received. And she listened to what people said.

She was interested to learn that Washington Hall, the oldest building in Central City, had been built in 1862 of hewn logs, by Sheriff W. E. Cozzens. Later he had covered the logs with clapboard siding and sealed the interior. Then he rented it to the county for twenty-five hundred dollars a year, to be used as a courthouse, a recorder's office and a jail, as well as for church services and all the social gatherings of the community. In 1868, the County Commissioners bought the building for ten thousand dollars and all county business took place under its roof.

At about that same time, she learned that Horace M. Hale had been hired to teach the school in a building that had been a bowling alley on Eureka Street that spanned Eureka Creek which ran through town to join Gregory Creek. (Mr. Hale's son, Irving, became one of the first cadets from Central City to West Point. He reached the rank of General, and later was a hero at Manila.)

On July 22 of that year, just before his election as President of the United States, General Grant brought Generals Sherman, Dent and Sheridan, and his own son, Ulysses, Jr., to Central City on a campaign tour. They came unexpectedly, on the stage in a driving rain, coming over the route Levinia remembered, with a shudder: across dangerous Guy and Dory Hills, through Mile Creek Gulch and into Black Hawk opposite the Toll Gate Saloon.

The distinguished party of winning generals had lunch in Central City, then went on to Georgetown and Idaho Springs and stayed all night. On the return trip the next day, they spent a short time in Central City, where Levinia caught sight of them on the street. It was an experience that meant a great deal to her, making a link to the east and a reminder that this was a free country, where the people themselves selected their own leader. Even Hugh became more certain that this was the right he wanted to have and wished the time was at hand when he could become a citizen.

The future seemed very bright and wonderful at that time. But on September 7, 1868, at the age of two years seven months and sixteen days, little Lillie died of pneumonia, plunging that glowing future into despair.

Hugh and Levinia just couldn't believe they had lost their second child. Reverend Vincent had left Central City, but came back at their call and assisted the resident pastor in the funeral services for their little girl. At his suggestion, Lillie's body was placed in a cemetery above Eureka Street and the remains of their first-born, William John, were removed from the churchyard and put beside his little sister.

Reverend Vincent stayed a few days to help them through their first despairing days, but it was Baby Edith, by her need of them, who did the most to bring them out of their grief. Her clinging fingers, her dependence, her laughter, her love, made them realize there was much in the present for which to be thankful.

Their great interest in the church helped, too. By that time, its walls were up and the roof was being put on. But with winter almost upon them, the members realized the building could not be finished that year, so they decided to finish the basement and hold services there. This called for special effort, in which the Champions took an active part.

The Daily Central City Register of September 19, 1868, gave the following item, which Levinia read with civic pride.

The first business block put up this season was that of M. M. Seavy, on the east side of Spring Street opposite Bridge Street. It is 25 x 65 feet on the ground and two stories high. The lower story is 15 and the upper story 12 feet high. Under the building is a cellar 30 feet square and 15 feet deep, which is a new thing for Central City. With thick, substantial walls, a tin roof and iron doors and shutters, the whole building is considered fireproof. But a thick, fireproof wall dividing off the rear 25 feet of the lower story makes a room 25 feet square and 15 feet high, almost absolutely fireproof.

On December 4 of that year, a festival was held in the uncompleted Methodist Church and netted $675.00 which helped a great deal to finish it.

On January 8, 1869, the basement of the church was completed. On January 15, the ladies held a tea party, serving oysters, fruit, confectionery and ice cream at $1.00 a plate, which brought in $270.00 for the church fund.

On May 30, ground was broken for a new school to be built of stone two feet thick on High Street, the street above Lawrence.

June 4th, the local paper ran the item: *An ox team arrived in town Thursday from New Mexico and unloaded at M. M. Seavey's store. Among the freight was one small item of 1,800 pounds of pinion nuts.*

On July 31, 1869, another boy, named William John after their first son, was born to the Champions. He was a light haired baby with dark blue eyes and an exceptionally long frame. Hugh was very proud to have another son, and Levinia prayed that this William John would live to grow into a man.

November 5th, the Post Office was changed from Mountain City to Central City, through the efforts of Colorado's Representative to Congress, Jerome B. Chaffee, a former quartz mill owner and operator in Lake Gulch, Gilpin County.

Mining rose at that period to near the one and a half million dollar-mark and Hugh was elated and proud and satisfied. By that time, Central City was established with comforts and institutions of contemporary civilization. The tastes of its residents ran to fragile French furniture and large brass spittoons, brought in by mule teams over the Virginia Canyon, or the "shelf" road from

Idaho Springs. The genteel antimacassar, which Levinia called "tidies," came into use to protect and decorate the backs and arms of sofas and armchairs.

The Champions didn't go in for French furniture. Lack of money and their decided tastes for more substantial articles, steered them from it and they had no use for spittoons. But Levinia began to make tidies for the one large chair they bought, a Morris-type, which Hugh found very restful after his hard day in the mines.

Up to that time it had been comparatively quiet around the mining camps. The different people there, for work and business, seemed to get along quite well with one another. Hugh was especially so well liked that he had no trouble at all with his fellow workers or those he met after working hours. He liked to be with other people, being less clannish than most Cornish. He had friends among other religions as well as different nationalities.

But with the influx of Irish into the county came unrest. There was a natural antipathy between the Irish and the Cornish, partly because of jealousy over the Cornish hard-rock knowledge and overseeing jobs in the mines, and partly because they came from parts of the Old World in which there had been trouble between them. The island and the British mainland had been at odds for a long time. Then, too, the different religions brought on some of the difficulty, for the Cornish were Protestant, mainly Methodists, and most of the Irish were Catholic.

There were fistfights and brawls when a few drinks made them more quarrelsome and many were somewhat injured. The habitually quiet community was broken by taunting, challenging voices. There were savage wrestling matches between the men to determine who was winner, and the Cornish and the Irish women avoided each other when they could. Even the children carried the quarrelsome attitude, copied from their elders. The Irish children sneeringly called the Cornish "Cousin Jacks" and "Cousin Jennys" and "Petticoats" because of former allegiance to Queen Victoria, while the Cornish offspring called the Irish "Black and Fightin' Irishers" and "Chaws."

Levinia worried about this entire disturbance. She didn't like trouble or violence and was glad her children were too small to get outside and into the midst of the children's spats.

Hugh took pains to avoid fighting, unless it was directed against him or his close friends. Then he made his presence felt; his powerful back and arms taking toll of his adversary and sometimes of the other Irishmen who joined in.

One bright summer day, Levinia took little Edith and the baby out on the front porch while she did some sewing just inside the door of her kitchen. Hearing some loud talking, she looked out and saw a burly Irishman coming down the street from the Parsons' saloon. When he got even with the house, he stopped and, reeling on his feet, began to curse her little ones, calling them Cousin Jack brats. Edith began to cry and Levinia ran out and snatched the children into her arms. Before she could reach the door, he had leaped over the low white fence and reached out to grab her. She screamed and tried to protect her babies from the clutching fingers of the drunken man.

Just as she realized she was no match for him, a German meat cutter ran from the store across the street, a large cleaver in his hand. He drove the man off and sent him down the street. Then he took Levinia into her house and soothed her fright as best he could, while Levinia assured herself her children were not hurt.

That evening, the German took it upon himself to tell Hugh what had taken place and Levinia gave her own version of the incident. Hugh knew the man as a troublemaker when he was under the influence of liquor. As soon as Hugh was sure he was sober, he sought him out and gave him a good, sound beating, and made him realize that he couldn't get by with molesting his family.

About that same time, many Chinese came to Gregory Gulch to placer mine in streams in the county. Natives from Austria and Italy came in large numbers as laborers. They could live on less and accepted lower and smaller wages, which threatened to cause trouble, even to the extent of starting an organization to protect the miners who were established there. Hugh used his far-reaching influence to try to bring about a better understanding. He joined his countrymen in a stand against the lowering of wages and demanded a square deal for the Cornish, with their superior knowledge of mining, a knowledge no other nationality had.

The trouble died out. The Cornish and the others got along quite well, made good citizens and raised their children together. But Levinia found the period a very anxious one.

Chapter 12

Bobtail Tunnel

That summer saw some improvement in the Central City domestic water problems. An excavation for a reservoir was begun in Eureka Gulch where water had been hauled from the springs. At one time, in a certain section of the community, a boy hauled water in a barrel on two wheels drawn by a burro, for seventy-five cents a barrel. Later, two barrels were mounted on a two wheeled cart hitched to a "stringhaltered" horse, whose stiff leg lifted awkwardly at every step he took. Each barrel cost fifty cents. Much later, a tank wagon drawn by a team of horses came to each dwelling and business and for the price of a dollar for three barrels, distribution was made through a long hose.

The Champion water barrels were in the open space under the kitchen which was called "the pit" and "depths," and water had to be carried up the steps and through the trap door for use in the kitchen.

So the work on the reservoir was a welcome event. Everyone waited impatiently for the water mains to be laid throughout the town.

The Bobtail Tunnel was the subject of much discussion and wonder during those days of looking forward. In the history of Gregory Gulch, the Gregory, Bobtail and Gunnel mines were the most famous. The Bobtail was the closest of the three to Hugh's heart because he worked there when he first came to the gold camp, and again when he left Nevadaville, in the first year of his marriage. In fact, he felt a personal interest in the Bobtail ever since he'd been in the vicinity.

The Bobtail lode had been discovered soon after John Gregory had made his own rich find, and was close to it. It was found and worked by the Cotton brothers, who had owned a docked-tailed ox which they hitched to a pronged fork of a tree covered with rawhide. With this they hauled the pay dirt down to the stream for washing. The mine that developed was known as the Bobtail and became the second richest vein in the district.

When Hugh came in 1861, the Bobtail was less than two years old and going strong. He had helped timber the opening shaft and worked in the mine rock until about the time he saved enough money to send for Levinia, when he had had a better offer in the California mine at Nevadaville and went there for a short time. However, he returned to the Bobtail before long because he had a close feeling for the mine and deep respect for A. N. Rogers, who managed it. Besides, the wages there were on a standard that made Hugh sure of getting ahead, which Levinia knew, was the topmost thought he had.

She knew that he understood that his growing family needed security and that the loss of his two older children demanded that he make good in order to help her bear her grief and to spare her the worry about money and how they would get along. Besides Levinia realized, he had to prove to her, and to himself, that he had been right in coming to America and in bringing her here. She was well aware that her husband was plagued by the fear that he would fail in some way and wouldn't reach the place he wanted badly to fill for her and their children. She tried to show him that she didn't mind working along with him and doing without some of the things other women had. She was happy with what they had, she needed only him and the children to make her thankful she had come to join him.

The Bobtail Tunnel, which Levinia heard Hugh brag about as though it were his own, was begun in 1871, after Mr. Rogers had succeeded in getting his company to consolidate the entire holding and work it as a single unit. This gave five hundred more feet of ground to the company and made about five miles of underground workings. With the purchase of a mill in Black Hawk, a short distance down the Gulch, the gold production of the Bobtail Company jumped to over $200,000 a year and plans were made for still greater efficiency in operation, for a larger yield.

The tunnel bore was started at the bottom of the hill near the gulch-like bank between Black Hawk and that part of Central City still known as Mountain City, to drain water from the Bobtail, Fiske and Gregory veins. The Bobtail vein was cut by it at five hundred feet below the surface and, with the tunnel driven through solid rock for twelve hundred feet, a large chamber was formed and machinery was set up there for deep-mine operation, which Hugh claimed was a most unique move in the history of mining.

He explained to her that the necessary power came from the steam of two large boilers, and that smoke from their large fire boxes traveled five hundred and twenty feet to the surface through an old abandoned mine shaft.

The main shaft of the Bobtail, sunk from the level of the tunnel floor, was sixteen feet long by eight feet wide and was divided into four compartments. Two of these were cage shafts. The third was for the pumping machinery and man-way ladders from the lower workings. The fourth was a bucket-way for sinking the shaft deeper. A smaller drum hoist was installed for this purpose.

Ore from the depths far below the tunnel level was hauled by mule power and in trains of steel cars from loading points to stations in the main shaft. Here a loaded car was wheeled onto the floor of the waiting mine cage and hoisted to the tunnel level where, after being sorted, the ore went to the stamp mill in Black Hawk. Later this trackway was extended to the mill and ore trains were unloaded into mill ore bins.

Hugh bragged specifically about A. N. Rogers' inventions: the steel cage and the two-ton steel ore cars. The eight foot long cars were mounted at each end on double-track trucks. Each car body divided in the middle and was hinged at the top. A latch at the bottom locked the two halves of the box in place. Releasing the latch made the two halves part, each half rolling in opposite directions, dumping the contents.

Chapter 13

Another Birth, Progress and Prosperity

On July 10, 1871, the second Lillie was born to the Champions. The new baby was like the first Lillie in more than her name for, being dark and plump and the very picture of health, she looked like the little one they had lost.

Hugh and Levinia found great satisfaction in their children, Edith almost four, William John about two, and the baby Lillie. They felt that the dreams and hopes of years before in Cornwall were at hand.

Good times were with them too, for the gold production in Gilpin County reached $3,237,364 that year and the town grew with substantial buildings while Cornish rockwork continued to appear on every level to terrace the steep slopes of the mountains for further expansion.

The new houses were of soft colors with lacy bargeboard or "gingerbread" trimming. Widows' walks had iron fretwork to decorate them. Even the new furniture was more durable and decorative, made of heavy walnut and mahogany on which flowers and fruits were carved.

Levinia noted with satisfaction that Central City was growing farther and farther from the temporary status she had deplored and was proud of her town's progress. More and more she considered this mountain settlement her home. More and more often she remembered Henry M. Stanley's 1867 description of the area, when he wrote about his trip there.

Nothing can be as idyllic as the lesser hills of Colorado as they stand hemmed in by the weather beaten peaks which loom above them in silent majesty.

Less and less she thought of Cornwall and life there. She had no wish to return and no thought of going back, even on a visit. Instead she thought of having her relatives come to the land she loved.

Already she had written her brothers and sisters of the country and was hopeful they would come and see for themselves. She wished she had money at hand to send them for passage and the fare for the ride across the plains. It was only in such an instance that she felt the lack of money.

At other times, she was sure that Hugh and she would get along, that the Lord would provide if they did His will and tried to do the best they could with what they had.

Late that year, the Methodist Church was finished and was pronounced the best stonework in Colorado Territory. It was built of native stone, the front was pointed and finished to look like hammered granite. It was 89 feet long and 45 feet wide. The tower in center of the front was 85 feet high. The Sanctuary, or auditorium, was 71 by 41 feet and 20 feet high.

The new church was dedicated by Bishop R. S. Foster. The solemn ceremony was a proud one to its members, and to Hugh and Levinia it seemed a personal achievement. It brought what they considered a good omen to their lives in the new world.

With great interest they watched the erection of another building, the Teller House. The progress of Central City and the surrounding vicinity had brought about a great demand for a better and more up-to-date hotel than the Connor House, the best in the community. Its owner boasted that the Connor House had real mattresses made in Chicago, instead of the "hay beds" usually found in such hostelries, but he too agreed that the city needed a better building than his.

The Teller House had grown out of this recognized need. In 1872, the new hotel was opened. It was advertised as having no transoms, which insured more privacy and safety, and there was a safety lock on each door. Running water was installed on each floor, brought through pipes from the Teller Springs in Prosser Gulch, for domestic use and to fight fires.

On Thursday, June 27, 1872, the grand Inauguration Ball was held there with some seventy-five couples of the elite attending. The next day The Daily Register printed the following.

The festivities continued until daylight, when, the large assembly retired to their respective homes. This notice ought to conclude with a grand display of rhetorical pyrotechnics, but charity toward our readers forbids. We have said the ball was a triumph; we now reiterate the declaration.

Levinia and Hugh read about the gala event in great detail from other newspapers and heard personal accounts of the participants. The location of the widely publicized brick Teller House opposite the Methodist Church which they attended, also gave the Champions a new realization of Central City's growth.

What touched Levinia personally at that time was the arrival of her cow and chickens, even a strutting rooster. Somehow, these possessions gave her a feeling of permanence and ownership, at which Hugh first laughed. But he fully understood after she spiritedly explained exactly how she felt about them. First, because they brought her closer to what she'd been used to having all her life and second because she was so sure she could help out by having fresh milk and eggs at hand. She maintained that she might even sell some of the supply if the project worked out as she planned and hoped.

Hugh kissed her and announced to the wide-eyed Edith and William John, that their mother was a very very wonderful woman which made Levinia's heart sing.

From that moment on, Hugh saw that there was plenty of hay and grain for Old Bossy, feed for the chickens and straw for their nests. However, Levinia told herself that he didn't take care of them in any way, didn't even try to learn how to milk the cow. But she was happy in every way about it. She loved doing it all, seeing that her children were cared for and safe in the house before she descended to the back yard to do what she termed "chores."

The mere fact of having the eggs she gathered and the pail of foaming milk repaid her in far more than the money she received from each small sale she made to her neighbors, and Hugh bragged expansively in her presence to his buddies.

That same year, 1872, the first narrow gauge railroad entered the district, penetrated the Rocky Mountains and was completed to Black Hawk. The depot was a stone mill at the lower end of Black Hawk, called "Porter's Folly" by the residents of the mining camps. The building had never been used as a mill because the company had gone broke before the milling machinery had been installed. It stood abandoned in the path of the railroad, and the canyon was so narrow there wasn't enough room on either side to bypass it. So the railroad purchased it and cut large doors at the ends so the entire train could be under cover. (It was used for six years until 1878, when a new depot was built closer to the center of Black Hawk.)

The railroad helped put Central City on the map, for it brought supplies, fresh vegetables and fruit from the plains, and took ore out of the district. In addition, it gave improved passenger service to the residents of The Gulch.

A rig, called a "hack," was driven to Black Hawk from Central City to deliver passengers to the train and to pick up others when the train returned. The "hack" was on the order of a small stage, with seats inside for protection from the weather, and a place in the hood and on top for the baggage and express.

It was drawn by a fast team that gave good service to the people above Black Hawk.

The narrow gauge passenger coaches were small but had red plush seats, a coal stove in one end, (set up on a low platform that held sand for the convenience of smokers and chewers), and was lit by swaying swinging overhead kerosene lamps. As the engine wound around the curves in the track along Clear Creek, it seemed to be coming back around to the coach, the curves were so short.

The biggest drawback any of the passengers found in the trip to Denver by train was the drift of heavy sooty, cinder laden smoke thrown off by the puffing wheezing, yet determined, engine as it labored over the steep grades. The black grime settled over every inch of the coach, covered the window sills and all clothing, smarting eyes at times and shutting off the view from the windows as it drifted by.

Hugh and Levinia were quite excited when their countryman Richard Pearce, (sometimes spelled Pierce) a metallurgist, found pitchblende, a source of uranium and radium, in the Wood Mine in Leavensworth Gulch, north of the town of Russell Gulch.

The mineral which was thrown away by the miners as worthless. As soon as he realized what it was, he got control of the Wood Mine and worked it for pitchblende only. He separated it from its impurities and shipped it to Europe, the only market there was for it at the time. It brought $1.00 to $20.00 a pound. The pitchblend was supposedly used by Madame Currier in her radium research.

Though this discovery didn't help the Champions financially, it added strength to their faith in their own Cornish people and proved to them that there were more and more possibilities in the land they now called their own.

Chapter 14

Fire and Miners' Strike

Around midnight, on January 26, 1873, a fire broke out in the Episcopal Church, a wooden structure on Lawrence Street. The fire burned this building and fifteen others down, among them the Tappan Hardware Store, where the skating rink was, a hotel called The St. Nicholas and three buildings belonging to "Aunt" Clara Brown,[9] a former slave. She was a firm Methodist and one of the most loved characters in The Gulch, a laundress, midwife, as well as a friend to everyone. It was she who, in the days when the Methodists were struggling to keep their church services alive, had held the meetings in her home.

Levinia admired Clara Brown and agreed with Frank Bedford, son of Judge Bedford (of Central City fame between 1870 and 1885), who described Clara Brown: "Clara Brown is black of skin, white of soul and golden of heart."

When the fire broke out in 1873, all the men including Hugh Champion, worked to save the town in the snow-laden wind that swept along the flames. Bucket brigades were organized and diligently and heroically manned. The National Hotel and the Baptist Chapel, opposite the burned church, were saved in a scene of wild commotion, as the fire raged up the street on both sides the rest of that night. Frantic parents on Lawrence Street moved their children and belongings in the dark up to High Street behind them. Dynamite exploded below them in an effort to destroy buildings before the fire, to try to stop it from coming up the street. When all this effort failed, the people and personal possessions had to be moved to Second High Street before they were out of the fire's reach.

---

[9] Aunt Clara Brown, a free slave, was a Presbyterian when she arrived in Central City. She was a charter member of that congregation. She became a practicing Methodist later since that church was avowed Abolitionists.

Fire and Miners' Strike

The J. D. Raynolds brick buildings on Lawrence Street, a powder store below and living quarters for the Raynolds family above, was supposed to be fireproof. But as the fire progressed around it, the tin roof curled in the intense heat and the wood frames of doors and windows were in real danger.

Mrs. Raynolds soaked blankets and sheets, even personal clothing, to protect the wood and the bucket brigade, with Hugh as a member, kept up a steady stream of water to keep the cloth damp. Her bravery and persistence, with the help of the filled buckets, saved not only the powder from blowing up, but her treasured piano which she'd brought with her on the long ox-trip across the plains in the early 1860s.

Eventually, the wind died down, the snow thickened and the fire was extinguished. Kate Raynolds was the heroine in the great loss and the terrible city fright during the night. But that fright and scare weren't enough to force Central City to take precaution against another such fire, a danger Levinia had seen and feared ever since her arrival.

In April President Grant, his wife, daughter and others came to Central City. The townspeople knew they were coming and put down silver bricks, which came from the silver mine at Caribou, for them to walk on from the street to the Teller House. When the President was told the value of the bricks beneath his feet, some $13,000, he could hardly believe it, or that the mine from which the silver had come, had just been sold for $3,000,000 to capitalists in Holland!

This aroused Hugh's interest in the silver strike at Caribou, near Nederland, and made him go there to look it over. But neither he nor Levinia could even guess what significance Caribou would have in their lives.

In the summer, the Episcopal Church members started a new church on East High Street, next to the new stone school. It was built of native granite in Gothic style, and was 64 feet in length and 34 feet in width, with a side tower 13 feet square, from which rose a spire 60 feet in height. The building seated some 300 people. It was opened for services on December 14, 1873.

The bell at the school building next door, called the Episcopal people to Sunday church services for years until the church received the bell formerly used at Christ Church in Nevadaville. This bell had been cast in Boston in 1867 and shipped to the Nevadaville Church, then being built. It had come by ox-team over the miles between the Missouri River and the gold camp.

Another structure, that showed the faith of the residents of Central City and their belief in their town's future, was the St. Aloyisius Academy on Gunnell Hill, behind the Teller House. A flourishing school was opened there by Catholic Sisters and continued over a long period.

In November, after progressive planning and building which was the result of the good times in Gregory Gulch, there came the most serious financial difficulty the county had ever known. It stunned the entire community, affected every family and almost plunged Hugh and Levinia into despair.

One of the principals in the trouble was A. N. Rogers, the manager of the Bobtail Mine and its properties. The other was George Randolph, who controlled several other mining companies in the vicinity. Together, these two men had charge of the lower Central City mining and represented the Eastern capital in that area. Until then their management had brought success and their companies had expanded and prospered for nine years. By 1873, a number of the mines had gone back into individual ownership as many companies failed or broke up.

The policies of Rogers and Randolph had proved profitable until that time. Now the factors joined against them, loans were called in because the increased depth of the mines made mining expenses higher. To save their companies' holdings a drastic step had to be taken, namely a cut in their miners' wages.

The first inkling of what was to come was given to Hugh on November 10. When he went to work at the Bobtail that morning he found notices on the shaft house and tunnel entrances. The notice stated that from that day the wage per shift would be $2.70 instead of the established $3.00!

Angry and indignant, he and the other miners talked it over and decided not to work at all at the reduced wage. They advertised their stand by marching through Central City to Nevadaville, made protesting speeches to all who were within hearing distance. Their angry action electrified the entire Gulch.

During the next few days Levinia was also torn between the two alternatives before the workers: to accept the mine owners' ultimatum or to stand pat against it. The rift between labor and management widened. Some miners working on contract weren't affected but joined the original strikers out of sympathy. The miners met at Turner Hall on Gregory Street in Central City under the leadership of big Tom Terrell, a Cornishman. Together the irate workers decided to form a union to protect their rights and to demand the full $3.00 per day pay.

At once, Rogers and Randolph called a council of mine and mill managers. In that meeting it was decided to set $2.50 as a new wage scale per shift.

Further angered by the abrupt drop from $2.70 to $2.50 per shift, the strikers put on a demonstration. They organized a band and marched up and down Gregory Gulch. They carried placards that said: "We will work for $3.00! No less!"

Other workers joined them until there were three hundred unemployed men. In addition, many "tribute pitch" or "tut-workers," which were really operatives rather than workers for wages, joined the union against the action of Rogers and Randolph. Then all those under contract to the two managers walked out and closed down all the mines in that section. Hastily, the managers made an appeal for substitute workers to keep the mines open.

Trouble came at once. The Sheriff and Marshall were called in and eight strikers were arrested for disturbing the peace. They were fined $200 each and bound over to the next term of court. This unjust decision against the miners made the workers in the Caribou silver district send $150 as a gift to the union to keep on fighting for their rights.

Day after day, the trouble went on and membership in the union grew. Three fourths of the strikers were Cornish and because of their clannishness they stood pat, in spite of what each individual man might have thought in his own mind. They refused to go back to work.

During this time, Levinia fretted and worried that Hugh would be in danger due to the tense situation. He was one of the best and loudest talkers in what he believed and absolutely refused to listen to her or to anyone on the other side. He even turned a deaf ear to Mr. Rogers, of whom he thought a great deal and considered as a friend, and was almost rude in his refusal when the manager wanted to talk to him man-to-man.

Levinia, while as loyal to her countrymen as anyone could be, saw that their vehemence had gotten them into pretty deep trouble and threatened to involve them even more if they kept on. Besides, she figured that there was a personal side to the difficulty and to the long period of unemployment. Money was scarce at best and with Hugh out of work so long, supplies to feed the children were at bedrock, with no chance to get any more. And to make matters worse financially, there was another child on the way.

Because of her fear that her little ones would go hungry if something didn't break up the trouble, she appealed to Hugh to start thinking seriously about his own personal problems. She pleaded that the drop from $3.00 wasn't so bad after all, when his family was being hurt, because he wasn't bringing any money into the home.

At last she got him to listen enough to get his reaction and let her see what he was up against. She could understand that one man, no matter how earnest he was, could do nothing against the large membership, and that principle and loyalty were involved. She realized he was torn between what he thought he should do and ought to do, and what he saw as a wish to do something about it.

Uppermost, she knew he was wrestling with the knowledge that he had no money to feed his family.

Her heart ached for him. She thought that life sometimes crowds a person into problems that make it impossible to stand alone.

She prayed that the end of the strike would come soon and that things would straighten themselves out before it was too late. She refused to look into the future that might hold dire need for her children. She had faith in God's direction and told Hugh of her belief that He would show them the way. But Hugh had little time to give her and less to think, for the union demanded that he take active part in its action.

It was a very strenuous and tense situation and grew worse as union membership grew and grew. There might have been a chance that The Gulch would have been taken over by the Union and the mine managers forced to adhere to the $3.00 per shift standard, if there hadn't been factors against the workers. Times grew increasingly bad, and men were laid off from jobs in other types of business in The Gulch and in Colorado. Men were even laid off from the local railroads. Narrow gauge construction was at a halt. People couldn't pay their taxes and lost some of their personal goods when the authorities decided to seize them as a pledge for payment due.

In addition, the Union was hampered by not being able to present a solid front, since Black Hawk and Nevadaville ignored their cause and enjoyed full-time pay. Then, too, very few of the Cornish, Hugh included, were naturalized. They had no answer when the mine managers argued that if they didn't like it in America and weren't willing to accept what their employers presented, they'd better go back to Cornwall where they belonged!

That brought Hugh and Levinia face to face with the truth. Even though Hugh had filed his intention to become a citizen, and was waiting for the stipulated period to elapse before he could become one, he wasn't one. This emphasized the fact that he, with many Cornish and other foreigners, was willing to accept all the good things that the protection of the United States offered without being an actual part of it.

The real turning point in the strike was an editorial in The Register, suggesting that each man choose for himself in the struggle before him. The article went straight to the heart of the matter.

The favorable circumstances which have enabled the Cornish miners to accumulate over a quarter of a million in the bank of this city and to return to England comfortably fixed for life, have been destroyed by this strike. The two classes cannot long remain in irreconcilable collision. We advise the miners to go back to work at the wages prescribed. Meet the mine owners fairly. They are entitled to as much respect as you are.

Levinia read the article out loud to Hugh, then laid the paper aside as she arranged her thoughts very carefully and made up her mind what to say to Hugh. She realized she mustn't push him too far, for Cornish wives are supposed to await their husbands' decisions in all matters. She knew she had already gone much further than tradition said was wise.

Finally instead of saying one word, she threw herself in his arms for a long silent moment. Then she started to fix some sort of supper from what she had: eggs from her pampered hens, milk from Old Bossy and a quick bread made from the very last of the flour. The children sensed that something serious was going on and were unusually quiet and subdued.

Hugh swallowed the meager fare in silence but she could see his indecision in the anxious glances he threw at her and the three children.

When the little ones had gone to bed, Hugh suddenly announced that he was ready to give in, but was pretty downhearted about going out to see what the others thought about it. Yet he went at once.

After he'd gone, she was glad she hadn't spoken out demanding that he do something about bringing home money to purchase food. She was glad she hadn't tried to take over any of his responsibilities as the head of a Cornish household.

Then she took herself to task for having even thought of influencing Hugh's decision. "I must be careful," she told herself, "to remember that Cornish wives obey without question, no matter the cost and they wait for their husbands to make all decisions and plans."

As the month of December swept down upon the idle men and suffering families with severe cold and heavy snow, the cost of flour, a real necessity in the making of Cornish pasties and many other dishes, rose to over $5.00 a hundred pound sack, while prices of other staples swung upward in proportion. All this brought the miners together in common suffering and they decided to go back to work.

It is very hard for a Cornishman to eat humble pie, to acknowledge he'd been wrong and to admit he'd made a mistake of any kind. Yet Hugh and the others did all three by going back to the jobs that reopened the mines. It didn't help their sober thoughts any to hear that six of their unmarried countrymen, who had leased the old Ophir Mine in Nevadaville, had made $100,000 each in twenty months and had gone back to Cornwall to become independent for life!

Hugh blurted out his bitterness to Levinia about the luck some men had. Some made all the money and others were not able to provide for their families as they wanted.

"Tain't fare! 'Em 'as try th' 'ardest 'n need et most, doan't make out's guld! 'Em 'ad guid luke at 'Vadaville,'em 'as naw'n to take care uv! 'Ee'r bachlers!"

She heard him out, thought over what he'd said before she spoke firmly, risking his reaction to her bold out-spoken and un-Cornishlike wifely words. She said that she'd thought he had come to America to help himself become independent, a free man, a citizen of the United States, instead of a subject of England. Without waiting to hear his criticism, she went on pleadingly, yet decisively, "Hugh, 'usband, w'en 'ee sent fer me t' come 'ere t' "ee, my 'eart came n' 'ead uv me. I wanted t' live 'th 'ee in th' new country, to 'elp 'ee 'n th' rest w'o live 'ere. I expected t' work 'ard 'n be a part 'f th' new land. I doan cum t' gamble 'n 't taake back 'ome w'at I caan git 'ere. N 'ee 'ave ben with me 'n all my plans. T'ese're 'ees plans, too, Hugh. T'at w'y I love 'ee mor'n ever, an' I tank God fer a' His blessin's."

As she waited, almost fearfully, Hugh seemed to study it all over. Finally, he smiled ruefully and said, "Vinia, 'ee said wa'at be troo," and his mood lightened.

But in spite of that statement, she knew he was not reconciled to the drastic cut in his wages and what hurt the most, was the fact that it had been thrust down his throat in such a way he had to accept it. Levinia felt that he had also considered some future move that took all his thoughts, rendering him so preoccupied, she was puzzled. But she waited in silence.

Chapter 15

Move to Caribou

Levinia soon learned why Hugh hadn't talked much. For in January of the next year, 1874, he announced that he was taking the family to Caribou to work in silver mine there. He said he had already spoken for a good big solid cabin in the town and that he had a good job that paid twice as much as he was getting at the Bobtail. He told her they were to move in two weeks.

Levinia was stunned. To be confronted with such a move in the middle of winter and to be told, without even talking it over, was more than she could take at the moment. She bit her lips to hold back her remonstrating words.

At last, wanting to be reasonable and understanding that Hugh was unhappy in his present job, she said almost lightly, "'N w'at t' do'th Old Bossy, n' chix, 'nth' 'ouse?"

Before he could answer, she added seriously, "Edith's in school, 'n moast 'alf 'er term's left."

She knew Hugh sensed her disapproval of his plan to move, for he shrugged with unusual impatience where the children were concerned, and gave no answer. He'd been anxious about Edith going to school, and proud that she could enter at five years of age.

Levinia wanted to scream at him for his seeming indifference and for his dictatorial manner. But his softened look as his eyes swept over her body swollen with a coming child, stopped her.

"A guid school theer," he said almost gently, "'N I be ready fer the baaby cumin.' 'Ee minin' comp'ny there 'as a doctor, 'a theer's a midwife in town. 'Ee'll luk af'er 'ee and th' childers."

Though this news relieved her somewhat, she couldn't forget that Hugh had gone to Caribou and had made all the arrangements, just as all Cornish males did in the same circumstances, without consulting their wives! But how could she have thought that Hugh would be any different from those others? How could she have hoped that he would do any differently when she'd been raised to expect exactly such high-handedness in Cornish husbands?

She severely reminded herself that she was the one who was different. She wanted to defy the Cornish customs in that instance. She longed to have some say rather than to take orders and accept. That thought was a sobering one and demanded self-examination. But not now, she admonished silently, and forced herself to speak agreeably.

"I'll go see 'bout 'avin' thin's taaken caare uv," and went to the house recently built next door on the left, where her dear friend Bessie Andrews lived. She bought milk and eggs when Levinia could spare them.

Mrs. Andrews promised to feed the chickens, gather the eggs and feed and milk Old Bossy.

"I'll look after your 'ouse, too," she volunteered and assured Levinia she'd be back home soon. "That 'igh country's worse'n Nevadaville. No un 'th good sense stays 'n Caribou long," she said with such conviction that Levinia, sad at leaving the home she loved so dearly and the pets to which she was so attached, took heart.

She was dubious about leaving Central City. Caribou, at 9,800 feet above sea level, was 1,300 feet higher than Central City's 8,500. She had heard the winters there were much more severe than in her home town, that the timberline silver camp was snowed in for long periods when a bad storm hit. Yet she knew she would be ready to take what came and stand by Hugh. Resolutely she made up her mind to do just that.

They were fortunate in having a nice day for the move to Caribou. The sun was shining brightly, melting the light snow that had fallen the night before. Hugh was cheerful and eager. He helped get the children ready. All three were excited by the trip they were to make. Seven-year old Edith could hardly restrain herself and five-year old Will asked questions about what he would see along the road as they drove. Even Lillie, at three, seemed to realize this was a very special day.

Levinia was glad they didn't have to take furniture and dishes and thankful the cabin in Caribou had everything except bedding.

Finally they were ready. The blankets and pillows were tied together and the food was boxed and fastened. Then Jim Mitchell drove up to the door in a two-seated buggy drawn by a team of horses. They were soon on their way, the children and Levinia on the back seat watched with only their noses visible in the scarves Levinia had tied around their heads. Jim and Hugh sat in the front seat discussing the ever-important topic of mining and the comparison between gold and silver mining.

Move to Caribou

They had almost completed the trip when Hugh informed Levinia that Jim would stay in their house while they were away and would put his own bed in the smaller bedroom upstairs.

She flashed a happy smile at both men when they looked back at her and let out a sigh of relief over the arrangement Hugh had made.

From Jim's placid look, she knew he'd thought she had planned this as she had planned for him to stay in the cabin when they'd started to Mexico. So she didn't tell him differently, although she did remark later that their house would be well looked-after with Mrs. Andrews on hand during the day and Jim in it at night.

The cabin in Caribou was what Levinia termed in surprise, as a real 'ouse! It had two bedrooms at the back and a very large room on the front. One end of that room was the kitchen and the other end a spacious living room.

Hugh explained that it was the home of a mine boss and his family. They had gone back east where the man had to undergo a very serious operation. He had a year's leave of absence to recover before returning to his job. Hugh said he'd made a good bargain when the owner agreed to let Hugh and his family occupy the cabin for looking after it for the year he would be away.

As Levinia walked through the rooms and took everything in, she saw that Hugh had been right about it being a good cabin. It was very well built and furnished better than any place she had lived, both in Cornwall and in America.

Both bedrooms were covered with good quality, wall-to-wall carpet and heavy throw rugs almost covered the sitting-room and kitchen space. A big kitchen range with a warming oven and a reservoir to heat water, gave off enough heat to warm the entire house and there was a big fireplace in the other end of the room.

There were pictures on the walls and ornaments on the mantle and tables in the sitting-room. There were "parlor" chairs and six dining room chairs around the family-sized table that divided the room into its two parts. The "good" dishes and bright cutlery warmed Levinia's heart. She had never been able to use, much less afford such fine quality!

She thought, "It's wonderful to live 'ere! I'll love usin' these beautiful things!"

She hated to bring in her old bedding and worn clothes but didn't voice her thoughts. Hugh was bitter enough about his failure to give her what he'd expected so she didn't complain in any way.

They had their first meal in the new home before Jim left to take the rig back to the livery in Central City.

After Jim had gone Hugh said soberly, "It'll be 'ard gettin' a man's good as Jim t'work'th." She knew he wished Jim had seen fit to come to Caribou with him and continue to work as his partner, the necessary arrangement among the Cornish.

Levinia knew that Hugh had someone in mind. Before he started to work in the silver mine, she met the man, a burly Cornish newcomer to America.

For several days, during which they got settled and laid in what groceries they had money to buy, the weather was good and they could see the rugged tops of the bare mountains above timberline. Hugh explained to the children that the abrupt line where trees and shrubs couldn't grow was because it was too high and cold and windy.

Edith started to school in the rooms rented for that purpose and readily slipped into the prescribed routine, but Levinia thought the child wouldn't do as well here as in the Central City school, where she thought Mr. Hale had set up such a wonderful system. Not that she knew much about schools. Hugh and she had had only a little schooling. Hugh had attended a "dames" school for a short while in Cornwall and then became a "helper" in a mine at the age of nine. She had had a better chance than he, for she had gone to school for some seven years and had taught Hugh after school, instead of playing all the time when they were together as children.

The Champions found the house in Caribou very comfortable. A very large store of cut wood in a shed built onto the house made them certain they had a winter's supply for the stove and fireplace.

Hugh said he liked his job and his partner and the men he worked for and with. Most of all, he liked the extra money he was making.

"Jim's a fool for 'angin 'ith old Rogers after w'at 'ee done to us 'bout the $3.00 a day," he declared. But Levinia felt that he was having a bad time with himself when he remembered that Jim had been loyal to Mr. Rogers, not only before the strike but after it was settled, while he had quit working for him as soon as he found a better job in Caribou. She realized that after the first indignant refusal to listen to Mr. Rogers, Hugh had been drawn by loyalty between Mr. Rogers and the Cornish workers in the Union. In her heart, she was glad Hugh's loyalty had been manifest, though she wondered if it had been shown in the proper channel. But that had been Hugh's choice. Unless she could help him, she would say nothing and would stand by him.

She tried to do that by observing, "Jim 'as no family, 'ee can work fer less." And the matter was dropped.

She didn't know until two weeks or more later that Hugh's increased wage was due to the extreme danger he encountered in the silver mine. She learned of it from the wife of one of the men who worked in the mine. She had come to call upon Levinia and told her that the rocks in this mineshaft weren't as solid as at Central City, so cave-ins were to be expected more often and were very hard to control. Hence, Hugh's higher pay as timberman here was an inducement when the dire need for an experienced and reliable foreman of the timbering crew had arisen.

Levinia prayed for her husband's safety, and she bitterly denounced to herself the fact that more money had driven him into taking the more dangerous job.

She told herself, "If I'd knowed the truth, I wouldn't've let 'im come 'ere," but admitted she couldn't have done anything about it. The Cornish, she reminded herself, are stubborn and unreasonable at times.

She made up her mind not to tell Hugh she knew of the danger in his job. Instead, she began to make wishful plans to go back home as soon as possible and to figure how she could help make up the difference in pay there so that Hugh wouldn't feel he had to accept this greater danger.

Putting Jim Mitchell's bed in one of the upstairs rooms made her realize that she could take in boarders and roomers by using the extra rooms in their home. She knew she would have no difficulty getting men to eat at her table. She already had a reputation as a good cook and there were many Cornishmen in the Mountain City community who would appreciate Cornish cooking. She planned this venture very carefully and silently while she waited for the arrival of the new baby. She decided that Hugh was not to know of her plan until the right moment. At that time, she would tell him how she could help out financially.

Chapter 16

A Difficult Birth in a Snowstorm

Six weeks passed. Her child was due.

She had contacted the midwife, a Mrs. Richards, who asked all particulars of previous confinements, how many and if quick or drawn-out, and so on. She seemed pleased to learn that all previous births had been absolutely normal and on the whole much easier than any even Levinia had heard about.

"The job of lookin' after you will be easy," Mrs. Richards said complacently, and lightly dismissed the coming event with the words, "You send for me when the time comes. I'll hold the date open." Levinia felt confident and didn't worry about how her children would get along while she was unable to take complete charge of them while Hugh was at work. The fact that there was a company doctor helped her too but the thought of a possible heavy snow made her uneasy.

She hoped the nice weather would hold until after the baby's birth but her wish wasn't granted. On the night of March 4th, her beautiful day, a blizzard descended upon Caribou. The wind, laden with snow, was high and whirled its burden into every crevice and low place, then leveled it out to bury everything beneath it and prevent anyone from going outside.

It blew all night. The next morning Hugh had to keep the lamps lit, even after nine o'clock. He remarked that it was a great blessing he didn't have to leave the house to get wood and announced that there was an extra barrel of water besides the one they were using, which he explained was over half full.

Though he couldn't go to work, and Edith couldn't go to school, he assured the children everything would be all right, but his troubled eyes met Levinia's questioningly. She knew he was worrying about the baby's coming while the weather was so bad.

She smiled to indicate she was fine and went about her kitchen work.

A Difficult Birth in a Snowstorm

Hugh tried to look outside. The snow had covered the windows completely, and when he opened the door, he found that the snow had drifted so tightly, it formed a front so solid that very little snow fell into the room. The doorway was a wall of snow! It was impossible to shovel a way out since there was no place to put the snow he would bring into the room. As far as he could make out, the drifts were even with the house, if not over it.

He stood on a chair and tried to look out of the window, just under the eaves. He couldn't see beyond the house.

Hugh's troubled eyes, met Levinia's. She smiled at him and he turned in relief to talk to the children who were excited by wind that howled around the house and the fact that they had to have the lights on in the daytime. Having their father at home when it wasn't Sunday was a reason for celebrating, which they did. They amused themselves with noise and play and drew him into it whenever they could.

Levinia was glad they were busy for she was beginning to feel uneasiness, a strange constriction above her waistline, the region where she was carrying the child. It was a dull fullness rather than a pain. She had never felt such a sensation before.

She didn't mention it to Hugh. It was nothing to do with childbirth, she was sure. But the baby had changed position and was higher than it had been the day before. She knew delivery would be soon.

She worried all that evening but kept it to herself. There was nothing to report, she told herself. But she was afraid the child was turning, or had turned in her womb, so that it wouldn't be in position to be born. She realized what a breech birth would entail. She remembered old wives tales about such births.

She then prayed for help and guidance and realized she had to prepare for any and every possibility. She faced the situation squarely. Neither the midwife nor the doctor could get there and Hugh had never been present when the children had come. He hadn't even asked her about childbirth. He had taken it all as a matter of fact. It was a woman's work or as she had heard him put it, a woman's privilege. So she knew he would be of little help except to carry out the instructions she might give him. She was on her own until the child came. Then Hugh would have to take over and do what she told him.

She thought, "I have the full responsibility. I can't shift that, not even the worry of what I almost know is wrong. Perhaps my life and that of my baby hangs on what I do with God's help."

Labor pains really set in and made her aware that the birth was at hand, though the child was still in the wrong position.

She told Hugh quietly, "The baby's on its way."

She could see that the statement bowled Hugh over. He swore to himself.

73

He looked as helpless as she knew he felt. He slumped into a chair, then sprang to his feet demanding, "W'at'll us do?"

She smiled at him as she did at her children when they were bewildered and turned to her for reassurance. She spoke very quietly and gave directions for each step in the anticipated event: a good fire in the stove and fireplace, water on to heat, sheets and cloths at hand, the protecting pad on her bed, sterilized scissors, string, oil, a receiving blanket, baby shirts, bands, and blankets. She deliberately omitted the fact that unless the child turned, they were in for great trouble, even death. It would be soon enough to tell him when she was sure.

Hours later, after much futile suffering on her part, she knew something had to be done to turn the baby. She went back over all the information she had from midwives' tales of such cases, nothing sure or authentic, but it was all she had on which to fall back. She had to try out what she had heard, and then had dropped aside as not worth retaining. Now, she recalled every bit of information she had heard from the women who had told the tales of difficult births from the same wrong position.

When she'd assembled the scant and inconclusive knowledge, she called Hugh close and told him to bring additional sheets and fold two of them into thick strips. She directed him to place them around her body just above the child and fasten them tightly, then to work gently with the strips to turn the baby's head downward, and its buttocks away from their present position.

Hugh leaned over her anxiously. "W'ats wrong, Vinia?" he demanded.

Bluntly, between the pains that racked her body, she explained what had to be done and why. He sensed her fear and fell to his knees beside the bed. He seemed to have lost his strength. She spoke sharply, the words ending in a moan she couldn't keep back, behind twisting lips, "Hugh, you've got 't'elp me! I can't do this alone."

He tried to do as she directed, manipulate the unborn child beneath the folded strips. But his fear of hurting her and the baby kept him from working with any effect.

It wasn't until she lay exhausted from her futile labor that she knew he realized she would soon be beyond help.

His frantic cry reached her dull senses. "Wake hup, Vinia! Tell me again'n show me w'at t' do!"

She revived and repeated her instructions. Then, encouraged by his efforts, she worked with him to use the sheets as pressures to push the baby about. Hugh worked faithfully. His broad back bent tirelessly, his big square hands gentle but firm, his eyes darted from her moist strained face to the task he alone could and must do in an effort to save her life and the child's.

A Difficult Birth in a Snowstorm

At last he told her the little body, maneuvered by his fingers with the sheet folds, had moved and guided her hand to prove it. She tried to smile, to show him he was right but the smile turned into a grimace as severe pain cut through her body.

From that moment on, it was Hugh's confidence that held her at her work. His gentle voice kept her informed of the child's different positions and made her understand from what he said that it would be a normal birth from then on.

She thought, "Now I know what to do." Her self confidence flowed back. In the seconds of respite from labor she told Hugh to build up the fires and be ready when she told him what must be done next.

By the time the birth was almost completed she had schooled him in minute detail, so when the baby came he was ready. Shaken inside as she knew he was, but determined and confident on the surface for her sake.

It was only after the child cried and Hugh had tied the cord in two places and cut between them as she directed, then wrapped the slippery, squirming little body in a warmed blanket and placed it close to the open oven door, that she noticed that the wind still howled. Somehow it didn't matter now. The baby was there, born March 5, 1874.

She gave Hugh further directions concerning her own cleanliness and care. She spoke in a tired voice she found hard to make loud enough for him to hear. She heard him ask questions. She knew he was doing what she told him, but she was hardly awake. It seemed to her that she was returning from a dream to talk to him. She knew he had said little Albert was asleep. She felt him draw the blankets up around her shoulders, his voice told her to rest, rest, rest. She roused herself a little when he buried his head in the pillow beside her and said, "I love 'ee, 'Vinia, wife."

Her hand, limp with weariness a second before, rose at once to his dark hair. "God 'elped 'ee save me and the baby," she whispered, then knew no more for several hours.

When she awoke, she was confused by the lights that were still on. She listened. She heard nothing. The wind had gone down. By straining her ears and lifting her head a little from the pillow, she could hear subdued voices in the big room beyond her bedroom, then the faint sound of dishes. She was about to call out that she was awake and hungry, when the door opened and a fair little head appeared as Edith peeped in. Cautiously, as though warned to be quiet and gentle, the child slowly approached, her big blue eyes meeting Levinia's anxiously.

Levinia called to her lovingly, holding out her hand to welcome her, but the little girl was still cautious. She stepped up to the bed with such sober restraint that Levinia had to laugh at her. "Kiss me, Edith," she said and held out both hands to draw her into her arms.

Over the child's head as she held her close, she saw Hugh and the other two children come into the room. Will hung back manfully, but Baby Lillie ran to the bed and began to clamber up to get close. Hugh lifted her so that Levinia could put an arm around her, then she called Will. The boy, seemingly reassured by his mother's voice and smiling lips, came swiftly to kiss her.

"Ave 'ee seen little Albert?" she asked him. He grinned with importance and said. "'Ee's so small 'ee can't play 'ith me!" Then he straightened up to show how tall and strong he was.

Levinia smiled up at Hugh, who explained to Will that at one time he'd been even smaller than the baby. Then he brought baby Albert to her. With her husband looking on proudly, Levinia thanked God out loud, for His help and care the night before and Hugh added a fervent "Amen."

The next day was also very vivid in their memories. Cut off from the outside and shut in by the snow, they wondered how and when they would get out. They talked about the mines and the school and wondered if the entire camp was isolated.

After still another survey of the situation, impatient Hugh noticed that the snow line had dropped a bit from the top of a back window. By standing on a chair, he could see bright sunshine on bare ground beyond where the storm's wind had blown the snow away to build drifts around the house!

He spread a canvas on the floor just inside the back door and then opened the door itself. He shoveled the snow wall at the door onto canvas, and then tunneled through to the bare spaces he'd seen beyond. From that position, he could look around. He realized that if he'd known the facts, he could have shoveled the door out and avoided the drifts around the house. He would have seen that he could have called the doctor and the midwife in when Levinia needed their help. At the same time, he wondered if either or both could have done more for Levinia and for little Albert.

He hurried to Mrs. Richard's home. He told her the baby had arrived in the storm and explained the complications of its birth. The woman was silent while she digested the facts and then said soberly that if she'd been there, she could have done nothing more, perhaps not as much. She had had no experience of that kind in all her midwife services or in all her own large family.

She went back with Hugh to take charge of his house. She first questioned Levinia about her condition and examined the baby, and found vivid marks on his body from the pressure, perhaps of Hugh's strong fingers trying to turn the delicate little form. She advised Hugh to have the doctor look the baby over and examine Levinia to see that she was all right. Then she went to work

A Difficult Birth in a Snowstorm

on the house and kept the children occupied with her activity, while Levinia rested and Hugh went for the doctor. The physician said Levinia was doing very well after her ordeal of the baby's prolonged birth. He found that little Albert hadn't been hurt, just a bit bruised during enforced turning. He told Hugh he thought he had saved the lives of his wife and child by doing what he had done.

"Ee tole me w'at t'do," Hugh said, motioning to Levinia.

The doctor asked where she had learned about how a baby might be turned in its mother's body. She explained that it had been more or less hearsay. She had known no real case, only heard simple talk, perhaps a bit of bragging by some woman who wanted to be thought an able midwife. He smiled with a somewhat superior air and made no comment.

When the doctor left, Hugh and Levinia smiled at each other. Now that the danger was over, they had an even better understanding and a much closer bond in their memories of that anxious night.

Later that day, Hugh checked on the storm's passage through the silver camp. He found that the mines had been affected very little by the storm's raging fury, but the school was not yet opened. All in all, there was but little damage to report and no lives were lost.

Chapter 17

Fire in Central City

Mid morning May 21, 1874, a bright sunny day in Caribou, a messenger sent by the manager of the mine where Hugh worked, arrived at Levinia's door. He told the families of the miners that a great fire was raging in Central City and the men had gone to help fight it.

The fire, rumor said, had started around 9:00 o'clock that morning in a shack occupied by a Chinese laundryman. He had been burning incense over live coals in a religious ceremony.[10] Levinia realized the great danger to her beloved city. She envisioned Dostal Alley on Spring Street, which led off from Main and Gregory Streets, where a number of Chinese lived in a row of tinder dry closely built, frame shanties and log cabins. She prayed for the lives of those the fire threatened, for saving their properties and for the safety of the fire fighters. At the same time she realized that even her own home might be taken.

She had to wait until Hugh, blackened and worn-out, returned before she could know how badly the fire had been and how it had spread. Hugh told her that their own home had been miraculously spared.

Hugh's story was very dramatic. The smoke from Dostal Alley was seen by downtown residents and businessmen, who rushed to try to quench it before it spread. The fire alarm was sounded and the bucket brigade called. But the creek was dry! There was no water with which to fight! The men tried to demolish the buildings to which the fire was spreading with axes, but the intense heat drove them back and they barely escaped with their lives. The flames increased in strength and became more and more intense! In fifteen minutes, the fire raced down Gregory Street at right angles to

---

10 Much maligned, the Chinese were blamed for starting the fire of 1874. However, it was generally accepted that the true cause was due to a faulty chimney flue.

Dostal Alley and Main Street, dooming the whole business section of town and threatening the entire city.

The people wild with fear of losing everything they had, rushed to save what they could. Main Street was piled high with goods to be taken away to safety. The few brick buildings along Main Street were thought safe, but the fire destroyed everything in front of it, rushing along Main Street two ways at once. It crumbled the brick structures without an effort and lapped up buildings across the street with fifty foot tongues of fire.[11]

Hugh explained that it looked as though the fire would turn the corner up Eureka Street and down Lawrence. So a council was held in the Teller House, where the manager had attached a hose to the buildings reservoir, which was fed by pipes from springs up the Gulch. There were two other wells a little farther up the creek that were also attached for use. Those at the meeting decided to make a stand at the Teller House and at the stone Register-Call-Masonic Building across the street.

When the fire turned the corner, its progress up Eureka Street was stubbornly fought for some three hours by sweating men. They guarded the two strong buildings by using the water from the Teller House.

At the same time, the fire's sweep along Lawrence Street proved even more threatening because it was started up Casto, or Bates Hill, where a residential district had been developed. The fire fighters destroyed some front residences to prevent the fire from leaping over First High Street and taking the entire hill.

As he had the year before, when the fire broke out in the Episcopal Church on Lawrence Street, Hugh fought at the brick Raynolds Powder Building, chosen as a stopping place on that street.[12] Once again Kate Raynolds and a bucket brigade, using water from a nearby well, saved the building though several others were burned in an effort to drive the flames back toward Dostal Alley, where it had started.

Levinia heard more about that awful day as separate stories came to Caribou. In one account she learned that the cashier of the bank at the Main and Eureka corner had put the bank's currency and securities in a large lard can. She then sent it with the Negro janitor, Henry Poyner, to his home on Second High Street, which seemed out of the fire's reach. The Negro, one of Aunt Clara Brown's twenty relatives she'd brought from the South to The Gulch at her own expense, buried the can under the porch of his house. He brought it back, intact, several days later. When the fire had died down enough for the cashier to open the vault into which he had thrust the scales, account books,

---
11 The only brick building on main street that survived the fire was the Roworth Block, built in 1864.
12 The Raynolds' building is constructed of cut stone, not brick.

and important papers, he found that the intense heat had scorched some of the papers, but not enough to destroy any one record.

Another story she heard was that a Chinaman who was thought to have started the fire in his religious zeal, had been cornered by irate citizens. He was abused by them, while they threatened to lynch him. He was saved by the quick thinking and bravery of some of the town's leaders, who stood between him and the eager crowd of would-be lynchers and held them off until he could be rushed out of town in a buggy drawn by a very swift horse.

There was a lighter vein in the story of men sent out to protect and remove the contents of Roworth's brick storehouse on Spring Street (the former Seavy Building, built in 1868) from a renewed threat of fire from smoldering ashes. Someone, either accidentally or with intent, opened a cask of liquor from the cellar of the building. The mob drank and went wild until overcome by drunkenness when they sank into a stupor. It was thought that some of the men had been driven to desperation from the loss of everything they owned. Others were over-tired from fighting the fire, and some were the usual run of drifters who took a drink whenever they could and under any and all circumstances. At any rate, the liquor took over and memory was blotted out for some for a time.

Eyewitnesses reported that those left homeless in the conflagration that night, moved to Gunnel Hill behind the Teller House and near the Catholic School, the St. Aloysious Academy.[13] That night they built fires to cook their suppers. Later, the refugees laid out blankets they had saved and rolled up in them to get what sleep they could. From that position on the hill, the victims of the fire could look down on the town where an occasional flame would leap up from live embers, reminding them of the terrible experiences they had gone through in the six hours the fire raged.

At the same time, the people in the town below who saw the flickering campfires on the hillside where the flames hadn't reached were thankful the fire had broken out in the daytime and that there had been no lives lost.

During the night the law officers had a great deal to do. The trains that had brought help and equipment to the stricken Gulch that afternoon brought others who intended to prey on the town in the dark hours of the night. The sheriff and his regular men, reinforced by deputies sworn in for the occasion, stood guard all night over safes and vaults and goods, and saw that the would be looters left town next morning on the very first train.

By the next night, the more fortunate residents of upper Eureka Street, and on the hills that had been out of the fire's range, or had been saved by the valiant efforts of the fire fighters, opened their homes to those who had

---

13 The Aloysious Academy on Gunnell Hill was built in 1875 and torn down in 1936.

lost everything. Meetings were held to discuss the future of Central City. The citizens were undaunted; their faith unchanged. They made plans to rebuild their stricken town.

Levinia and Hugh, thankful their little home and belongings had been spared, took the children and drove over from Caribou to see what remained of Central City. They were appalled at its ruins. There was very little left of the business section. They looked with awe at the Teller house, The Register-Masonic Building the Raynolds Powder Residence, the bulwarks of defense against the ravishing flames and at the Raworth Storage building, which still stood.

As they drove about in the desolation, Hugh told her more of the terrible moments he had gone through in fighting the fire. He had been sent with others to the worst danger spot at the moment, Lawrence Street, to help prevent the fire from taking the residences on the hill above that street.

Central City after the fire.
Photo courtesy of Denver Public Library, Western History Collection.

"Fightin', sweatin', tighten' more, never stoppin' never givin' hup, even when the fire burned 'ee's 'ide through the clothes 'ee wore," Hugh said soberly. Levinia put her arm through his as they sat on the seat of the rented rig with Edith and Will in the back seat, Lillie in front between her parents and baby Albert on his mother's lap. They stopped at their own home to see how things were and to show their new son to the neighbors, but they didn't stay long. Levinia remarked that she felt quite formal, like society folks, in making such short calls.

She knew Hugh understood her great love for her home and pets. They stood in the back yard beside Old Bossy and among the chickens. He looked up at the house and smiled, then said, "Tis hour hown 'ome." His eyes were soft as they met hers, which told her he loved the modest place.

It was the moment she'd waited for. She spoke quickly, her heart in her words. "Hi want to come back 'ome, Hugh, as soon as 'ee can bring hus. Hi can keep boarders and roomers to 'elp out the difference hin wages hin Caribou and 'ere. Hi 'ope hand pray 'ee'll give hup that dangerous job and come back 'ere to work. Hi fear fer 'ee in the silver mine. Please, Hugh, bring me hand the younguns 'ome for good soon."

She could see that he welcomed neither the idea nor the offer but he didn't refuse. Instead, he seemed to be thinking deeply. He put Edith and Will, who were reluctant to leave the old home and the pets, into the buggy. He stood and looked at the house a long time. He walked down the street to look back as though studying the side of the house. But he didn't explain what he'd been sizing up nor what he was thinking. He merely got into the rig and drove off toward Caribou.

When the older children talked about what they had seen and thought about their home, Hugh silenced them with a motion of his hand, all it took for obedience, and the family rode on without conversation all the way back to Caribou.

Levinia was glad for the silence, for her thoughts were galloping over what she'd said to Hugh. She worried he would take her words as an acknowledgement that she thought he couldn't provide for his family, that she wasn't pleased with the home he had obtained for her in Caribou. She asked herself if he thought she was trying to interfere with his job and if he considered her an off-track Cornish wife by speaking out and making plans without his first mention of them.

She thought, "I don't want to be the kind of wife the Cornish is at home. I want to carry half our load. I want to think things over for myself without waiting for Hugh to map out every move we are to make.

Yet she admitted, she wanted to be the wife Hugh wanted and needed.

She was unable to reach a conclusion that would solve her problem. When Hugh lifted her and the baby down in front of the house in Caribou, she was still troubled. Hugh smiled at her and looked under the shawl at the sleeping boy, then helped Edith and Will out of the rig.

Levinia was surprised to find Mrs. Richards there to welcome them. There was a fire in the fireplace to drive out the chilly evening air of the high altitude. The teakettle sang on the stove, supper was ready, the table set and the chimneys on the lighted lamps were clean and shining.

Her heart lightened at Hugh's realization that she would be very tired after her trip, so had had things made ready when she arrived. She looked at Hugh, who smiled in understanding and nodded, well pleased with himself, when she murmured, "'Tank 'ee, Hugh."

Hugh made two more trips to Central City that summer. The first time, he went without explaining why. When he returned he didn't say one word about his trip, but she could see that he was very thoughtful and preoccupied, so she knew he had a serious reason for going. She also knew that the trip hadn't turned out as he had hoped.

She realized full well that if things go well, the Cornish are on top of the world in spirit. If there are reverses, their down-hearted moods betray them. Yet, on the whole, she knew they are willing to face any danger or any threat to themselves or to their loved ones. Loyalty is one of the most important traits in their character.

So, Levinia understood that her husband was trying to bring about something that wasn't going smoothly and waited for his serious mood to change.

After the second trip to Central City, as unexplained as before, he returned in much better spirits, and entered the house with happy words of greeting for each member of his family. Then, abruptly, he announced that they were packing up and going home at once. He had a job at the Bobtail and had made arrangements to have the Caribou house lived in by a new manager of the silver mine, where he had been working.

When Levinia looked at him in surprise, questions on her lips, he said, "We'll be 'ome this winter and the children'll start to school t'ere."

Levinia felt relieved, for Will would go to school next year and Edith, she felt sure, would do better in a larger school.

"Mr. Rogers?" she dared to ask. "'Ee said 'ee's glad't 'ave me back," he answered and she knew he was pleased.

She thought she'd better mention taking in boarders and roomers before she began to pack. So she volunteered, "Jim can stay upstairs and I'ave 'is meals'th us."

He nodded. "Ee knows that. I told 'im," he said. Then he added, "Hi'm afraid it'll be 'ardon 'ee, Vinia, takin' Jim in hand all, but we'll be 'ome again, as 'ee said 'ee wanted t'be." He stopped and eyed her soberly.

She went to him and, clinging to his arm, looked at him. "Work's never 'ard on me, Hugh. I'm hall right again after Albert. I do want t'be in our 'ome again, and to 'elp 'ee with the livin' expenses make me 'appier."

He patted her shoulder, but she realized he could not make enough at his job to keep her from taking on the extra work that would be involved.

She decided she'd better not say anything about having more men than Jim. Jim's staying was enough for a starter. She planned to let Hugh into the idea gradually and went about packing with happiness in her heart.

There was quite a celebration in the community when they moved back. The neighbor women, with their husbands and children, came in with prepared dishes for supper and remained until bedtime, filling the three rooms to overflowing. After supper, they sang Cornish songs, and the men talked mining, pro and con, in the parlor, while in the kitchen the women discussed their children, who were playing in the bedroom.

After the happy return, things got back on their former footings. Hugh went to work at the same mine, Edith resumed her school routine and Levinia was busy with her household, her children and her pets. The only changes were Will's entering school, walking up the steep slope with Edith and Jim's presence as a boarder and roomer.

It was Jim who, realizing that Levinia wanted to include more men in this project, suggested at supper one evening that he tell three Cornish bachelors they might get room and board with the Champions.

It was as simple as that. Hugh made no objection, so Levinia told Jim to report that the three could move in as soon as she was ready.

Now that the move was made, Hugh scouted around at once and got two second-hand double beds and put them in the large room upstairs. Levinia got blankets, made up the beds and laid in extra groceries and supplies.

The project worked out well. The children were fed earlier in the evening and sent to the parlor to amuse themselves, while Levinia reset the table and fed the men.

After the meal, the boarders went upstairs or out for the evening. This left the family together for Bible reading and prayer which was the habit Levinia had formed from the very beginning of her stay in America.

The older children helped with the dishes and cared for the younger children. Edith, now eight, was a regular little mother to the baby and watched Lillie, while Will, six, brought water and wood from the cellar before and after school.

Chapter 18

Grasshopper Plague, A Child Nearly Dies, Another Birth

At that time, Hugh told Levinia boastfully, that the Bobtail Mine Tunnel had grown into a smooth running gold-producing industry with over thirty miles of underground work and three stamp mills. The company had had a gold production of three and a half million dollars since 1864. With A.N. Rogers at its head and the five hundred men hired, they produced a hundred tons of ore each day!

Hugh also reported that Hill's Smelter at Black Hawk had been enlarged by the addition of three more smelters and seven more calcining furnaces, which made Hugh say, "'Eee's place bound to get ahead and grow much more."

He was right. The smelter grew to a maximum of eight groups of buildings and seventeen furnaces. It occupied four acres and had a capacity of fifty-two tons of ore per day.

In comparison, the other mines and mills were doing very well indeed, making Central City a growing town with an enviable future.

But the good times were blotted out that summer by the worst plague of grasshoppers the region had known. Grasshoppers migrated from the plains in greater numbers than in 1864 and 1867, each of which had been considered a real calamity.

In The Register, Levinia read. As the sun reached the meridian, countless millions of grasshoppers were seen in the air while the atmosphere for miles high was literally crowded with them. They sailed by under a light East wind in vast billowing clouds, the lower strata falling in a ceaseless shower to the ground covering the streets, the sidewalks, the exterior of buildings, jumping, crawling, crushed by every passing foot, filling the eyes and ears, covering the garments of pedestrians, swarming everywhere in irrepressible currents.

In late August, The Register commented: There is nothing left for the grasshoppers to eat but quartz.

The Denver newspaper reported that, in addition to Colorado, Kansas and Nebraska, there were other states east that suffered as much from the grasshoppers as the Colorado prairies did and the Federal Government made a "grasshopper appropriation" for the destitute farmers. It was quite some time before the farmlands recovered and crops were raised again. In the meantime, the gold camps suffered with those areas on the plains from short supplies, which had to be shipped in from the East or from California. Residents in the mountains were thankful they had the railroads to bring supplies to them.

September presented a glistening new business district to Central City. The fire of May had brought an entirely different appearance to the streets. As agreed upon for the town's new growth, brick and stone were used, and uniformity was realized by making the buildings two stories in height instead of the high and low lines of the former structures. The Great Fire was indeed in the past and Central City boasted substantial and spacious erections on the old sites.

Even though it was past history, the fire lived in the memories of the people to the extent that for years May 21 was a day of celebration in commemoration that no lives were lost and many homes saved.

For the first year's celebration, there were contests between volunteer firemen's units that had been organized and trained with determination that their town would never go through such an experience and loss again. There were several such teams, among them the "Alert," "Rough and Ready," "Rescue," "Number 2 Hose" and "Hook and Ladder." These fire teams were a colorful part of the celebrations with their contests, bright uniforms and parades.

There were two kinds of races in these contests: Hook and Ladder and Hose. For the Hook and Ladder Companies, the test was to run 200 feet and put a man to the top of a thirty foot ladder. A world record was made by a Denver team that finished the race in 22-1/2 seconds.

The test for the Hose Companies was to run 500 feet to a hydrant, lay 200 feet of hose and get water through the nozzle. A new world record in this event was made in Colorado when the Bates Hose Company made the run in 31-1/4 seconds. Besides this "wet" race, there was a hub-to-hub or straightaway run for the fire teams.

Central City had her share of racing and winning teams throughout the years and their records were very good in all events.

(In the book Colorado History, by Hafen and Hafen, Central City is given credit for holding the first Annual State tournament in 1875, the year after the Great Fire. The next one was in Denver. Later places included Georgetown, Colorado Springs, Silver Cliff and Trinidad. The book states that these tournaments and the Firemen's Ball financed the volunteer fire companies of the area.)

A personal event for the Champions occurred in May, in Will's first school year, and only a few days before Levinia expected her seventh child. That morning after Hugh and the boarders had gone to work, Tommy Adams, the boy who took Old Bossy (one of several since the first Old Bossy) with other cows to a day pasture on the slopes outside of town, asked her if Will could go with him for the day. Tommy was in the tenth grade in school and had taken Will with him before quite often while he herded the cows. So Levinia gave her permission and packed a lunch for them.

When they left, driving Old Bossy ahead of them as the first cow to be picked up for the tramp to the grassland, Levinia didn't watch them leave. To the Cornish, it is bad luck to see a loved one vanish from sight. So she hurried into the house and began her housework. But she didn't sing, as usual. Her mind became uneasy, though she couldn't have explained why. Being Cornish, she was absolutely sure something was going to happen. All her people believed in premonition of this sort. They are sure a warning is given before accidents and death.

Her uneasiness persisted until she wished Hugh and Will hadn't gone that day. Somehow, she became sure Will was the one she worried about. She wondered if she shouldn't ask a neighbor to look after her children and go to where the boys had gone. But she wasn't positive whether this was the day Tommy took the cows north or south to graze above Black Hawk. So she had to remain at home and "stew," as she called her worry, which she did and she became more and more nervous as time went on.

Long before it was time for the boys to bring Old Bossy home, she began to look for them, going to the back door again and again, watching down the alley where they would appear. Edith, who noticed her uneasiness, asked what the matter was. Levinia smiled down at the questioning child and turned the query aside by remarking that Cornish mothers were always anxious when one of their children was away from home.

After that, because she didn't want Edith to become more concerned about her behavior, Levinia didn't allow herself to watch from the door. So she didn't see Tommy run into the yard with Will in his arms. The first she knew of their return was when Tommy shouted her name frantically, over and over.

No Wealth for Levinia

She and Edith rushed to the door! Tommy stood in the yard below looking up at her holding Will on his outstretched arms. Tears ran down Tommy's white cheeks as he gulped out words. "He fell in an old well when we were almost home! There was water in it! I got him out . . . I'm sure he's dead, Mrs. Champion."

Levinia also was sure he was. His head hung down over Tommy's arm. His body was limp. His arms swung down without life. His feet dangled like ropes in the wind.

With an anguished cry, with no thought of the child in her womb, she ran down the long flight of steps to the yard. As she pulled her apron off and wadded it into a roll. She dropped it and her shoes, kicked off in the moment she took Will from Tommy and laid the boy face down on them, then began to try to pump water from his lungs, telling Tommy to run for the doctor.

She worked desperately, steadily, but no water came from his lips. She turned him over and looked at his deathlike face. She was sure he was in shock. What was she to do? What could she do while she waited for the doctor?

She prayed for some sign for action. As her sobbing breath formed words of prayer, she remembered such an instance in the Bible when a child appeared dead. Elisha had revived him by breathing into his mouth. In her subconscious mind, she repeated the words in verse 34-35, Chapter 14 of Second Kings. *Arid he, Elisha lay upon the child, and put his mouth upon his mouth and stretched himself upon the child, and the flesh of the child waxed warm, and he breathed.*

She didn't consider that Elisha was a prophet, a disciple, a man of God. She believed God had shown her what to do for Will. She breathed into Will's mouth steadily and kept it up until she felt the boy move slightly and there was a convulsion in his throat. God had helped her save her son!

When the doctor came from his office across the street, Will was breathing normally. The doctor seemed skeptical when she happily explained what she had done, giving the information in almost disconnected sentences. But his eyes were approving and admiring, as the two knelt by the boy.

"He's all right, Mrs. Champion," he said, and she didn't care whether or not he believed her desperate method had had anything to do with her son's recovery. It was enough for her to know God had answered her prayer.

The physician helped her to her feet and steadied her while she regained her balance after her long position on the ground. Then he told Tommy to help her into the house.

"I'll bring your boy in," he told her and reached down to lift him.

It was then that Levinia noticed that Edith wasn't in the back yard with her. She raised her eyes to the door of the house.

Grasshopper Plague, A Child Nearly Dies, Another Birth

The little girl stood there with Lillie's hand in one hand and Albert's in the other. She watched and waited, her wondering eyes were enormous, her lips aquiver; the little mother watched over her two charges. Levinia's heart was lightened by the little girl's care, but her mind was too full to think clearly.

In her stocking feet, with Tommy's help, she got her weary, heavy body up those seemingly endless steps. Now that she knew her son was alive, her reaction from working over him and the fear that she had lost him, made her so tired she could hardly move. But when she got into the house and saw wide-eyed Edith standing with the little ones, she pulled herself together and smiled in an effort to restore the children's confidence.

"Get mama's shoes from the yard, Edith," she said calmly, and drew Lillie and Albert close to her as she showed the doctor where to put Will, weak and trembling after his near brush with death.

When he was stretched out on the couch in the parlor, they took his damp clothes off and bundled him up in blankets. As he shivered, he tried to tell his mother he hadn't known the well hole was there. He'd walked over the same spot many, many times before, without its lid giving way.

"You are a bigger, 'eavier boy now," she told him quietly. Will accepted her explanation and was willing to swallow the medicine the doctor took from his fascinating black bag. Edith brought her mother's shoes and helped her put them on.

The physician gave Levinia medicine too, telling her she'd be better off if she did so. Levinia did as he said and sat in the rocker he indicated, and then answered his question about how she felt. She realized he was concerned about the effects of the shock she'd had. She smiled at him reassuringly and told him she was all right now that there was no worry about Will.

He made her promise to let him know the minute she didn't feel well, an expression she knew he was using because the children were present. She was fully aware that he thought her fear and exertion might bring the child at once or in a short time.

When he was leaving, he turned and asked her what had made her breathe into the boy's mouth. She took the Bible from its usual place on the parlor table and pointed out the verse that had come to her mind in her great need. He read it and the look he gave her was mixed with awe and disbelief, then he nodded and went away.

Levinia felt no serious physical result from the experience. She went about her work, though Mrs. Andrews and another neighbor took turns staying with her and helped cook for the boarders, while Levinia saw that Will got the rest the doctor had prescribed.

Hugh was stricken dumb when he learned of Will's narrow escape and, as soon as he found out that all was well with him and Levinia, he went to talk with the doctor. Levinia knew he went because of her, even more than the boy, who was demanding something to eat.

When Hugh returned, she was sure he shared the doctor's expectation that the baby's arrival might be hurried by the circumstances. She turned that anxiety aside by remarking that Tommy Adams had done a wonderful thing to get Will out of the well and bring him home so quickly. Hugh agreed and went to look at the well cover that had given way under Will's weight. When he returned, he reported that the wooden lid had rotted and the dirt at its side was damp from a recent shower, which explained why the boards had gone down the well when the boy stepped on them.

Tommy told Hugh that when Will disappeared down the hole feet first, he had called out that there was water at the bottom. Tommy had found a length of solid old timber close by and told Will to stand aside as best he could when it came down. He lowered it carefully until it hit bottom, which fortunately was only a short distance from the surface. He told Will to climb up the slanting timber, but Will had fallen further into the shallow water and couldn't make it. So Tommy had gone down and found Will, as he thought, dead. He had brought him up by climbing with one hand, holding the limp boy in the other arm, then ran with him to the Champion home.

Hugh thanked the boy sincerely and told his parents they had a very fine son. But Tommy was concerned about Old Bossy and the other cows that had wandered away after the accident, though his father and Hugh told him they would come home when it was time for them to be milked and fed. He accompanied Hugh home and was pleased to find Old Bossy at the back gate, lowing for attention, and Will eager to know exactly how it had happened. He seemed to remember so little after going down the hole.

On June 2, 1876, Emily was born to Levinia without complications of any kind, though the doctor had been called as soon as Levinia was sure the birth was at hand. Emily was a small child compared with the others Levinia had brought into the world, but she was a full-term baby. She arrived the very day Levinia and the doctor had figured the little one would put in an appearance, if the shock of Will's accident didn't hurry matters.

Emily had lots of thick dark hair and dark blue eyes, fringed with long eyelashes. She had a ready smile for everyone and a sweet disposition. Levinia told Hugh the patient child made so little fuss she hardly knew she was in the house. "'T would be easy to neglect 'er" she added soberly. Hugh smiled broadly and Levinia knew he'd been amused by thought that she could neglect any child, which made her happy in his trust in her.

Grasshopper Plague, A Child Nearly Dies, Another Birth

The parents were very happy as they realized that, when they needed him, God had been with them. Their daily and nightly prayers came from full hearts.

On July 17, of the year 1876, the people of Central City filed patent for their own town site in the United States Land Office there. On August 1, 1876 Colorado was admitted to the Union as the Centennial State, one hundred years after the Declaration of Independence.

Hugh and Levinia studied the Denver, Colorado Daily Rocky Mountain News, of Wednesday morning August 2, 1876 that contained the Proclamation of Colorado's admission.

Colorado Proclaimed a State yesterday by the President in Washington, August 1, 1876. The President, in accordance with the provisions of an Act of Congress, approved March 3, 1875, has issued his proclamation declaring and proclaiming the fact the fundamental conditions imposed by Congress on the state of Colorado to entitle that state to admission to the Union have been ratified and accepted, and the admission of said state into the Union is now completed.

The Champions joined the other proud Central City folks who helped celebrate the great occasion. The entire state was happy over the fact that the "Mile High" State had been admitted to the Union.

To Hugh and Levinia, the proclamation brought new information about the Colonies and the War for Independence called The Revolutionary War. They realized more than ever the intent of the writers of the Declaration of Independence. They felt a new and greater pride in the country they now considered their own.

Yet, when it came right down to the fact that Hugh could take out his final papers that would make him a naturalized citizen of the United States, he put it off. In spite of Levinia's cautious reminder that the time of probation was over, he let it slip by without appearing before the proper authorities. Levinia felt the urge to insist but forced herself to drop the matter until Hugh was ready to do the studying it would take to be able to answer questions that were necessary. But it worried her a great deal. She wanted her children to be citizens of the United States.

Chapter 19

Cycle of Life and Death Continues

The following summer, a circus came in five trainloads to Black Hawk and started up the long steep climb of three miles to the most level spot that could be found, Gunnell Hill, sometimes spoken of as Academy Hill, because the Catholic Academy was there.

The climb, with the heavy wagons of cages and equipment, was so hard that several of the horses gave out. Some of the members of the circus were overcome by the altitude and the exertion getting everything to the chosen site.

The company played performances to capacity crowds of three thousand both afternoon and evening. During an evening show, due to the slope of the hill where it had been erected, a section of grandstand collapsed and a large number of the frightened audience was thrown to the ground. Fortunately, no one was hurt.

Among those who fell, was a pious elderly Cornish woman everyone lovingly called "Granny Moyle." The Champions had known Mrs. Moyle since 1870, when she came to the gold camp. At that time, she attracted the attention of everyone by riding out on a horse whose eyes were kept straight ahead by blinders, so that he couldn't see the parasol the woman held over her head to keep from tanning in the sun. As she grew older she was always in the limelight because of her eccentric attire and actions, which brought smiles and remarks from an admiring group wherever she went, though they didn't always agree with her outspoken opinions.

Now in her advanced years, she still held a firm conviction that the devil was in all frivolity and especially in stage performers. Against her judgment, she had been persuaded by her younger relatives and friends to attend this one circus show, just to please them.

Cycle of Life and Death Continues

As it happened, Granny Moyle was sitting in the section of grandstand that collapsed and when she found herself falling, she like many others, thought the end had come. In her belief that this was her punishment for having come to the "sinful exhibition," as she called it, she screamed loudly in her fright, "Dear Lord, 'ere hi come an' killed in a cir-cuss!"

When it was discovered that neither she nor anyone else had been hurt, the incident of Granny Moyle's participation and her words were never forgotten in the community.

Hugh had taken Edith, Will and Lillie to the performance, while Levinia, heavy with her eighth child, stayed at home with Albert and Emily. The children had watched throughout the entire period of the show's climb to the spot. They had counted the long strings of wagons as they went up Lawrence Street in front of and beyond the Champion back door and were agog with excitement by the time they were seated in the big tent. Though they weren't in the same section of seats, they had seen the accident and heard the screams and curses of those who were thrown to the ground, some to roll downhill on the steep slope. Among the cries of fear and terror, they heard Granny Moyle's message to her Lord.

Edith, who knew and loved Granny very much, was very concerned over what Granny had said in her fright and what she'd expressed in her usual frank way. She had asked her Mother what Granny had meant that evening when she'd cried out above all the others. Levinia tried to show the thoughtful worried child what had been uppermost in Granny's mind at that moment, and when Edith stopped asking questions and seemed as happy as before, Levinia had taken it for granted the child understood.

But two days later, when Edith came down with a high fever and tossed and turned in her bed in delirium, she often muttered parts of sentences in which Granny Moyle's name occurred, given in terms of fright and fear that showed that the impressionable child hadn't really understood. Edith was ill only a few hours. From the very first the doctor had been with her but he couldn't reduce the consuming fever in her tortured body. She died July 17, 1877, at the age of nine and a half years.

Hugh and Levinia were prostrate with grief at the death of their third child. It didn't seem possible that Edith could have been so well and active, and then have gone so soon and in such a way. They couldn't understand that, nor reconcile the fact that they'd lost all three of their first-born, William John, Lillie and now Edith.

After the touching service in the beautiful Methodist Church, Edith was laid away in the cemetery lot with her brother and sister. As Levinia got into the rig to go back down the long grade to her home, she turned and looked back where her children lay. Her heart was broken, her life torn, her faith tried.

In her despair, she questioned aloud God's will in this, and told Hugh bitterly there could be no reason in the loss of their little ones. "How can there be a just God?" she cried, and said she wished she was not bringing another child into this cruel world!

Hugh held her close in silence until they were almost home, then he said quietly, "Ee still 'as four children and one more almost 'ere. If 'ee's a girl, we'll call 'er Edith for the one we left up there on the 'ill."

She was comforted by his sensible words and calm manner and finally admitted that he was right in looking upon their remaining children as blessings. She kissed him gratefully, and when she entered their home she saw William John, eight; Lillie, six; and Albert, three, standing in the door waiting. She thankfully gathered them to her, then went in and bent over Emily, a little over a year old, asleep in her crib. She straightened up, looked at Hugh and nodded to show him she'd been wrong in her outburst against God. Then she fell to her knees and asked His forgiveness for her rebellion because she'd lost Edith.

When she arose, she said simply, "God don't explain 'is actions," and Hugh nodded in understanding. The days that followed were hard ones to bear. Edith still seemed to be everywhere in the house and in everything they did. They missed her so much! At first, Levinia thought she missed her the most, for she had been with her nearly all the time, as she had helped her mother in all she did. But she soon realized that Will's loss was almost more than the little boy could take. His older sister had taken the lead in everything. She had helped him in every way, abetting him in what was good and seeing that he didn't go too far off the path their parents expected them to follow.

Gently, unobtrusively, as she understood Will's feeling, Levinia urged the slender lad to take over the direction of Lillie who showed great preference for him, now that Edith wasn't there to look after her and play with her. Levinia explained to Will that Lillie was lonesome for Edith and his attention would help her very much, while she as well as all the rest of them, was getting over Edith's leaving them. Will accepted what she said and he received comfort in Lillie, as his mother had known he would. At her suggestion, Hugh took an increased interest in Will and made him more of a companion, which in turn gave comfort to the father as the boy was helped.

That sharing and working thoughtfully together got them over the worst days after Edith's death. Slowly they adjusted to her absence and she became the beautiful memory Levinia taught them all to consider her.

On November 25, 1877, almost ten years to the day when the first Edith had been born, the second Edith, as fair and blonde as her predecessor, came

Cycle of Life and Death Continues

into the world. She was their eighth child, the fifth of their living children. The family rejoiced.

On Christmas Eve a fire broke out in the Bobtail Tunnel and, though the firemen thought they had it out, Hugh was kept on by the mine management to watch that it didn't break out again from the ashes. (The Bobtail was at Gregory Point, about half a mile down towards Black Hawk from the Champion house.) So he was away from home when the fire alarm sounded for the second time in a short period and before the fire fighters had reached their homes after the Bobtail blaze.

Levinia and her older children, afraid a fire had broken out again in the tunnel where Hugh was, ran to the front porch and looked down the street toward the Bobtail. There was no sign of a fire there. It was Will who first saw the flames reaching skyward from behind the Benallack grocery store across the street. He screamed and pointed up Packard Gulch, which opened from Gregory Street across the "square" from the Parson's Saloon.

Levinia's heart leaped in fear as she realized the first or the second house in Packard Gulch was afire and that they were just beyond the grocery, which would go next. For in the slight wind that was blowing down the Gulch, the house was in the direct path of the fast moving flames! From the grocery, it would be easy for the sparks to cross Gregory Street and get her home!

From a distance she heard the man-drawn fire cart jolt along and come around the corner from the firehouse but her mind and body seemed paralyzed until she realized the fire fighters were on the job. She prayed thankfully but feared the fire might be more than they could handle with their scant water supply, so she sprang into action.

She took the children back into the house and sent Will to open the back gate from the yard into the alley and put Old Bossy outside where she could escape if the fire took the house and barn. Next he moved the chickens to an old shaft house across the alley by Gregory Creek, then hurried back to her. Levinia worked frantically to get her things together. She moved all the clothing and bedding belonging to her family and the boarders into a pile on the back porch to be moved across the alley if it became necessary.

Then she held her little brood, wrapped up against the bitter winter wind, ready to flee from the house if the fire reached the grocery store. Will had Lillie on one side and Albert on the other, holding tight a hand of each. Levinia had both babies in her arms as she prayed God to spare her home.

At that moment Hugh, almost out of breath from his frantic run up the hill, burst into the house and told her he'd heard where the second fire was. He had asked to be relieved as watchman at the Bobtail, so he could run home to move his family from the threatened spot.

When he saw that Levinia had things well in hand, he took Emily from her tired arms and held her while they watched the progress of the fire. The flames were less by that time and more smoke arose from the vicinity behind the store. They could see men working to wet down its roof against the sparks.

Jim Mitchell came hurrying from the fire soon afterwards and told them the fire team from that section of the city had checked the fire very effectively. They held it back to the two houses in Packard Gulch without the help of the two other fire teams that came from upper Central City.

But Jim's news contained the sad fact that two persons had lost their lives in the fire that had burst out suddenly in the second house up Packard Gulch. Jim said no one knew how it had started. There were two theories. One, was that someone had knocked over a lighted lamp during the Christmas festivities, and the other that a Christmas tree had caught fire from a lighted candle on a branch and the house had been ablaze at once, trapping the couple. The house next to it and some sheds were burned to the ground, but all other buildings in Packard Gulch were saved by pouring water on them.

When the beds were remade and the children, reassured by their parents, were in bed, Hugh and Levinia knelt side by side and thanked the Heavenly Father for His protection. Then Hugh went back to his job as watchman.

The next morning, even before the children had gathered for their Christmas under the tree, Will and Lillie let Old Bossy, lowing and protesting relentlessly at the gate, back into the yard and brought the tame chickens, clucking noisily, from the shaft house.

Just before Levinia dished up the Christmas dinner, goose with Cornish "trimmings" and plum pudding, there was a great commotion on the stairs of the second floor bedroom. It came to a stop when something hit the wall of the small landing at its foot.

Hugh and Levinia rushed to the high door in the corner of the kitchen, opened it and looked inside. One of the boarders, who loved attention and was delighted to be called a contortionist, lay on the landing on his back, stunned. His feet were up around his neck in the favorite position he assumed to climax his boasted ability to twist his body at will.

When Hugh removed him, the man was still unconscious.

The other boarders had come down as far as they could from the bedroom above and crowded on the landing. When they took his feet from their unnatural position, they found his left leg broken below the knee. His entire body was bruised from its free and rapid descent to the landing. He had lost control in the bedroom above during his performance and had tumbled, end over end down the stairs.

Christmas dinner was delayed a long time. The doctor had the abashed victim carried back upstairs to his bed, where he set his broken leg. The accident was a painful one and the victim lost a lot of time from work because of it. However, the other miners laughed and laughed as they remembered the victim for own foolishness, his legs folded about his neck, rolling down the stairs and knocking himself out when he landed.

Levinia had more work in caring for the injured man. The hardest part was the extra trips upstairs to wait on him. The once-discarded step stool Hugh had made was brought up from the cellar, cleaned off and used for her to get up onto the landing with a loaded tray or an armful of clean bedding for her charge.

Before the week was out, she had another patient upstairs.

A boarder had frozen his feet in a snowdrift during a Christmas hunting trip. All ten toes were removed by the doctor, who broke them off like brittle sticks, before he could treat the rest of the man's feet. He was able to save all except the toes and, after a long period of idleness, the miner went back to work at a restricted job.

While making more work, all this made more money for Levinia. Her countrymen, being frugal, had money put away and were able to pay their debts to the doctor and to Levinia, whom they called "the nuss," and their bedroom "the 'osspittle."

The year's close brought the report that all the production figures in mining were up over the previous year and gave the assurance that Gilpin County's place in gold production was secure. Its mineral output was a third of a million dollars higher than its closest rival, Clear Creek County, of which Georgetown was the county seat. What pleased Hugh and Jim immensely, was the fact that the Bobtail was $200,000 ahead of any other mine in the entire district!

But Levinia was aware that in the back of Hugh's mind was the gnawing knowledge that the California, the mine in Nevadaville where he and Jim had worked when she came from Cornwall, was rapidly coming to the front. Its shaft had been driven over 2,200 feet and was giving outstanding results at that time.

She heard Hugh and Jim discussing the California one evening and she was concerned when Hugh said they would have been better off now if they had stuck with that mine. After all, Hugh argued, Nevadaville had upheld the standard wages during the strike that had helped bring on the panic of 1873, and had gone steadily ahead ever since it had been operated.

When Jim remarked that they'd never know whether they should have stayed with the California or not, she heard Hugh reflect bitterly how easy it was to look backward and see some moves as damned mistakes he could do nothing about now.

Levinia couldn't help countering with the words, "Tis useless t' look back when 'ee finds fault'th 'eeself. Regrets," she went on earnestly, "can pull 'ee away from makin' real success out of w'at 'eels doin' now. I mean stickin' 'th the Bobtail! Let the California do 'ithout 'e. The Bobtail's the mine 'ats done most for us, and 'ee knows it! Hugh, I was sure'n 'ee thought the Bobtail's the best mine of all. 'Ow can 'ee forget it?" Hugh grinned in surprise at her outburst, and she knew he understood what she meant, while Jim nodded that he agreed with her.

Afterwards, when she thought it over, she was glad her speaking out hadn't angered Hugh. She had, she admitted to herself, run that risk when she'd spoken without thinking it all out ahead of time.

Her contemplation of the matter made her see again that Hugh was troubled by the realization that his judgment wasn't always for the best. He wanted so desperately to make good, yet seemed to be powerless to get ahead as he had hoped. She was very gentle and thoughtful in her words from that moment on. She gave full appreciation for all he was able to accomplish for her and the family, while showing her love in a more demonstrative way than the Cornish wives usually did.

Chapter 20

Opera House Opening, Colorado Central Railroad Completed

The last large structure built during boom times was the Opera House. It was the result of the community's great music and drama needs and was erected through personal efforts of the residents, not through gifts from people wanting to elevate their own personal standing. The building fund was subscribed to by individuals who put up over $20,000 collectively. It was built on the site of Tom Pollock's livery stable on Eureka Street, opposite Washington Hall, and spanned gurgling Eureka Creek.

Levinia, going through the finished building with her proud husband, observed that the four double doors that opened directly on the sidewalk, led to a foyer on Eureka Street, the width of the building. From the foyer, two stairways rose to a large balcony swung across the rear of the auditorium. Here were the unreserved seats, wooden benches, where the miners usually sat during performances. From this section, Levinia was sorry to see, some of the miners dropping peanut shells and other such debris on the bare shoulders of the elegantly dressed "society" women seated on the main floor below the balcony. On either side of the foyer, other steep steps ascended to the parquet and dress circles, where the seats were sturdy hickory chairs. Beneath the auditorium were four large dressing rooms and ample space for stage "properties."

The theater itself was so beautiful, so glowing and so colorful it almost took Levinia's breath away! The ceiling was decorated with graceful frescoes of red, blue and gold, and it featured a proscenium and front panels. The drop curtain showed a balcony scene on the Rhine, with a river and a castle in the distance. The whole interior was illuminated by a crystal chandelier with its many gaslights that showed a beauty of which Levinia had never dreamed.

The opening of the Opera House on Monday evening, March 4, 1878, was given in The Register-Call next day, March 5.

If ever the people of Central City had reason to feel proud of the energy and enterprise of the first city of the mountains, it was last night upon the opening of her magnificent Opera House, which today stands the finest Temple of the Muses west of the Missouri, and far ahead of anything of the kind projected in the Rocky Mountains. The beautiful frescos work, brought out in bold relief by the scintillations of a hundred gas jets,[14] the handsome drop curtain and the house filled to its utmost capacity, was a sight seldom seen, and certainly not soon to be forgotten in these mountain regions. A slight history of the beautiful building which now graces Eureka Street may not be uninteresting to the readers of The Register-Call. Ever since Central City has been known as a city, she has been famed throughout the state for her musical talent. Something over a year ago, the Amateur Society of Central City produced for their own as well as their friends' amusement, Rolfe's Opera, the "Bohemian Girl," the different characters taken by some of our most respected citizens. And such was the complete success of the representation that its fame soon spread over the state and it was stamped by all, and especially the Press, as the most successful amateur musical performance ever given in Colorado. This success stimulated our amateurs to still nobler efforts, and at the same time showed the necessity of having some first-class place; a hall or theater; for such productions, and opened the eyes of some of our capitalists to the need of an Opera House. The impulse once given it was immediately resolved to erect a lasting monument to the honor of the city and the state. Just one year ago, March 5, 1877, a party of enterprising gentlemen of capital organized a company; plans and specifications were drawn; sufficient money subscribed to purchase the present site, and work immediately commenced under the supervision of the architect, Mr. R. S. Roeschlaub, of Denver. The walls (four feet thick), which are built of solid granite taken from our grand old hills, arose as if by magic under the direction of Messrs Mullen and Sartori, who had the contract for the masonry work, and in a short space of time the building had assumed shape and was closed in. The masonry work being completed, the building was immediately turned over to Messrs McFarland, and Company, who had the contract for the carpenter work. The frescos and scenic work was done by Mr. Massman of San Francisco. How well all these

---

14 One official in the Gilpin County Historical Society and Museums recalls that somewhere it is written that the gas lamps were fed by gasoline and two men in the basement worked a hand pump to expel fumes from the building. Electric lights were installed in 1896, according to William Axford author of "Gilpin County Gold" (1976).

gentlemen performed their part of the contract: the building itself, the most substantial in the state bear's testimony. The furnaces, hot air pipes and heating apparatus, furnished by Bacon and Sons of Denver, work like a charm and make the building very comfortable. The size of the building is 55 by 115 feet, with a stage of 43 by 52. The dress circle and parquet will seat about 500 persons. The gallery will seat about 250 persons. It may be safe to say the entire building as it stands now costs between $20,000, and $25,000.

The Denver papers commented: No town or city in Colorado can compare with Central City in the line of musical and dramatic talent.

Reporters gave glowing accounts of the two nights' opening performances.

The first, March 4, mostly musical, the second, March 5, mainly dramatic; and of the gathering that marked these openings: special trains, carriages, and hacks that transported guests from Denver, Golden, Boulder, and Idaho Springs. The press mentioned names of the guests and told what each wore on these evenings, and of those who performed for their pleasure and entertainment.

But the account Levinia treasured most was that given by Theatre Arts Monthly, Volume XVI, in which Charles Bayly, Jr. described the opening. This writing seemed to express her own feeling about the new building and what it meant.

The Central City Opera House opened on March 4 and 5, 1878. The building 55 x 115 feet, is built of masonry, plain but impressive, with walls 4 feet thick. A large and comfortable gallery swings across the rear of the building, but is not carried down the sides. The floor of the parquet and dress circles slopes gently to the stage, giving a good view of the performers. It is well lighted and heated and has a beautiful central chandelier.

There isn't much "gingerbread" or woodwork of any kind in the interior, which is neat, not "gaudy," and the frescoing is very fine; as elegant in its line as anything in the country. The artist seems to have been more "at home" in the theatre than in a church. The ceiling is splendid! The centerpiece is an "open dome," and one can imagine that he was looking through the roof to the sky overhead, with angry clouds hurrying by, en route to Georgetown direct, without change, as the railroad guides say. The drop curtain is also very fine, representing a Rhine scene, shown through the parted drapery. The stage, 43 x 53 feet, is handsome and adequate. The parquet and dress circles seat 500 and the gallery 250. The Opera House in Central City stands as a unique and fitting and a beautiful thing! No other decoration can equal it in America! It makes you realize you are going to, or are in a theatre! It seems to have the rarest of qualities and one least expected in a mining camp in the heart of the Rocky Mountains - the quality of style!

However, the Opera House enjoyed only three short years of such highly satisfying results, for Leadville's rich silver strike broke in the early 1880's and created a great rush to that vicinity. H. A. Tabor of silver fame, built an Opera House in Denver which drew the highest talent.

On May 21, 1878, Gregory Gulch celebrated the commemoration of the Great Fire and the completion of the extension of the Colorado Central Railroad from Black Hawk to Central City. This extension was called the "High Line" and the "switchback" because it covered a distance of four miles and went up a very steep grade! Its construction along the mountainsides was considered a real engineering feat. It ran over bridges and trestles, going backward and forward into Central City, depending n the make up of the train on each trip. Sometimes it was necessary for the locomotive to push instead of pull the little coaches as they climbed between the two Gulch towns, to gain the elevation necessary.

Included in the difficult construction, was a great iron bridge across Gregory and Selak Streets in Black Hawk to carry the train over the town from Bates Hill to Bobtail Hill. From there the track followed a long switchback down the North Fork of Clear Creek and up Running Creek, in order to gain altitude to make the grade possible for a locomotive. It was necessary, too, to build trestle over Running Creek and one over Packard Gulch. The cost of the extension came to $100,000!

In celebration of its completion, the city mayor and his helpers planned a full schedule for the day and night, a parade, a firemen's tournament, and a ball at Turner Hall on Gregory Street.

The day before, in spite of the rain that steadily fell, the town filled up with visitors. They came by stage, by private rigs and a special train brought two hundred excursionists. There were delegations of firemen, civic officials and citizens from Cheyenne, Wyoming, and firemen from neighboring towns.

The next day, May 21, which turned out to be a bright, sunny day, more people arrived by special trains. Golden brought their team of firemen, the Excelsiors, filling two trains. Another train brought two hundred from Georgetown with two fire teams, the Lopes and the Alpines. By noon, nine hundred had registered at the Teller House and the crowd in town was estimated at ten thousand, among them Hugh and his two oldest children, Will and Lillie. Levinia, though wanting to see the activity and have a part in the coming-of-the-rail-road celebration, had thought it wise to stay at home with the three little ones. So she waited until Hugh and the children got home to hear about it.

The parade, she learned, had included the Fire Department, Hose Companies, Hook and Ladder teams, officials in carriages and six bands. It formed on Main Street, marched down Lawrence, went across Gregory, turned right to Main Street, then up Eureka Street to a wide spot at its crest. Here the marchers circled and came back to the Opera House to file in through its wide open doors to hear a welcoming speech.

After dinner was served in every hotel, restaurant, boarding house and residence in town, the races were held and Hugh took the children back from their lunch at home to see them. From every window along the street, watchers looked down to see the competition between the fire teams. In one of these windows, Hugh had obtained a space ahead of time for Will, Lillie and himself, so they were able to see almost everything that went on.

The teams made their individual runs down Eureka Street, pulling the hose cart and hoisting a ladder at an indicated spot. Central City's team, the Rough and Readies, captained by the popular deputy sheriff, Andy McFarlane, made the best time and won first place. That made a fitting close to the celebration, as far as the Champion family was concerned.

Another colorful Central City event that year was the Union Ball held at Amory Hall, the home of the Emmet Guards, a branch of the State Militia. Next morning after the ball, Levinia read the account in a Denver paper.

As early as 9:00 o'clock last evening, Amory Hall began to fill up with members of the Guard in gay, brilliant uniforms, escorting fair ladies in the height of fashion. The music of the Centennial Band that played for the four hundred in attendance could be heard far down the street until the wee small hours of the morning.

In June, the Hill Smelter was moved from Black Hawk to Argo, Colorado, and two miles from Denver, because of the increasing difficulty of obtaining fuel. The hills were denuded, and there was too much expense to bring fuel in by railroad. Hugh said the loss of the Hill smelter was a bad omen.

About that same time many fashionable families moved down mountain to Denver and many others left Central City for Leadville and different parts where they hoped they could do better than they could in The Gulch. This also depressed Hugh, but stubbornly positive, the vicinity held its own.

On November 24, 1878, after making the required declaration of intention and filling the necessary period of probation with serious study and prayer, Hugh Champion became a full member of the Methodist Church. Levinia considered this a real achievement. Her materialistic, matter-of-fact husband was very pleased and proud.

Chapter 21

Hugh's Mysterious Disappearance, A Crippled Daughter

But that winter, she wasn't proud of Hugh. He suddenly left her and went to Cornwall, taking every cent she'd saved from taking in boarders and roomers; the entire sum they had agreed to set aside for a "rainy day." They had lived on Hugh's wages entirely by sticking to a budget Levinia called a "makin' do."

There had been no indication that he was going back home. She didn't even dream he had any such plan in mind, and he didn't give her any chance to voice her disapproval or to ask why he wanted to leave her and their children. One morning, instead of going to work as usual, he announced that he was taking the train that was leaving Black Hawk within half an hour. Then, before she could speak after the shock, he announced that he needed the money she'd put away in the old teapot in the cupboard. He was taking it to pay his way back home to Cornwall! Stunned, she watched him take the money, count it out loud and put it in his pocket. Almost before she realized he was actually going, he left the house and entered the hack he'd had stop for him on its way to the depot in Black Hawk.

She sank into a chair. Her heart was too heavy to even think about what had happened to her. Later, she forced herself to take stock of the situation and face her problems. She'd been deserted! She had no money. She didn't know why Hugh had gone, leaving her with five children, the oldest one nine. Leaving his children hurt her the most.

She was glad the boarders had had breakfast, picked up their lunch buckets and had gone to work before Hugh made the announcement. She was thankful that the children were still behind the closed kitchen. That gave her a little while to compose herself and to face the immediate problem of dealing with the children. What should she tell them? What could she tell them? She decided not to say a word this morning about their father's absence. In her heart she hoped Hugh wouldn't take the train, that his better judgment would prevail and bring him back home. He just couldn't leave his children, his wife and his home! He was too good a father and husband, he told herself hopefully. Yet, when she faced the fact that Hugh didn't do things without thinking them through before acting, she sank back in despair again. She had to accept what had happened and set herself to go on from that moment.

By the time Will and Lillie came out for breakfast, she had herself in hand to the extent that they didn't even guess anything was wrong. She sent them off to school and took care of the younger children, then cleaned her kitchen, made the beds and began the laundry. She was glad she could keep busy, that the children kept her thoughts from the dire situation before her. Yet, she realized she had to have some explanation ready when it came time for Hugh to come home from work. Then she would have to give the children some reason for their father's absence and the boarders would have questions she must answer. She made up her mind to tell the truth about Hugh's going to Cornwall. She didn't have to explain he'd gone without a word of farewell and didn't give a reason for his going. She resolved never to admit he'd deserted her.

It worked out so that the children, the boarders, her friends and Hugh's believed only what appeared on the surface. Hugh had had a sudden idea of going to Cornwall to see his mother. That, she figured would take care of the immediate questions. She would deal with whatever developed when the time came. That would be soon enough for anyone to know. Besides, if Hugh came to his senses and came back, she had the course laid out to save his pride and hers.

She had no difficulty in having her explanation accepted, for other Cornishmen had gone back, and then returned to Central City. Only Jim Mitchell gave her any trouble. He asked outright when Hugh had made up his mind to go, and expressed his opinion that going now, when the children were so little, and money was scarce, seemed pretty foolish. She had to put on a brave front that turned aside his questions and discouraged the discussion of Hugh's action.

Her greatest difficulty was with the children, who couldn't understand their father's sudden, secret departure. Over and over they asked her why he hadn't even mentioned going away, why he hadn't said goodbye to them, and why he had gone before they got up that morning. She satisfied them, at least partially, from day to day for fifteen months. Although not a day went by without them bringing up the subject of his absence, tearing her heart as they talked about him, and asked the inevitable question, "When is Papa coming home?"

Those fifteen months were endless, filled with despair, worry and prayer. She heard no direct word from him. However, letters from her own brothers and sisters contained the information that Hugh was at Hayle, their hometown. They said he looked somewhat drawn and sick, that he was staying at his mother's house and that he didn't talk much about anything or anyone.

Levinia worked hard and long. She took in another boarder and roomer, who slept in the big room upstairs, making two men in each double bed. And, to help her with the expenses, Jim Mitchell took another Cornishman into his bed and room, making six men in all.

She did very well in feeding her children and keeping them warm and comfortable. She very carefully counted every penny, making each go as far as she could. She was doubly thankful, now that she had her cow and chickens to help out with grocery bills. She planned many of her dishes around the eggs and milk and had enough of a flock of hens to kill one now and then for the table.

Custard puddings and pies made delicious desserts for the main meals, and Devonshire cream, which Levinia called "scalded cream," was a welcome addition to the Cornish fare.

"Scalded cream" was made by putting the fresh milk into shallow pans which were then left at room temperature for several hours. Then the pans were placed on the stove to heat very gradually until the cream rose to the top and thickened as the milk almost reached the boiling point. The pans were then removed from the heat and allowed to stand until thoroughly chilled.

Then the thick heavy golden cream was skimmed off and used over pies, even spread over bread, as butter. The skimmed milk was given to the children, who loved its delicious, somewhat different flavor that came from its near boiling treatment while the cream was being "scalded."

Added to the worry of not knowing what was before her, in regard to her absent husband, she had a new and despairing fear. When little Emily finally began to walk, (she was almost three years old before she even tried) Levinia noticed that the child as developing quite thick shoulders and there was thinner space along the little back below them. She called the doctor who looked very grave before he told her it looked as though Emily had a thickening growth on her back along her shoulders.

Later, when the shock had subsided into calmer acceptance of the possibility of "curvature of the spine," Levinia learned that very little could be done about it. The doctor advised her to wait until they were sure. Then, as he watched the otherwise perfect child bring herself to her feet and try a few steps, he spoke warmly, "Emily will walk in spite of what else may happen."

He tried to turn aside Levinia's anxious question of whether she might have injured the unborn child when she'd tried so desperately to bring Will back to life, when she'd feared he was dead. The doctor couldn't or wouldn't answer. He merely shook his head, leaving her with the belief that she had crippled the child that day, a thought that tore at her heart until she was almost beside herself. She longed to have Hugh to help her with this new fear. Her prayers rose from her anguished soul.

Day after day, she watched the determined little girl struggle to her feet and use her lower limbs. She made up her mind then, that aside from the growth at her shoulders, the child was absolutely normal. She talked even sooner and better than the other children had at that age.

Emily had the best disposition of any of them. She was sweet and patient and very independent. She seemed to know and understand one's thoughts and was quick to carry out instructions. She was an integral part of the family with a great deal of influence on the rest. All her life she was a strong help to Levinia. The two seemed closer than any other child and Levinia, even though the mother made no difference between Emily and the others.

As the girl's curvature became more apparent, Emily became even more important to her family and friends. She was loved by everyone who knew her, admired for her bravery in ignoring, as much as was possible, the fact that she was a cripple. Though she could do almost everything other children did, she never admitted there were some things she couldn't do. She never allowed helplessness to stand out in any way. She didn't want to be pitied, and she wasn't.

Chapter 22

Hugh Returns, A Birth, A Death

Hugh Champion came back as suddenly as he'd gone. One afternoon in early June of 1879, Levinia looked up and saw him enter the house and stand looking at her. She was at the table having lunch with the children. Hugh's eyes held hers and then he turned and studied the children. There was a smile of pride on his lips as he turned back to her. He then waited, as though wondering, what she would say and do.

The children settled that. Will and Lillie sprang to his side, followed by Albert, and were held tightly in his arms. A little later, he went to the table where Emily and Edith sat in high chairs. They didn't make as much fuss over him because they had been over a year younger when they'd seen him last, so couldn't remember him as well. He lifted each little girl in turn and kissed her, while the other children kept exclaiming, "Papa's home!"

As Levinia looked on, her heart beat fast with the knowledge that Hugh did love his children, even though he'd left them for a while.

When Hugh came toward her, his eyes pleading, she said, "Welcome home, Hugh," and stood in his arms, held close. It was a moment for them alone. Her prayers rose from her thankful heart.

Hugh gave no explanation for his absence and she didn't ask him about it. It was enough to have him back and to see him replace every cent of the money he had used. He soon explained that he'd worked hard in Cornwall and saved his money.

Later, he remarked that his mother had been very glad to see him and had thought he had come back to stay. "But I tole 'er 'ome is 'ith Vinia and our younguns," he said simply, and the matter was dropped.

He went back to work at the Bobtail and fit into his former place there and

Hugh Returns, A Birth, A Death

in the community. But he had to take a new work-partner, as Jim had teamed up with another when Hugh left.

Levinia was glad she had refrained from any talk which might have revealed that she'd feared Hugh had gone for good. She was well aware that Hugh had been worried about what he might find on his return, for he had been restless until he found out from the boarders and friends that she hadn't discussed his absence at all. In their frank questions about Cornwall and his family there, he knew they had considered his absence as the visit she had intimated.

Hugh told them Cornwall was about the same. The mines didn't pay much, jobs were hard to get and he hadn't even thought of staying there. He said his mother wanted him to do that. She fought all mention of her other two sons going to America, as they were planning to do. Hugh had assured them that there was more opportunity in the new world and promised to have jobs for them when they arrived. Their mother, Hugh explained, would have their sister to look after her until the future was worked out for her.

Levinia's brother, George, was coming too, but he didn't want to work in the mines unless he absolutely had to. He maintained that men who worked there paid with their health, as sooner or later silicosis would kill them.

Though Hugh made light of her brother's wish to work at something else, Levinia sided with George, because she knew that miners lived only as long as their lungs kept a section open with which to breathe. Miners lungs filled with dust quartz particles and death often came at an early age, sometimes in their early thirties.

Levinia had watched the miners in the community drop out of work because they were short of breath. With apprehension, she looked at Hugh and Jim. Hugh was a strong robust man and seemed to be in good shape. But Jim, never as hale as Hugh, took on that pallid color that showed lack of oxygen, while his body assumed the familiar "stoop" that came with the lack of lung power due to silicosis. The miners called this "The Con" or "The miners" or "bad on the lungs" and "rocks in the lungs."

Jim had to stop working soon after that, and went back to Cornwall to live out his days. They missed him terribly, and Hugh seemed to take his leaving as a warning, for he talked to Levinia with unusual sober consideration of silicosis and his own ability to withstand it.

Out of that first discussion came the realization that he knew she would have to go on without him some day. He said no one could foresee how long he could continue to bring in money earned at the mine. He brought up the subject of adding more rooms to the house, and she learned that he'd entertained that idea ever since they'd lived at Caribou. She remembered that he had surveyed the house that day five years before, when they had come in to see the ruins of the Great Fire.

Quietly she said they needed more rooms anyway, for the children should have more than the one bedroom. If they used the upstairs for the family, the boys could have the small room and the girls the larger one.

They discussed the matter thoroughly. Hugh gravely said that later it would be sensible for her to keep on with roomers and boarders. That way, he went on, although she would have to work very very hard to keep the family fed and clothed, she would be at home with the children instead of going into "service" work in the homes of those who could afford hired help.

"The younguns soon be able to do a lot to 'elp 'ee 'ith meals and beds," he said, and she knew he was looking ahead to the time when he wouldn't be there.

Though the thought wasn't expressed, they realized the rooms should be added while Hugh was able to see to it and could help after work hours. Levinia 's heart saddened more and more every time the inevitable death of hard-rock miners came up. Each time she could see that Hugh was facing the truth as something that would come sooner or later in the mining industry.

He was forty-four, older than most miners. He said he'd lived that long because he'd done some open-air work around town, building stone fences and walls, and had sometimes timbered the mineshafts instead of working continuously in the quartz dust. He encouraged her to look upon the future as hopefully as she could, reminding her a bit boastfully, that he was stronger than most men, so might live to see their children grown. But they both knew this couldn't be expected.

It took much planning and maneuvering to even start to build the new rooms, for they didn't have the money to pay for the material and labor outright.

Hugh arranged with the bank for a loan to cover most of the estimated lumber, and planned with his Cornish friends to have a "Bee," or as the Cornish called it, "a raisin" to put up the framework.

While the building was going on, another child, a son, John Sherman, was born February 11, 1880. Though he was a plump healthy breast-fed baby as all Levinia's children were, and seemed to be thriving, he died suddenly on April 21, 1880, of bronchitis, at the age of two months.

The sorrowing parents put him into a little white casket and held it on their knees as they rode in a rented rig up the long steep hill to the family lot in the Knights of Pythias cemetery. That lot then held four young Champions, their three first-born: the first William John, the first Lillie, the first Edith, and now the youngest, Baby John Sherman.

Hugh Returns, A Birth, A Death

There were several other cemeteries on the mesa above Central City: Bald Mountain, Catholic, Masonic, Dory, Odd Fellows, Foresters and The City. The majority of the headstones revealed the dates of the death of children and young men.

On that sad day when they came down the hill after the burial of John Sherman, Levinia thought bitterly, "The children of this community die before they have a chance at life, and the men are taken when they ought to be in their prime."

Losing a child who fed at her breast caused Levinia a great deal of suffering from swollen milk glands. She developed a high fever and her nipples almost became open sores from the outer eruption. Her physical condition was very serious for a few days.

As though the death of their child had been an omen of the end of an era, the year 1880 showed that the Little Kingdom of Gregory Gulch no longer led the Colorado mining camps. Leadville and Aspen had taken away its title. Though the mines were still running full time, and their output climbed from one and a half million dollars in 1875 to more than two and a half million in 1880, the vicinity was changing in ways not easily apparent to the residents of the county.

After so many first families left to live elsewhere, and the Opera House no longer held its glamorous place in the town and state, the community suffered, even though it remained busy and active. As someone put it, "It's just different now. It's only another mining community, not the leading one."

But its growth didn't stop, nor did it go backward. Progress continued, though it was longer on the "Queen Camp" basis. One of the optimistic changes was the takeover of the first telephone lines out of Denver by the Western Union and Bell Telephone Lines. Another change was the school district purchase, in 1881, of the now unused Congregational Church, to be used for the first four grades. This was to ease the overcrowding of the stone schoolhouse on the street above.

A personal change was the acquisition of a sewing machine for the Champion home. With so many to sew for, Levinia simply could not keep up with the sewing by hand, as she'd done up to that time. So the sewing machine had become a necessity. But Levinia didn't learn to run it. After a lifetime of hand-sewing at home and in her dressmaking establishment in Cornwall, it was too much to try to change that habit. So it was Lillie, industrious steady Lillie, who was taught by the seller to operate the wonderful machine. Levinia cut and fitted and Lillie sewed the seams after school, and on Saturdays, but never on Sunday.

For the Cornish believed Sunday was the day of worship, God's Day. Every Sunday morning the Cornish children went to the Episcopal Church, whose services were arranged for that hour, as were the Sunday school activities. This was worked out so that churchgoers could take in the services held in the Methodist Church in the afternoon, with the Young People's Services in the early evening, followed by Church Services.

Taking in these gatherings of the two Protestant Churches kept the Cornish busy on the Sabbath and was a fine family routine to help the children get a good, solid Protestant Christian background. Their Sundays were so filled there was no time for mischief.

But even if it happened that for any reason, they couldn't attend Church or Sunday school, no work was done at home or in the mines. It went even further than that. Not even a button could be sewed on Sunday, nor a stitch in repair taken, much less sewing on garments on that day. All cooking and preparation was done the day before and readied with the very minimum of activity on Sunday.

Chapter 23

The Tenth Child Born, Hugh Becomes a Citizen, Changes to the Opera House

The new addition to the Champion house was finished in 1881. As had been planned, the three rooms were primarily for the boarders and roomers, leaving the old part of the house for the family.

One of the new rooms was a long large kitchen, built outside the door of the old kitchen, and down four steps on a different level on the slanted lot. That room had an outside door exactly opposite the old kitchen door and led to a long outside walk or narrow porch, railed in for protection. That porch ran the entire width of the new addition, from which some twenty steps with a sturdy banister, led to the back yard where Old Bossy and the chickens had their own buildings. There too, were the clotheslines and the "privy" or "back house."

Around to the right, the railed-in porch extended several feet along the old kitchen to the front street, from the back door of the new kitchen, so that the roomers could enter there instead of going into and through the family part of the house. Along the left side of the big kitchen was a room almost as long. The only part cut off was room enough for a narrow stairway rising from the kitchen to the floor above. This second largest room was the dining room. It had two windows, placed side by side, overlooking the back yard, and there was quite a large pantry, or storeroom, under the stairway.

A large Charter Oak stove (very much like the well-known Bismark of that period) was put in the new kitchen. It had a hearth and a reservoir for the hot water. It stood on sturdy legs that looked from the front like those of a fat god, offering something on a tray (the hearth), grinning at you through the ruddy grate behind the doors that opened like gates above the hearth.

At one end of the firebox, there was a door that opened to allow quite large sticks of wood to be pushed into it. Emily said this opening was the side-mouth of the god, used for gobbling up its victims which she added, was put at the side instead of at the front, to fool those victims. A second door at the side, below the firebox, was used to take the ashes out, a job given to Albert.

A long strong homemade table was placed below the double windows that looked out upon the Andrews house next door. There were cupboards for groceries, dishes and for the pans of milk standing for the cream to rise before "scalding." One cupboard had glass doors that revealed the contents inside. The girls were kept on their toes keeping it neat and the glass shining.

Behind the back door of the new kitchen, Hugh put a homemade piece of furniture that served the purpose of a "sink," where the men washed before eating or going to their rooms. It was about 2x4 feet and had a five inch board around all sides and on the top. This "railing" and the top of the tablesink were covered with oilcloth, carefully pasted down to keep all water from going through. In the extreme end of this piece of furniture, there was a round hole through which the wastewater from the washbasin was poured into a large pail that stood below, hidden from sight by a curtain on a string. The pail had a handle or bail, by which it was carried outside to the porch where a pipe was set up endwise. This pipe had an old tin dishpan with a large hole cut out fitted over it, which served as a funnel to take the wastewater through the pipe to the flume that ran to Gregory Creek across the alley from the back of the Champion home. Levinia was very proud of Hugh's installation of the "sink" which saved her so many steps.

In the dining room of the addition, there was a heating stove and a large table where the boarders ate. In the upstairs room, reached by the long and very narrow flight of stairs from the new kitchen, were double beds set up in rows, making it look more or less like a barracks. There were drawers in which the roomers could put their clean clothing and extra garments and there were wall hooks for coats and hats.

As Levinia surveyed her new working quarters, she thought she had a very handy convenient and comfortable place for the men to live and for her to work, while the family was more or less alone, yet under her thumb at all times. They ate their meals in the new kitchen, before she sent them to the old part of the house.

In the old kitchen, up those four steps from the new one, they had kept the old coal stove for heat, and the big table for study and games. The parlor became the "parlor" again by adding a few pieces of furniture. There was a small table and some chairs, and the old couches were recovered, while a few bright pictures the children had cut from advertisements or from magazines were in place on the walls. On the small table were the Bible and a coal oil lamp that allowed Levinia to see to read the "Book" each evening before the children went to bed. At his bedside, each child knelt and repeated a prayer he had been taught.

Will and Albert occupied the small bedroom and the double bed Jim Mitchell had left. The girls had the big room, Lillie one big bed to herself and Emily and Edith slept in the other.

Hugh said he'd never expected to have such a large house with Levinia. He rejoiced in its possession even though they owed for part of the new addition and would be in debt for quite a while.

On January 6th of the next year 1882, Mabel, a fair little dumpling, and the last of the Hugh Champion family was born. Levinia, then forty-five, thought she had passed the age of childbearing, but welcomed the little one gladly.

Hugh said proudly, "Ten younguns born to us, Vinia, and six of 'em alive and healthy and active."

Then he sobered and Levinia knew he was thinking of Emily, the only child with a defect. She said defensively, "Emily isn't unhealthy! She can do all her sisters do!" And Hugh nodded that she was right. Yet, they both knew Emily was a cripple. The "hump" on her shoulders was becoming larger. They feared that as time went on she might have trouble from it and from thoughtless children when she went to school. So they decided to keep her at home until Edith, a year younger, started to school. That way, Edith would be with her and in some ways protect her, at least report any slurs that might be given about her deformity.

In 1882, fifteen years after he'd made his Declaration to become citizen of the United States, Hugh Champion fulfilled the requirements of the Government for the granting of that citizenship. Through testimony of his residence by Richard Harvey and Robert B. Hathway, Hugh became a naturalized citizen of the land he had chosen over his native Cornwall. His Allegiance to Queen Victoria of Great Britain ended.

Levinia wept with joy when she read the paper that made the entire family citizens of the United States. She had waited so long for Hugh to do it and had done all she could to hurry that act.

That same year several Central City families listened to music transmitted by telephone wire from Georgetown, in their homes. Hugh and Levinia and the older children were invited to listen at these homes and found it hard to believe what they heard.

Soon after, news came concerning their beloved Opera House. Since the changes from top billings in drama and opera, it had become a different sort of entertainment house having minstrel shows, Cornish wrestling matches, high school graduation exercises, political meetings and boxing exhibitions. J. L.

Sullivan gave one of these and action-picture slides of the Corbet-Fitzsimmons prizefight were shown there.

Even that status was threatened in 1882. The Opera House Organization and the directors, who had put up the bulk of the money, were in financial straits and possession of the property was now doubtful. The value of the Opera House was set at only $8,000 and it became necessary to refinance it. Horace M. Hale, the head of the school system, had advanced $2,000 out of his own pocket to try to help keep the organization alive.

For years after that, the Opera House was nothing more than a Community Hall, but the residents of the community were pleased because it was at least open. Finally, it was bought by the County commissioners for use as a Court House. When it became known that this transfer would necessitate the elimination of the theater section, the citizens protested. After careful consideration, the commissioners offered to sell the building for $8,000, the exact sum they had paid for it. In December 1882, the structure was purchased through the efforts of those who wanted it preserved. For many years it was operated as a theatre under lease to resident managers by the Gilpin County Opera House Association.

Later, it fell into the hands of the McFarlane family, which had played such an important part in the original finishing of the structure, when it opened a half century before with such gala recognition.

Much later, in 1931, the Opera House was given by the heirs of the McFarland family to the University of Denver as a memorial to the pioneers of Colorado. This arrangement stipulated that after its restoration, the building would once more maintain the high standards of music and drama which had been expected of it in 1878. On July 16, 1932, the old Opera House was opened with "Camille." It was a grand success.

Central City Opera House Reopening.
Photo courtesy of Denver Public Library, Western History Collection.

Since then, except when it was closed by necessity during the war, the Opera House in Central City, Colorado has held a six-week Summer Festival which is known throughout the entire United States and in many foreign countries as well. Thus the old building in a former gold camp was restored to the glamour it had held in its heyday a half century before.

Because of the restoration of this old Opera House and the interest of the University of Denver, the historic gold camp of Central City has come back into a well-known spot in history. Town properties have been purchased and renovated, summer business has grown and the entire community holds a special place in dramatic and musical circles with the Opera House as its center. Fine roads now carry the thousands and thousands of music and drama lovers and tourists to this historic center of the "Richest Square Mile on Earth."

Chapter 24

Hugh Has Silicosis, Another Flood

Hugh Champion's brothers, Richard (Dick) and Tom, came to Central City within a few months of each other. Dick and his wife, a childless couple, didn't stay very long. Hugh and Levinia knew they went back to Cornwall because he didn't work at the job Hugh obtained for him at the Bobtail. He loved to get out with "the boys," and spent a great deal of his time drinking with them in saloons. His wife, red-headed Lizzie did not approve. Armed with her rolling pin, she would search until she found him in a saloon and take him home. She told Hugh that in Cornwall she could control Dick's drinking better and make him work more.

Levinia was glad Lizzie went back home, for the woman was very adventurous and dared go to places Levinia thought a lady shouldn't go. For instance, Lizzie never missed attending the public hangings held far up on Bates Hill. She stood close to take everything in and then reported every gory detail to Levinia's children.

Tom, Hugh's other brother, had lost his wife in Cornwall and had married again. He came to Central City alone and took the job Hugh had waiting for him in the mine. As soon as he was established in a house in Central City, he sent for his wife, Bess, a son two years old named Albert, and three children by his first wife. Emily Jane was about sixteen, Tom Jr. fourteen, and Richard, eleven.

Tom, an industrious and steady worker with very outstanding Cornish characteristics, was a fine citizen. He liked the new country because it offered more opportunities for him and his family. He was about Hugh's height and weight and, like Hugh, dark stalwart and energetic, willing to do his part in all circumstances. Their families became very close.

George Perry, one of Levinia's three brothers, came to Central City bringing his curly-haired wife, Christina, whom Hugh's children were taught to call, "Auntie Perry" and their two half-grown sons, George Jr. and John. George Sr., tall slender and light complexioned like Levinia, went to work as a miner when he couldn't find other employment. He was a gentle man, understanding and quick to see another's viewpoint. He was a good friend to everyone, but no match for his wife's planning and directing.

He and Levinia got along very well, and Hugh tried to help as much as George's wife would allow. The Champion boys tried to teach their Perry cousins the new ways and methods of America but they realized that "Auntie Perry" and her sons considered themselves above their American cousins. So, the Champion brothers called the Perrys "stuck up" and "toney" in Cornish terms.

Levinia knew this difficulty between the boys came about in part because George Perry, Sr. had been able to bring some money when he came to America, a fact that placed him on a different scale from Hugh, who always had to struggle to meet his bills. Auntie Perry refused to live in the same area of Central City where the Champions lived and moved her family into a house on Casey Avenue, a section considered quite choice and restricted. The young Champions accepted the move with scorn and made it uncomfortable for the Perry boys at times by pointing out their attitude as "big headed."

Another thing that set the Perrys apart was the fact that George Perry, Jr. never worked in a mine. His mother saw to it that he got a job she called "employment" in Hawley's Mercantile, on Main Street in Central City. He did well there, stayed on and married a Hawley girl. Later they moved to Denver, where George continued to be associated with the grocery business.

In her heart, Levinia thought Auntie Perry was right in seeing that her son didn't enter the mineshafts. She wished her son Will wasn't interested in going to work with his father at the Bobtail. She feared the dread disease, silicosis. It wasn't because she wanted Will to be above mining, as her sister-in-law insisted her sons were.

George Sr. found "employment," as Auntie Perry reported, in the railroad yards in Denver and he and his wife moved there. After that, the two families grew apart, although Johnny, the second Perry son, stayed around Central City, working at different jobs, and never put in a day in the mines. He often visited in Levinia's home, ate her Cornish cooking, and was closer to her family than his brother was. But because Johnny liked to repeat what he heard and tell what he saw, his cousins avoided telling him much about their affairs. After several years of quite close friendship, John Perry moved to Pueblo, Colorado, where he married Bessie Polkinghorn of a prominent family, a fact which in her heart made Levinia very proud.

By the time 1883 came, investor capital had been diverted from Gregory Gulch to the booming Leadville area, where silver was leading Colorado in metal production. The mines of Gilpin County were neglected by investors, causing the output of gold to drop from the two and a half million dollar record to one and a quarter million.

This drop didn't affect the Hugh Champion family as much as one would expect, for the mines were still running and all the miners wanted were jobs that paid enough to keep their families fed, clothed and comfortable. Of course, if they could make enough to save a little they were well pleased, but they weren't greedy, just very fugal and conservative while being thankful.

Hugh worked every week at the Bobtail Mine but, Levinia saw with apprehension that he was slowing down physically. He wasn't as active as he had been. He had given up the outside diversions he loved: wrestling, foot-racing and the drilling contests. And he didn't sing at home as he'd always done. She learned from the men he worked with that he didn't sing out happily with his strong voice as they marched double file when they descended from the mines to the town, dropping off each man at his own gate or street.

During that winter, Hugh had a cold he couldn't throw off. He became worse and developed a cough that became more and more troublesome. Will, then an observant fourteen, noticed it and discussed it with his mother. They realized that Hugh wasn't well, though nothing further was said about it.

The next development was the fact that Hugh couldn't sleep in his bed and he would get up and sit in his chair and doze there. The upright position seemed to help his breathing and ease his coughing. These indications pointed out to Levinia that the dreaded silicosis had taken a firm hold on her husband.

In private, she shed many bitter discouraged tears. But in front of Hugh and the children she maintained a cheerfulness that never faltered, not even during the next year, when he became gradually worse. He kept on working, and forced himself to keep on with his job. Mr. Rogers, manager of the Bobtail, realized Hugh's physical condition and eased his mine duties until, by the end of 1884, Hugh became night watchman at the Bobtail Tunnel.

It wasn't long before he had to give up all thought of working in any capacity. He couldn't even walk up town, so he couldn't attend church services unless he rented a rig or rode with someone who brought some kind of conveyance. The pastor and members of Hugh's Sunday School Class and Bible Study, held extra sessions in the Champion home so that he could participate in the church work he had grown to love so much. Members of the Church dropped in often to see him and Cornish friends came to sing to him. All this attention did him a lot of good and he remarked that nowhere did anyone harmonize better than Cornish voices.

Hugh Has Silicosis, Another Flood

The presence of Hugh's brother Tom helped both Hugh and Levinia. Tom and Hugh spent a good many hours reminiscing about Cornwall, their boyhood and the family they had shared there. And there was a great deal of discussion about their aged mother in her far away Cornwall home. They were glad that Dick had gone back and that he and their sister, Jane, were near her to look after her.

To Levinia, Tom Champion was a considerate and understanding brother, far closer to her than her own brother, George Perry. Tom was a staunch friend as well to her and her family, who loved him dearly. To Will, he was an advisor, understanding and very patient, always ready to help in any way he could.

One day in 1884, Hugh suddenly suggested that Levinia and he have a photograph taken. He reminded her that they hadn't had a picture of any kind taken in all the twenty-one years they had been married.

So, on the day she made the last payment on the house addition, using the last wages Hugh was to earn, she made arrangements with the Central City photographer. The picture was taken in the Champion home because Hugh couldn't go up town to the studio.

When the photograph was shown to Hugh, he said the "pitcher" didn't show them as they really were. He declared that he couldn't believe the stiff, unnatural-looking couple was Levinia and him, seated side-by-side on chairs with carved backs and fringed bottoms brought by the photographer for the sitting. Albert, ten years of age, cocked his dark head and studied the likenesses critically. Then he said, "Both of you look sad and cranky." The other children agreed. But Will, fifteen, complained thoughtfully, that they looked just like that on Sundays when they were in church, or when they soundly scolded any of them. Then he said, "Pictures never show people as they are every day," and his smile was warm and loving.

Levinia could understand what the boys meant. She thought the couple in the photograph much too posed and too dignified, their faces too sober, their bodies held in an unnatural prim position. Yet, when she examined the likenesses very closely, she liked what she saw. Although she had to look beneath the unnaturalness that struck one at first glance, to realize that the photographer had caught some very important things she wanted to have impressed upon her mind.

First, she studied Hugh's appearance. He was dressed in his very best; a dark suit with his coat open, showing the vest and white shirt. He wore square-toed boots with heels over an inch high, as was the custom of that day. She wondered if his lips beneath the "General Grant" type of beard were as set as hers, which showed so plainly in the picture. Then she noticed only the extreme ends of his black bow tie showed beyond his whiskers. What she

No Wealth for Levinia

Hugh and Levinia, 1884

liked best about Hugh's photograph was that it showed his thick heavy, dark hair and large capable hands, with his fingers bent at the first joint to rest on his legs above knees, as they always did when he sat empty handed.

Curiously, she looked at her own likeness. There was a feeling of sadness and disappointment because it reflected a Levinia Champion she didn't know. The face was set, the eyes stared coldly in a determined "do-or-die way," the lips were held so rigidly she actually looked stern and forbidding. The hair, parted in the middle and drawn back severely into a bun at the back of her head, carried out the appearance of unforgivable relentlessness the face betrayed.

Dismayed, she told herself she wasn't really the person the photo tried to say she was. She thought, I'm not like that inside. Not even on Sunday do I feel like the woman in the picture looks. She wished the happiness she felt most of the time could have been shown. She regretted that her love for and the pride she felt in her husband, her children and her home, could have been reflected in the likeness she was studying.

For an instant, she thought of the curls she used to wear, and she smiled. Hugh had loved those signs of "lightness," but she hadn't even missed that old custom of wearing curls. It had been dropped when her busy life had no time for them. Their love, she concluded, had needed no curls, no adornments. How lucky they both had been! How wonderful their years together!

Her eyes returned to the photo. The fine work displayed the dress she'd made for herself and that pleased her very much. It was heavy black silk, made with an over-skirt. The bottom flounce, with wide silk fringe, touched the floor as she sat. The upper flounce with fringe half as wide, was some four inches above the lower flounce. The dress had long sleeves of ordinary fullness, with ruching at the wrists. The neck had a ruche of the same black material, a white ruche above it, next to her face. Covered black buttons were placed in front from the neck to the upper flounce of skirt. At her throat she wore a cameo brooch and from her neck a fine gold chain fell in double strands to her lap. The chain's ornament, a small gold ball, was hidden by her left hand which rested on her right one. The fingers of both hands were bent in a position she wasn't conscious of ever assuming!

She had a swift thought that her hands looked very strange, resting like that, for they were seldom idle. She worked all day and did her sewing in the evening. Only when she read the Bible were her hands still. Oh, yes, she amended with a smile, "I rest my hands when I nurse my babies and rock them and when I pray." Then she noticed that in the photo, her hands looked larger than Hugh's square ones. When they measured them, they found it was true. Her hands were as wide as Hugh's and her fingers were longer.

Will remarked that her hands had grown large because she milked the "smelly" ole cow. The boy was fastidious and disliked animals, while Albert loved them all: cats, dogs, even burros, but horses were Albert's real love. He spent all the time he could in the horse barns. He helped feed and tend the horses that drew the ore wagons. He loved being with them so much that he unwillingly, at first, accepted the pay the barn keepers insisted he had earned.

Levinia closed the subject of the reason her hands were large by putting the photograph away. She whimsically thought that wringing out so many garments on washday every week for years and years could have had its influence on the size of her hands.

Later, she brought the photo out again. This time to settle a point that had troubled her. As they sat there, she looked three inches taller than Hugh, when the truth was they had been the very same height when they were married. Close scrutiny showed that Hugh really looked shorter. Her heart contracted painfully as she realized that silicosis had shown its influence; that he who had been so erect, so strong and had carried himself so proudly, couldn't hold his body straight now. Silently, she rebelled against what she knew he faced. It was cruel!

Hugh's condition got worse until he could no longer draw a deep breath. His breathing became more and more shallow and labored. What little sleep he got was while he sat in a straight chair propped up as straight as possible in an effort to get his breath. The quartz particles he'd breathed in and swallowed as dust, had filled his lungs and sealed his air passages.

It was during those last inevitable stages of silicosis that a flash flood came roaring down Packard Gulch one afternoon, opposite and above the Champion home. There had been many floods from that Gulch during heavy summer showers. Those floods had deposited gravel and silt from the steep slopes of Packard Gulch onto Gregory and Miner Streets and in front of their house until all the low places had been filled. Gradually, those repeated deposits had filled in the space in front of their house until, instead of going up the original seven steps to the front porch, the porch was now about level with the street.

In this particular flood, there was no place to deposit the load of gravel and fine dirt as it was swept down, trying to reach Gregory Creek below and beyond the Champion house. The water overflowed the flume to carry off the run-off between the Andrews and the Champion houses. The floodwaters broke into the Champion cellar and dropped most of its contents there. Then, with no more space to fill and no area to cover, the

Hugh Has Silicosis, Another Flood

water crept higher and higher toward the front door of the Champion kitchen, which was almost directly in its path.

Levinia, in the upper kitchen with all the children around her except Will, sixteen, who was at work in the Bobtail Mine where his father had obtained a job for him, heard the deep, resounding thunder and the sharp cracks of lightning that accompanied the summer deluge. She watched anxiously as the water ran down the Gulch through an open space between the Bennallack Grocery and an empty cabin. With fear, she saw the angry stream increase in volume and force as the hard rain continued, pelting the roof of the house so loudly that speech was almost impossible to be heard.

When she realized the flume wouldn't carry the floodwater, she knew it would pile against the house and come in or over it this time, as it never had before. Already she could see that the roaring, tumbling stream was coming higher and higher toward her home, heading for the door. If the storm continued, the house would be swept away!

She had to save the children and Hugh, who sat in his chair in the parlor with a rug over his knees and a shawl about his shoulders. Should she send the children out the back door, and command them to go to higher ground? Hugh couldn't do that. There was no chance to get him to safety. There wasn't even time to consult him.

In an instant, she decided to stay in the house and to keep her family with her. If the house went, they would go with it. Neither the children nor she would leave Hugh. But if the water went through the house, in the front door and out the back door, maybe it wouldn't back up and take the house when it broke through.

Albert, eleven, was her only help, her sole hope! She gave him quick directions to run down and open the back door of the new kitchen and fasten it with the big hook behind it in the wall, so that it couldn't close and allow the water to back up and drown them.

"'Urry, Halbert, and run right back to me," she ordered, and then she prayed silently that he'd have time to get back.

Next, she ordered Lillie, fourteen, to put Emily, nine, Edith, eight, and Mabel, three, on the landing to the upstairs, and tell them to hurry to the big room above as fast as they could. Then she ran to Hugh, who was watching the storm through the window. His eyes were anxious, but his voice was quiet when he told her she'd better put all the children upstairs. "Water might come in," he finished, and held her hand to reassure her.

Levinia told him the little ones were upstairs. Then without explanation, she, Lillie, and Albert, who came bounding into the room from his errand, picked Hugh up, chair and all, and carried him to the landing off the kitchen. His chair was set on it, the two children were sent upstairs, and she climbed onto the landing beside him, crouching close, their arms around each other. Just then the water came up to their front door, crashed through its frame, and spread over her kitchen floor. She just had time to snap shut the door to the landing when she heard the flood waters tumble over the four steps to her lower kitchen, then through the opened back door to the yard below.

The Champion father and mother prayed in the darkness. The storm continued. The water rushed through their house, but there wasn't even a tremble in its structure. Later they seemed to hear the thunder from a greater distance, and the lightning became less sharp, which gave them hopes that the storm was abating. In the darkness, shut into the small space together, time seemed endless.

Levinia kept one hand along the bottom of the door from the landing to the kitchen, so that she could feel the water if it came that high. She heard Hugh say the house was well-built and strong. She felt his arm about her shoulder, giving her comfort through its confidence.

Lillie, watching from an upstairs window that faced the street, called down to them that in the flashes of lightning that pierced the darkness the storm had brought, she was sure there wasn't as much water coming down Packard Gulch as there had been! Levinia thanked God, waited a few minutes, then reached in front of Hugh to open the door a crack so that she could look out into the kitchen below the landing. The light was very faint, but she could see that water was running slowly over its floor, in what she guessed was about three inches deep.

She squirmed about, wanting to go down and examine the damage, but Hugh cautioned her to stay where she was until they were absolutely sure the storm was over, and there was light enough for her to see clearly. So she sat impatiently, the door open now through which they could see the room come into view with all the mud and silt. Her heart was torn between discouragement at what she saw, and thankfulness that her home still stood as a shelter for her husband and their children. She stooped and looked at the watermark along the wall beneath the door to the landing. The water had risen within an inch of its floor!

They stayed where they were until no more water ran along the kitchen floor. Then Hugh agreed that it was all right for her to go down and look around. The storm clouds had dispersed. The early evening was bright, showing the effects of the flash storm. The children were impatient to come down. Albert insisted that he had better get out there and see what had happened. Hugh said the "nipper" could help her.

Levinia took off her shoes and stockings and descended gingerly into the mud. Albert and Lillie, barefoot at their mother's suggestion, joined her. The three little girls sat on the stairs behind their father's chair and waited, their tongues busy with questions and expressions of their eerie experiences in the dark upstairs while the storm raged. Little Mabel snuggled as close to "Papa" as she could, his arm holding her comfortingly.

Levinia was surprised how little real damage had come to their home. Of course, the water had left sediment, even some good-sized pebbles on the floors of the two kitchens, and the walls as high as the water had reached were dirty from the mud. But very little water had entered the parlor and none had flowed to the bedroom behind it. The dining room below had fared the same way, just some "side water" had spilled into it from the main volume of the floodwaters, as they rushed to get out the back door on their way to Gregory Creek.

Albert went down into the back yard and reported that Old Bossy was in the barn. The floor was pretty wet, and the chickens were on their roosts, very damp, but not at all harmed and not a one was missing!

Will came home from work early, before they could get much done; even before Albert could report the damage that had been done to the property. Will lifted his father and his chair down and set them on the side of the parlor the water hadn't even reached. Then he carried the little girls to stay with him. Levinia heard the big lad order them to keep out of the mud and heard Hugh answer that they would. Then Will joined her and Lillie in the upper kitchen and they mapped out a plan to clean the house and see to the boarders' supper.

Fortunately, the meal had been planned and started before the storm came. The pies were baked and placed on the dining room table to cool. So were the pasties and the saffron cake for the lunch buckets next day. The water hadn't reached that table! They stood in a proud array that lightened Levinia's heart. But the roast beef, in the oven when the storm broke, was completely ruined by the muddy water that filled the oven. The stove itself, just three feet from the back door, was covered with mud where the water had splashed against it, and there was muddy water and silt in its reservoir! The teakettle was gone, so were the homemade rugs from both kitchen floors.

The water reached the lower cupboard shelves and every bit of food and staples there was ruined. The milk standing in the pans in the cupboard was mixed with muddy water. In another cupboard every pan and the milk in them had been removed by the force of the floodwaters and had disappeared. But all in all, Levinia was thankful so little had been carried away or destroyed.

When the boarders came from work, they pitched in and helped remove the mud from the floors. Others, from Will's and Albert's age groups, joined in the cleaning up and the final scrubbing.

The women of the community took over the supper problems. The meal for the Champion family and their boarders was served at one home with the food gathered from several homes to supplement that left intact at Levinia's house.

That night the Champion family was separated for the very first time, for it was thought wise not to have them sleep in the damp house. Hugh was carried across the street and he, Levinia and little Mabel stayed in one neighbor's home, the three girls in another and the boys in a third.

The roomers said they'd stay on in their own beds in the upstairs rooms of the new part of the house, though they did accept the offer to have breakfast at a neighbor's house, and to pick up their lunch buckets at a second.

The next day was bright, sunny and warm. Levinia and her helpers, who insisted upon working with her, threw open all the windows and doors to allow the house to dry out. They cleaned the stoves where the water had left marks in the two kitchens inside and out, and put the kettle on for tea. They washed down the walls to remove the high water lines and smudges, and worked until they were satisfied with the cleanliness of the rooms where the water had been. As they worked, they ate some of the food Levinia had prepared the day before and finished off with cup after cup of strong tea which Cornish consider an absolute necessity. Next they brought in a new supply of groceries from the store across the street to take the place of what the water had taken or ruined.

But Hugh wasn't allowed to return home for another night and a day, for it was decided he mustn't risk getting a cold from the dampness that might remain in the house. So Levinia stayed in the neighbor's home with him, but all the children moved back in the charge of Will and Lillie.

After serious consideration, it was agreed that the greatest damage the flood had done was underneath the house. Up to that time, with the exception of the inevitable sediment that water had left there from small run-offs and from seepage in the cellar, the entire space under the house was open. Beneath the older part of the house, there was space set off for the storage of fruits and vegetables to prevent them from freezing in the long and very cold winters. This was the space just below the door between the two kitchens, where the water barrels, the wood, kindling and coal were kept.

Beneath the new rooms the wood and coal for the cook stove in the kitchen, and the heater in the dining room where the boarders ate, were stored. There was also room for the water barrels used in the newer part of the house. But the last flood had filled the entire space under the house with rocks, gravel, and silt, burying the fuel centers, the water barrels and the vegetable cellar. Will and Albert, assisted by their friends, dug out enough dirt to make room for the supplies of fuel and water, and made a new cave for a cellar. They wheeled all that deposit to the creek in wheelbarrows, a back-breaking task that took weeks!

That particular flood stood out in the memories of all the Champions, except Mabel, who was too young to remember how horrible it was and how much worse it might have been.

Chapter 25

Hugh's Death on New Year's Day, January 1, 1886

Hugh Champion didn't live long after that harrowing experience. Little by little, during the next few weeks his breathing became more and more labored as he struggled for air. He suffered terribly. Levinia realized that nothing could be done for him and that the end was near and tried to maintain a calm composure in the face of what she really felt, steeling herself to conceal her anguish and schooling the children to be cheerful. She stayed with him constantly. She turned over the cooking for the boarders, the cleaning of their beds and rooms and the care of the children to Lillie and Aunt Bess, Tom Champion's wife.

After one last futile effort to get his breath, Hugh died in his chair January 1, 1886, at the age of forty-seven years, three months and twenty-four days, one of the very few hard-rock miners to reach the age of forty. Most of them died in their early or middle thirties.

As the doctor covered Hugh's face, confirming Levinia's fear that Hugh had left her, her first thought was that she couldn't wish him back to suffer as he had. Then she fell to her knees beside him in the chair and sobbed wildly, relieving herself of the stern self-inflicted composure she'd maintained for Hugh and the children. The doctor let her cry until she was able to control herself somewhat, then drew her to her feet and took her out into the upper kitchen where the children waited with Tom and Aunt Bess. To them he announced gently, "He is beyond all suffering now," and seated Levinia in a chair among them.

Tom Champion took charge at once. With Will, he made all arrangements with the undertaker for the burial which, because all bodies were taken care

Hugh's Death on New Year's Day, January 1, 1886

of at the home instead of at an undertaking establishment at that time, couldn't be put off any longer than was absolutely necessary. The interment of Hugh was a very difficult one, for a heavy snowstorm occurred at the time of his death. The snow drifted into every low place. It filled the streets, the Gulches and all the roads that led out of town, making it impossible to drive about unless snow was removed by snowplows.

On the day of Hugh's death, knowing that it would take some time to dig a grave in the frozen earth of the family lot at the top of wind swept Cemetery Hill, Tom knew he had to make immediate plans to get around the difficulty. He first contacted the snowplow crew and efforts were made at once to remove the snow up the Eureka Gulch road to the cemetery, so that the hearse and funeral carriages could get through. Next Tom, Will and volunteers from among Hugh's many friends went by foot up the long hill to the gravesite, to pack the drifted snow as much as possible.

Finally, after trying to dig in the frozen earth, Tom found he would have to use dynamite to loosen the dirt. Those with him agreed but were afraid to set off the explosive, which was brought by a man dispatched to town for it. They feared the blast would disturb the graves of Hugh's children, so close to the spot indicated as the last resting place of the father. So Tom had to do the blasting himself. His skill, knowledge and great caution prevented any damage to the graves, and Hugh's grave was made ready.

The next day the road up Eureka Street to the bottom of the hill in Eureka Gulch was only partially opened, while the hill just below the cemetery was covered with such deep new snow it simply couldn't be cleared in time for the funeral. Tom and the undertaker consulted with others concerned. The undertaker declared bluntly that he couldn't hold the body any longer than the next day. So it was decided that the hearse and carriages would go as far up Cemetery Hill as possible, then the body would have to be carried the rest of way to the lot, by men struggling through the snow.

In her grief, Levinia hardly realized the plan. The casket containing Hugh's body was carried by his closest friends through the little white gate, which opened from the house to the street, and placed in the black hearse drawn by coal-black horses, waiting in front of the house. All she was able to understand at that moment was her Hugh was leaving his home for the very last time.

As in a dream, she went with Tom and her brother, George Perry, to the first carriage behind the hearse. She was aware that Will, Lillie and Albert joined them in that carriage and she knew the other children were with Aunt Bess and Auntie Perry in the second carriage. But her thoughts were with Hugh, her husband, who had gone from her forever.

At the church George reminded her that the service was about to begin. She got out of the carriage, went up the outside steps to the first floor of the church, then climbed the beautiful, long steep, circular stairs that led to the Sanctuary. She went with the others down the long auditorium to a seat in its front, quite close to the casket, already in place. As if from a great distance she heard music and knew the service had begun. Though she seemed to know the pastor spoke words of comfort to her and the children, she couldn't really follow and the words he spoke directly to her made little impression upon her stunned mind.

But in the solitude of her own room that night, she could understand all that had happened at the services. She could appreciate the beauty and the simplicity of those solemn moments in the church Hugh had loved and for which he had done so much. And she was deeply thankful that it had been done as Hugh would have liked. The realization comforted her.

Because of the difficulty experienced after the church rites, memory of that cold winter day was to remain with her forever. When the body was placed in the hearse at the church, and the mourners and friends were in the carriages again, the funeral procession left the church and proceeded up the street to Cemetery Hill as far as the snow had been cleared away. At the foot of the first rise to the mesa where the several cemeteries are located, the hearse was forced to stop with just enough room to get the horses around and for men to take the tongue of the vehicle out of its usual place in front and place it at the back of the heavy hearse. This was the emergency position planned for in just such a case. In this way, the horses can draw the hearse back down hill without turning it around, an impossible feat when the snow is so deep.

The casket was removed from the hearse and the pallbearers, spelled by volunteers for the really difficult task of getting the body to the burial lot, carried it on their shoulders up the hill and across the mesa, where the winds swept snow with icy particles into their faces. The last few feet, between the cemetery gate and the lot, were the most difficult, for the snow had drifted since the grave had been opened, covering the path.

It was impossible for Levinia and any of her children except Will and Albert to go with Tom, George, and the pastor, who followed the pallbearers. She sat with Lillie in the carriage, which had been turned around to go back down the hill. She couldn't see her husband laid in his last resting place. Nor could she help bring him to the children already there on the bleak hill in the blinding snow.

In the days that followed, Levinia was more and more thankful for the presence of Tom Champion. It was he who stood between her and the many heart-rending circumstances that surrounded her in her great loss. Even with his help, as well as his understanding wife and family and that of her own brother and his wife, she could hardly stand her grief. She found that even the loss of her first-born children couldn't be compared with the complete and absolute loss she felt when Hugh was taken from her. In the agony of giving him up, she thought she just couldn't go on without him. He wasn't there to bolster her courage, to help her face the great empty void. Only her faith and staunch belief in the hereafter, when she would again be with Hugh and the others who'd gone before, carried her through the hours, days, weeks, months and years that she lived after Hugh's death.

Those twenty-six years she lived without him comprised an entirely new life for her, a life built without his help, his approval or criticism. A new life was built by her own planning and efforts. Though it was shared by her children, to whom their father became a fond memory which Levinia kept clear and proud, she was the pivot upon which their lives revolved. She prayed for help to make her strong and steadfast and to keep her healthy and able to work to provide for her children.

Chapter 26

Mining Improvements, Family Makes Plans for Life Without Hugh

Shortly after Hugh's death, the news came of an accomplishment he had watched and waited for, hoping it would come about before he died. It was the report in The Register-Call of May 5, 1886.

The Consolidated Bobtail Company has commenced driving ahead a diamond drill hole in the incline shaft in order to guard against any accident that might possibly occur from the tapping of water in old workings of the Gregory lode west of the present heading of the incline shaft. The drill will be kept 100 feet in advance of the shaft heading. Steam pumps will be used for drainage purposes, one of which will soon be in place. The foundation for the hoisting plant of machinery will soon be in position and enclosed in a building.

A week later, in the same publication: *The incline shaft of the Gregory lode has attained the length of 700 feet from its initial point and possibly a depth from surface of 500 feet in the Gregory lode, the present driving of the incline southwest being four feet a day.*

Under the date of May 28, 1886, The Register-Call reported: *Last evening, thirty pounds of nitroglycerine was fired in the diamond drill hole sunk from the end of the incline shaft on the Gregory-Bobtail lode, Black Hawk. At 2:30 that same day; the joyous tidings have just been wafted over the telephone wires in this office from the company's office, that the tamping had been removed from the drill hole, and the water came out with a rush, and is now mingling itself with the water of Clear Creek. The people of not only Black Hawk, but of the entire county, rejoice with Mr. A. N. Rogers and his able associates in the successful consummation of this long-looked for objective.*

Mining Improvements, Family Makes Plans for Life Without Hugh

Levinia read the report with streaming eyes and thought what a fitting close to Hugh's life this news would have been. If only he could have lived to know that his great hope for the Bobtail had finally come true, that this achievement had actually come about.

Because of an interest created by his father in the Bobtail, the mine which he had worked so long, and where Will now worked, Will was very enthusiastic over the news. He showed Levinia that the personal feelings of the Champions had been instilled in their son, and that the Bobtail was more than a mere mine to him, as well.

On July 23, of that year, 1886, water mains were laid on Main Street of Central City, and plans were made for extension to other parts of town.

About that same time Frederick Kruse, a member of an old pioneer family, organized the Gilpin County Tramway Company and started to lay track from a depot north of Black Hawk up Chase Creek to the mines around Central City, Nevadaville and Russell Gulch. Levinia listened to Will's excited explanation. It was a diminutive two foot gauge railroad designed to transport ore down to the mills at Black Hawk or for shipping on the Colorado Central Railroad to the Hill Smelter at Argo, Colorado.

Following her son's growing interest in mining, Levinia recalled his father's own enthusiasm, his beliefs and his knowledge. Thus, she was able to converse intelligently with Will about mining in general, and its history in and around Central City. Will was much surprised. She knew he hadn't thought her capable of having the actual knowledge she had.

Levinia realized, too, that much of Will's information had come from Hugh's training of his older son. As was typical of Cornish fathers, Hugh had instilled in his boy the belief that women, while dear and precious, and worthy of the highest esteem of all men, were not supposed, nor expected to be intelligent. They certainly weren't to show the intelligence they acquired in any way. Women were supposed to be docile and, if not obedient in the strictest sense of the word to their husband's wishes and directions, they were expected to listen, but not talk. In silence, they were supposed to listen as their husbands expounded to their hearts' content.

She knew, too, that Hugh had taught Will that the eldest in a Cornish family is the most important possession of the Cornish father. She was well aware that no other son, no matter how many he might have, could take the place of that first-born, or eldest boy. This position Will occupied because of the death of the first William John.

Levinia spent many hours thinking about that fact. Now that Hugh was gone, and she was both mother and father to the family, even to Will, she studied what she could do with him and the others in regard to his having been raised as the most important in the entire family. He was, of course because he was older than the others, her mainstay in the future she faced. But Will needed help and guidance. She wouldn't even suggest that Will consider his Uncle Tom as a substitute for his father, not entirely that is. Of course, there would be many questions she wouldn't be able to answer for him as well as Tom could, many occasions when Will would need a man behind him. In that case, she admitted thankfully, there was no one she wanted to call in but Tom.

Already Tom had shown his interest, his willingness and ability to advise Will, yet Levinia felt she mustn't allow Will to depend too much upon him. At the same time, she had to let the boy develop without her domination. After long consideration, she decided to try to show Will that she would listen, then when the opportunity came, she would try to help him in the things she felt she could.

With their common interest in mining and its important place in Central City and in the county, she found a way to become closer to him. She discovered that he was old beyond his years and experience. In taking on a man's job at the Bobtail and trying to keep up with what his father expected of him, he now expected to take on the responsibility of the family his mother had to raise: four children under twelve and Lillie fifteen, while he was only seventeen, himself! Speaking carefully, grateful to the point of tears, she showed him that he wasn't to be fully responsible for her and the younger children. She reminded him that his father had planned for and had seen to the addition of the three rooms on the house, so that she could support herself and the family by taking in roomers and boarders, while she stayed at home and took care of the children.

By actual figures, she showed him that she could make enough to support the smaller young ones without his financial help, that is, if she kept her health. Then she told him of the plan she had worked out for the family, a plan in which each child was to do his part to help himself and the rest of the family. Each child, she explained, was to have his own tasks and shoulder his own load in holding the family together.

Will's part, she told him gratefully, would be to act as her advisor because he was the oldest child. She said she expected him to show his authority if it became necessary in a decision where she and he had to stand together for the good of everyone.

Will didn't say a word when she finished, but she could see he was impressed by what she'd said. She felt that she surprised him greatly by releasing him from what he'd thought of as his responsibility now that his father was no longer there. She thought he looked relieved as well, and was

Mining Improvements, Family Makes Plans for Life Without Hugh

glad it was possible to lighten the mental load the boy had been carrying because of his father's illness and death.

She waited for a few days so that Will could think matters over. When he came to her and suggested that the family be told her plans, she called them all into the parlor, and they held the first family meeting of the many that were to follow throughout the years. She was the main speaker. However at her suggestion, Will put in a few words now and then, until the others got the idea that Will and their mother were standing together for their good, and that they were to listen and pay heed. They understood that they had to work as a family unit to get along without their father.

When they went to bed that night, it was understood that Lillie was to quit school entirely, so that she could assume her duties as her mother's full-time helper to make a living for them all by keeping boarders and roomers, as they did now. Albert was to stay in school, but would work more steadily with the horses at the barns, and earn as much as he could in doing so. Emily and Edith would have the dishwashing and some of the house cleaning as their projects.

The only member of the family not to have specific duties was four-and-a-half-year-old Mabel. But Levinia singled her out as the one person who was to pick up around the house, and keep things in place. They all laughed as the little girl shrugged and smiled at her own importance and then promised to put her toys away and help everyone.

So Levinia had laid out the pattern for each member to make their own contribution to the family's budget. Though it was in truth, almost the same routine they'd been following since their father's illness, it now had a real and different aspect. They were now on their own, banded together in a group showing strength that gave Levinia an assurance that deepened as time went on.

The Gilpin Heat and Light Company was incorporated in 1887, and electric lines were installed the following year, when electric lights were put in on the streets and in business houses. It was expected that in the next year or two the homes in the vicinity would be illuminated by electricity.

In 1888, trains on the tramway were drawn by Shay locomotives, and gave enormous aid hauling in the ore from the mines in the region.

Another great change that year was the extension of water pipes to the residential districts of Central City. To the Champions it meant a water hydrant in the right hand corner of the kitchen just at the foot of the steps from the old part of the house. It was a great convenience indeed, and meant a lot to Albert especially, whose job had been to carry water upstairs from water barrels in the space under the house.

Chapter 27

Improvements in Central City, Difficulties with Albert

The appointment of Horace M. Hale, the head of the school system, to the presidency of the State University at Boulder, Colorado, that year was a personal loss to all the residents of Central City, though it was a real step for Mr. Hale. The residents were proud that he had been selected for the high position, although they regarded his leaving a district loss.

Emily, twelve, and Edith, eleven, considered his departure almost a calamity. For days they could talk of nothing else. Mabel, in her first year of school didn't miss him, and Albert, fourteen, wasn't at all concerned, for school and Albert weren't on the best of terms. While the girls were good students and loved to attend class, Albert considered going to school a distinct waste of time. The last three years, he had dropped out of school more and more until, as he argued earnestly with his mother after his father died, "There wasn't any use in trying to keep up 'th them smart uns," who liked to study so he might as well stay out entirely, and get a steady job to help her more.

As Levinia and Will listened, trying to decide what was best for the boy, Albert told them he had a mighty good job already, driving "whip," so they said he could try it and see how he made out. Albert certainly did well as "whip." His early love of horses and his close association with them when he helped feed and care for them in the barns had given him an understanding that stood him well in the job he took on.

Driving "whip" meant driving a horse on a hoisting contrivance called a "whip." After the shaft of a new mine became too deep to use a windlass to bring the ore and waste rock from the bottom (usually when the hole is more than 100 feet deep) a tripod of logs or timber called a "whip," some ten or fifteen feet high, was placed over the shaft collar. One pulley was hung from the apex of the tripod with another pulley at its base through which the hoisting was threaded. A horse or mule, usually driven by a boy, was used to hoist the bucket which holds up to 500 or 600 pounds, and the empty bucket was returned by gravity to the shaft bottom, its speed of descent governed by the brake on the "whip." After quite a bit of experience driving "whip," Albert was promoted to a more complicated and elaborate horse-operated engine called the "whim."

A "whim" consisted of a drum or spool on which the hoisting rope was wound and unwound. The drum was connected by means of a bull gear to a boom, or pole. Hitched to the boom's end, the horse, plodded patiently around a circular track, hoisted one bucket, then stood patiently while it was emptied and lowered again by gravity to the shaft bottom. Erected above the shaft collar was a stout, securely braced "gallows frame," of eight inch timbers or logs, 15 feet high, at the top of which was a grooved pulley called "sheave" which carried the hoisting rope. later a steel cable was used in place of the hemp rope from the drum to the ore bucket. Finally, if the mine continued to show promise of paying, this primitive equipment was replaced by a steam hoisting plant compressor to generate air for the machine drills.

If and when a mine began to pay by the use of the "whim," Albert's work was over with that particular mine and he sought another "whim" to drive in another prospector's hope for success. Albert always had a job. In fact, he sought out jobs ahead of time and filled each place so well that he was trusted with the horse he worked in each case. Later, when he was older, he drove an ore wagon. His horses were well-kept and well-trained, and in time Albert became an authority on horses and their training.

Levinia was thankful that Albert had such a deep interest in horses and that he was given a chance to work with them, for the boy had been a problem. He had never liked school. He hated to study and in idle moments had been in trouble, though not of a very serious nature, running the streets, carousing with similar irresponsible boys.

Now, as she looked back on Albert's early boyhood, she came to a half conclusion that a second son was at a disadvantage. The first-born boy was a companion to the father and trained by him. Each son after the first-born was allowed to go on his own more and more until he somehow showed that he needed attention, usually because he had gotten into mischief or had behaved in a way his father didn't approve. Then he was curbed suddenly and severely and made to feel that he had disgraced everyone, especially his father.

Will never caused his parents one minute's worry. He was considerate and cooperative. He knew what was expected of him and kept close to it, striving to live up to his parents' wishes, wanting to have his father's full approval.

But Albert had always seemed thoughtless and his parents were forced to regretfully believe "devilish" at times. He didn't try to do what they wanted him to do. Instead, it seemed as though he liked to see how far he could go before they would check and punish him. He was determined to go out on his own, defying them even when he was punished (and Hugh Champion laid the rod on him very hard). Albert took the beating quietly, refusing to show he'd been hurt by the punishment, and not even once had he said he was sorry he'd caused his father trouble. Levinia remembered the boy's eyes as they met hers after the lashing he'd received, a fleeting glance that seemed to show her he didn't include her in the punishment. Before long, he had earned correction again.

Seeing that severe punishment didn't make Albert any more thoughtful or obedient, they'd tried shutting him in his room upstairs. He made a rope of the bed sheets and swung down the story and a half to the street below. Then he ran away to join his companions who were as curious, energetic and reckless as he, and relied upon his leadership in all they did.

One day the boys went to a large slaughter house far up Eureka Gulch and watched the men butcher sheep, hogs and cattle. It fascinated them and they planned to try out what they had learned. In due time, they were ready. When several families in the community missed their pet cats and searched everywhere for them, they found them butchered and dressed out, hanging in a shed exactly the same way the boys had seen at the slaughter house.

For this cruel and needless killing, they were severely punished by their fathers. They were warned and threatened by the law, which sobered them all completely and for a time they were so subdued they walked the narrow path laid out for their behavior.

During that period, Levinia talked to Hugh and other parents about her belief that the energy the boys had needed to be directed toward some common interest they could and would develop. It was decided that sports might fill the bill. So contests in running, jumping, wrestling, and ball playing resulted, and carried Albert and his young friends through boyhood and early manhood. They developed an intense interest in sport events. Chief among these events were baseball, wrestling and fire-team participation. Albert was active in all three and made quite a name for himself as a wrestler and as a valued member of the Alert Fire Hose team throughout his manhood.

Sometimes, when she thought about this change in Albert, she believed that his work with horses had done a lot for him. She also realized that his interest in them was now secondary to his love of sports. But she wondered if he would ever be as reliable as Will.

From that question, she went on to ask herself if one child could be any dearer to a mother than another. She was very sure that couldn't be. But she thought a mother's love would reach out with more visible strength when one child needed more understanding. That concern, she told herself, would make it seem that she was more devoted to one child than another one who was stronger in character or more able to stand on his own, as Will did.

She believed that Albert needed her concern and understanding, just as Emily in her affliction, needed a certain warm approval and backing. She resolved never to fail either of them, and to stand by any other child who needed special understanding or consideration or both. Seriously, lovingly, she considered each child and realizing their individual differences prayed for each in turn. Then, strength seemed to come to her and she knew she had God's help in facing the raising of her children without Hugh.

She made it a special point to gain Albert's confidence, or as much as she realized a boy would confide in a woman. For she was well aware that he considered too much open association with a mother or any other female, would tend to show him up as a "sissy," a term he declared the most degrading of all the names he could be given.

But Levinia saw some little changes come over him. He anticipated many of her wishes and carried them out before she could let them be known. And sometimes her chores would be done before she could get to them. The boy's crooked grin and sly wink of pleasure became a bond between them. But he made no show of waiting on her; all his helpful acts were performed quietly and unobtrusively. She knew that he hated open praise and shunted any demonstration of appreciation, even from Emily. Levinia allowed her approving smile to tell him he had made her happy by what he had done for her.

Little by little, through such quiet changes in the former inconsiderate boy, Levinia came to understand Albert well and they grew very close as the years went by. But he still spent a great deal of time away from home and didn't explain where he'd been or what he'd been doing. She knew better than to ask and, though she couldn't help but worry about his secretiveness, she told herself sternly that as long as he kept within the law; she wouldn't try to interfere with anything he did.

So she prayed that he would remember her love and her hopes, and that no trouble would come between him and Will, who at times tried to give Albert advice. Albert, she knew, became angered whenever Will pointed out any slip, however small, that Albert made in the pattern the Champion family had laid out for their behavior when their father died. She was very glad when Albert went to work in the Bobtail with Will. That association, she hoped, would whittle down the five years between their ages, a fact that Will had always felt was a very good reason for him to tell Albert exactly where he was wrong, an attitude that Albert dubbed "damned bossy."

Levinia trained her girls very carefully to carry out the rigid routine of housekeeping she had worked out for her household. Sunday was, of course, given over to church. There was no work done in the home on the Sabbath. Though it was, in reality, the first day of the week, she planned it to be the last day; the day to which the preceding days had led. On Monday, the clothes worn on Sunday were cleaned and pressed and hung up, ready to be worn again. On Monday the washing was also done. On Tuesday they ironed and mended. On Wednesday, the mending was finished and the sewing of new garments begun. Thursday the upstairs was cleaned. On Friday, the downstairs was gone over thoroughly. Saturday was baking day; pies, cakes and breads were turned out in quantities for Sunday and for the boarders' lunches on Monday. Then meats and vegetables were cooked for Sunday, for nothing was left to be done on that day except to boil water for the tea and heat the food for the meals. The only exception to not cooking on the Sabbath was boiling of the soaked codfish for Sunday's breakfast.

Because of this careful planning, Sunday was the culmination of a busy week and brought a day of rest from all labor. Even the mines were closed on that day unless there was a need to keep a few men on duty for a special reason.

During the week, in addition to the extra or special work assigned to a particular day, the Champion household ran smoothly under the regular duties assigned to each person. Each girl did her own work, and kept up the sewing, mending and daily cooking made necessary by the large family and the boarders.

Levinia was an excellent housekeeper and a splendid manager. She was particular and firm. No one got away with neglect of one's duties. No one was allowed to shirk. The older girls had charge of the younger ones, to a certain extent, but each was responsible to Levinia, who kept a strict rein on them all. Her word was law, but her love was warm and she showed them she appreciated everyone's cooperation.

Sometimes Lillie, now almost seventeen, complained that she was never without her sisters, that she couldn't go anywhere without one or more, or all three. She asked her mother why she always had to take Emily and Edith with her. Levinia answered calmly and firmly, that the two girls, so near the same age, couldn't go anywhere alone, nor could they be separated. They had to have someone older go with them to look after them. Then, too, she reminded Lillie there was safety in numbers and explained that the three girls could go many places where she couldn't go at all unless she had them with her.

"'Ee see, I'm too busy to go with 'ee or the girls, so 'ee, as y oldest girl, are my representative and 'ave got t'see that the girls are safe and behave, while they make 'ee safer, too."

Lillie seemed to get the point and agreed, though reluctantly, to say no more about it. Levinia was sure she knew she'd rather have her sisters tagging along than stay at home. Levinia wouldn't allow Lillie to go out with anyone else, nor to have what she termed "boy hangers-on." Lillie was too young, she thought, and she didn't want her to get any ideas. Marriage, she told herself, was too serious a matter to be settled before a girl was old enough to know what she wanted or was in line for, and she drilled into Lillie the fear of choosing the wrong man.

She talked to her family in a group about the love of God and God's work. She told them she could see no excuse for any failure to do what they could to help in his work, and spent as much time as she could, working alone with each child.

To herself, she admitted that while she made herself stronger and better by the help she tried to give each child, she was also becoming sterner and firmer than ever, less and less like the warm and carefree mother she wanted to be most of the time.

Sometimes she felt worn out and discouraged, unable to cope with the problems of making her way and providing for her family. Even with the help Will and Albert gave her in the way of money each month for board and room in her house, she found it hard to feed and clothe the girls and keep the household free of debt, a fear that hung over her, driving her on. She prayed that her health would continue to be good. At times, exhausted and weak in body, perplexed in mind, and on the verge of defeat, she wept alone in her room. But after prayer the next morning, she found the strength and determination to go on for Hugh's sake, taking care of his children. She faced her family bravely and serenely, giving no indication that she had been momentarily discouraged.

Chapter 28

Marriage of Daughter, Lillie, to Samuel John Hoskin, Birth of Granddaughter Amy Hoskin

Three years passed since Hugh's death in 1886. The Champion family was still together. Levinia was 52, Will 20, Lillie 18, Albert 15, Emily 13, Edith 12, and Mabel 7. All were well and working hard and cooperatively.

Levinia had all the roomers and boarders she could take care of and was doing quite well financially. She was able to remain out of debt.

Her work was hard and confining. There could be no change in a day's routine, and there was little time for pleasures outside of her home. In the evening she did her sewing and made rugs to cover the floors so that the cold would be felt less on winter mornings. Besides, rugs made walking easier than bare floors, a fact of which Levinia became more and more aware, for her feet gave her trouble at times. There were so many many steps to be taken each day in her work, up and down stairs, crossing the entire work space over and over, that her feet had very little rest. But she gave it all just a passing thought. She was thankful she was able to work as she did, and achieve so much.

It was at that time that Levinia first noticed the mutual interest between Lillie and one of the new boarders, a young man named Samuel John Hoskin, whom everyone called "Jackie." He had been in Central City about three years. He came from Perranporth, Cornwall, England when he was twenty-one to join his brothers, Will and Walter, who batched over the hill from the mine where they worked. Levinia suspected that Jackie Hoskin had sought board and room at her house because of Lillie.

At first, she was displeased by the discovery that there was keen attraction

Marriage of Daughter Lillie to Samuel John Hoskin, Birth of Granddaughter

between the two young people. She felt that Lillie was far too young and inexperienced to become interested in a man.

Besides, she didn't want to lose Lillie and her excellent help with the house and the children. She asked herself how she could get along without Lillie.

She pondered over the matter and kept a keen eye on the two while she learned as much as possible about the young man. Believing very strongly in family background, she invited his two bothers to supper so that she could see for herself what kind of men they were.

William Hoskin was tall, slender and fair. Walter was some three inches shorter and dark, like Jackie, and about his height. They seemed to be quiet and well mannered and told her all about their widowed mother, their other brother, Alfred, and three sisters, Ellen, Celestine and Amy, in Cornwall.

From inquiries she had Will and Albert make, Levinia learned that the three Hoskins were good workmen, knew hard-rock mining very well, and held down good jobs. Jackie was a "surface boss," staying in the shaft house for the most part, instead of working in the depths of the mine, as his brothers did.

Jackie was energetic, steady and cautious and fit in very well with the other Cornishmen in her house and with her family. Will liked him very much and the two were often together in the off hours from the mine. Will told her that the Hoskin boys were nephews of Stephen Hoskin, a mine manager and promoter, who had made good in the community and was actively engaged in the vicinity. Being related to Stephen Hoskin, the well-off, well-thought-of mining authority, didn't harm Jackie's cause one bit in Levinia's mind.

Albert found Jackie interesting because he liked sports and dogs, horses and chickens, and had a gambling streak which appealed to Albert. Jackie's gambling, however, was confined to betting on fighting gamecocks, a sport very important in the community among the Cornish.

The younger girls adored Jackie. He paid a lot of attention to them and sang with them almost every night before Bible reading. He developed Edith's strong, sweet soprano voice, which blended beautifully with his tenor. The Champions loved this singing and Levinia welcomed it, for since Hugh wasn't there to lead them, their singing had dropped off almost completely. Now, in Jackie's presence, there was a new evening interest to hold them together.

After due consideration, Levinia came to the conclusion that she thought not to discourage the romance between Lillie and Jackie. She admitted that he was a good, kind man. He went to church every Sunday and to prayer Meeting on Wednesday. He worked in the Sunday school and was interested in the boys' sports. Her main thought was that he would provide well for her Lillie.

She thought of the many beautiful articles of handwork Lillie had laid away in her hope chest, which Albert termed her "hoping box." He told Jackie about it at great length, which brought Lillie's anger to the front, until he had to run out of the house while Jackie laughed. Levinia made plans to add to the chest's contents; there were so many things a girl needed when she went into her own home.

So, when Jackie asked Levinia for permission to marry Lillie, she gave her consent and they were married in the Champion parlor.

The Register-Call announced. *Married at Central City, April 19, 1890, at the home of the bride's mother, Mrs. Hugh Champion, Reverend A. L. T. Ewen officiating, Mr. Samuel John Hoskin and Miss Lillie Champion, both of Central City.*

After the wedding, the young couple went to Nevadaville to live, for Jackie had a better job offer there.

Levinia thought it strange that they, too, were to begin married life there, just as she and Hugh had. Memories flooded over her as they drove away at that moment, Hugh seemed so very close. She went to her bedroom and had a good cry. Her children couldn't know that her tears were divided between memories of their father and the life she had known with him in their youth, and Lillie's departure from home.

When she went to Nevadaville for the first time to visit Lillie and Jackie, she had another bad time. Seeing there the ruins of the cabin Hugh had fitted out for her was almost too much. But when she really examined the quite-nice, three-room house Jackie had rented and the good furniture he had put in it as up-to-date as the times called for, she was struck by the great difference in the place Lillie lived and the pine cabin with its home-made furniture she had had twenty-nine years before in the same vicinity.

Her thoughts turned to Hugh again and while she admired the new home, of which Lillie was so very proud, she wept inside. But later, when with less emotion, she considered the matter, she felt that Lillie was happily married and she began to hope for a grandchild!

Perhaps the greatest loss Levinia realized in Lillie's leaving was the fact that Lillie had run the sewing machine for her. Because the girls seemed too young to learn, it was arranged that Lillie would come down from Nevadaville to do the machine stitching when Levinia needed her. In the meantime, the younger girls would be taught by Lillie to operate it.

That same year, 1890, saw business expand until 3/4 of all the homes in Central City were lighted through the Gilpin Heat and Light Company, incorporated in 1887. To Levinia, this was real achievement for her town and she wished Hugh could know. She regretted that she couldn't afford at that time to have electricity her own home.

A somewhat sad note to the "old timers" and to the younger set as well, was that in November of 1890, after eighty years as a daily and a weekly paper, The Register-Call came out as a weekly only, under the name of "The Weekly Register-Call." Levinia missed the daily very much and waited, almost impatiently, for the weekly, so that she could keep up with the personal events she couldn't hear about otherwise.

The first of the New Year found Lillie back in her mother's home awaiting the birth of her first child, which carried Levinia to great heights of pride and expectation. Lillie was in labor over two days and nights, during which Levinia prayed and did everything she could to bring the birth about. The doctor, called in by Jackie in frantic fear, could do very little to help. Finally, a tiny daughter, weighing a bare five pounds, was born. She was named Amy after Jackie's baby sister in Cornwall.

When it was all over and the child and the mother were resting, Levinia told herself she'd rather she had given birth to the baby than watch Lillie's seemingly futile efforts. But her pride in having a grandchild put the memory quickly in the background and she declared herself the happiest grandmother in the entire world!

At once she began to regret that Nevadaville was so far away and that she couldn't get up there as often as she would like to see the baby. She began to plan how to get around that drawback. She climbed the steep grade to Nevadaville as often as she could take time from her work to visit with Lillie and little Amy. She was more anxious than ever to do away with going so far. Will and Albert solved the problem by declaring

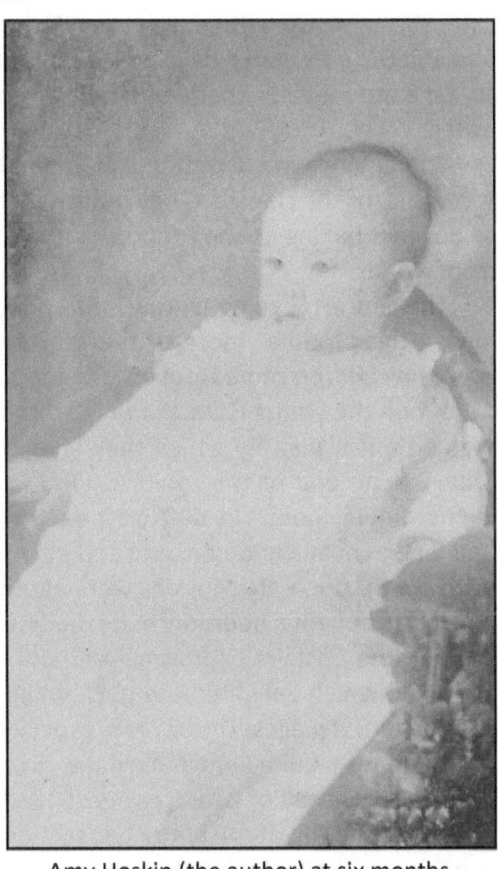

Amy Hoskin (the author) at six months.

she wasn't able to walk that far up the long steep hill and still carry on her work at home. They pointed out that she was having more trouble with her feet since the baby's arrival. They came up with a plan that would bring the grandchild nearer, and would make it easier for Levinia to make money for the maintenance of the household. The plan was that she discontinue keeping roomers and boarders and rent the three lower rooms to Jackie and Lillie. The boys argued that sooner or later Jackie would work in the mines close to the Champion home, so they would move to the vicinity where the work he liked as "surface boss" was to be found.

Levinia was dubious. She said the rent Jackie could pay wouldn't be as much as the beds and meals would bring in and declared that she wouldn't have Will and Albert give her any more than they did for staying in the old home.

She thought it over and counted carefully what she had to have to run her household and figured what Jackie would pay as rent. To be absolutely safe, she came up with a way to make up for any deficit that might occur. She and the girls would bake pies, cakes, and bread for the bachelor miners to take home with them, and perhaps bake "pasties" and saffron cake on order.

The family agreed with this plan and the miners who lived in her home were told of the change. They moved out, but made arrangements with her to do their baking as she proposed, and picked-up food when they came by from work.

The new arrangement grew into a good business, and the family enjoyed having their mother more to themselves, for the baking was done by the time the children came from school and the boys from their work.

When the young Hoskins moved into the lower rooms, Levinia and Lillie worked out a plan by which they shared the lower kitchen. Levinia put a table in one end of the room to feed her family and Lillie used the table in the dining room. In that way, each family was separated at mealtime, and when Levinia and her boys and girls went to the upper rooms after the dishes were done, the Hoskins were alone.

Jackie bought a bedroom suite, bedstead, bureau and commode, and put them in the upstairs bedroom. The new furniture was a beautiful polished light oak, which delighted the girls, while Levinia thought she'd never seen such beautiful pieces. The bureau, especially took her eye. It had a full-length mirror above a quite large table base. To the left of the table was a complete division composed of two drawers divided in the center by a deep shelf with a door. At the top of the entire left section, there was a flat surface the same size. Below the table and the left hand section were two large drawers.

Little Mabel said the bureau held as much as a room and was very nearly right. The commode was flat on top and had two compartments below. In one, Lillie kept the "chamber pot," one of the three pieces of a ware her brothers had purchased for her bedroom: a large washbowl, a tall bulging water pitcher, and the covered "chamber." Will placed the chamber in the commode and said, "There, Lillie is your sugar bowl all handy!" Albert remarked, "The handiest place for that pot is right under the bed."

The new arrangement at Levinia's house pleased Jackie very much, for the yard gave him a place to raise Cornish Game Cocks for sale and to train for fighting. When Levinia's hens quit laying, they were put to work sitting on eggs from which baby Game Chicks were hatched. The hens made very good mothers and Jackie's project did well in one half of the yard, while Levinia's layers had the other part.

The entire family was interested in the Cornish hens and roosters but Albert was the most involved. He watched the growth and the increasing ferociousness of the cocks and helped Jackie to train them to kill the cocks that fought against them. They sharpened long spurs that were the weapons of war. They washed and greased the red combs and wattles. They trained the birds to use strong wings to challenge the enemy and to shield themselves against ttack.

To go with Jackie to see the combat, itself, was a real thrill for the boy. Of course, no women went to the contests. Levinia shuttered whenever she saw the readied birds. She didn't believe in turning them loose to fight until one or the other was vanquished or killed. To her it seemed cruel and useless. But she couldn't do thing about it, so she ignored the matter as much as she could.

Chapter 29

Marriage of a Son, Levinia Is Unhappy

Though Levinia was pleased and happy about Lillie's marriage, she was shocked when she discovered that Will was courting Annie Stephens, who lived next door in the small building that had been the Taylor shop when the Champions bought their house. Not that she had anything against Annie or her family. It was the fear that Will would leave her home and establish one of his own. She learned of Will's real attachment when she called at the Stephen's home to check on Annie's bad cold, which had confined her to her room and bed. When Mrs. Stephens took her to the girl's room to see for herself that Annie was much better, Levinia found Will sitting by the girl's bedside!

Levinia was surprised and unhappy when she saw him there. Until that time, she had been confident that Will was not really interested in any girl. Now, in Will's calm words as he told her Annie was almost over her cold, and in the girl's happiness at his presence, she read the deep feeling between them. The fact Mrs. Stephens had allowed Will to go into the girl's bedroom and sit by her bedside, told her that Will was an accepted suitor.

She was hurt, almost angry, but managed to conceal both. Later when she questioned Jackie and Lillie, they said they had known the two were good friends, but hadn't guessed it had gone that far. When she asked Albert about it, he grinned that almost sly grin that told her he knew far more than he was going to tell. Finally she got him to remark, "Old Will took long enough to find a girl he actually wanted to kiss and make over. Gosh, he's over twenty-three and hasn't been in love afore! It's time he learned what he's been missin'!" The frank words of her eighteen-year-old son shocked her.

Though she had asked for his views, had really insisted that he tell her what he knew, she was unprepared for what she read in reply. His frankness confirmed the bits of information she'd heard dropped here and there, which told her that Albert wasn't shy, nor the hard-to-please boy Will had always been. Now, she had to admit to herself that Albert had many girl friends and in his indirect way, he had boasted of the fact.

Albert brought her back to the present situation in regard to Will when he said soberly, "Ma, the only thing that's kinda bad 'bout this is because Will don't know if Annie really is the girl he wants for his wife. How could he know when he hasn't compared her with any other girl? She's the only one he's ever been interested in."

Levinia thought back over her own choice, Hugh was her only love and she his. There hadn't been another in either of their lives. Then she remembered that Lillie hadn't had a chance to compare Jackie with other men.

She tried to explain to Albert, but the boy smiled knowingly and declared, "When I get married, if I ever do, it'll be to the one girl I've picked out of hundreds. I'll know she's the right one!" She got nowhere when she tried to make him see that marriage was a chance at best, even if one thought his choice was a good one, and that marriage wasn't as cut and dried as it appeared. Each person had to give and take to achieve real happiness in marriage.

Finally, she realized that Albert was restless and wanted to get away from the seriousness she had put into their talk, so she ended wistfully, "I hope Will will think it over a long long time before he decides to get married." Albert actually snorted. "He's hooked, Ma! He won't do any thinkin'. You wait and see! Will's a good catch for any girl, and Annie's caught him!" He wouldn't elaborate, he darted away.

In the next few days, she learned that Albert had been right. For Will came into her room one night after she'd gone to bed, the best chance she knew to talk to her alone. He told her outright that he was to be married to Annie in the next two weeks, that Annie had set the date that very evening. She was to have a big wedding at her mother's house. Edith was to be her bridesmaid, her own sister would be matron of honor.

Levinia's first thought was that it had all been arranged without Will's own mother knowing anything about it! She hadn't even been sure there was to be a wedding. She had only feared, dreaded and hoped against it.

She wished Hugh could have talked to Will. The two had always been close. If Hugh had been alive, he would have seen what was happening and would have advised Will. Annie and her mother couldn't have had it all settled without Will's family knowing. Yet, she asked herself, could Hugh have known? And if he had, would he have had any influence?

Her thoughts raced to the belief that Annie's family had advised Will not to tell his mother until the date was set! She was deeply hurt, yet she had to admit that if she had known she might have tried to interfere and Will might have resented it.

As from a distance, she heard Will say eagerly, "Annie and I will give you the same amount each month as I'm paying you now. We both know you need it to get along." She shook her head, her eyes holding his. He said pleadingly, but his face was firm. "I won't let you down, Ma, even if I have a home of my own. I'm the oldest child and Pa held me responsible for you and the kids. I'll keep on with that, Ma." Then more strongly, "I love Annie. We're going to make a real home together."

She nodded, the tears close, but she refused to let them fall. Her son was still hers, though Annie would have first place, as the Bible said. Somehow, she was able to say, "I understand, Son. You are grown up. You've been a wonderful son. You'll be a wonderful husband. I hope you and Annie will be very happy."

Will hugged her in an unusual demonstration of affection. His voice was husky as he said, "I want the kind of home we all had when Pa was with us, and the kind you've made for us since he left us." When Will left her room, she was sure he believed he'd have that kind of home with Annie. She prayed that he would. She wanted his complete happiness. She resolved that if Annie allowed her to, she would do her best to help her.

During the next few days, she saw the Stephens furniture taken from the building next door, and moved to quite a large house on Bates Hill, almost directly opposite her own home.

Albert told her the Stephens family had moved there so that there would be room for Annie's wedding. He said, too, that Will had rented the four-room house on the same hill, but below the one now occupied by Annie's folks, and was buying new furniture for Annie out of his savings.

With new interest in the house, because Will would live in it, Levinia looked at it carefully from her back porch. It had a front yard built up by Cornish rockwork. She wished she could remember whether or not Hugh had put up that retaining wall. She had visited friends in the house, so knew the position of the rooms in it. She pictured how it would look with Will and Annie and the new furniture in it.

With mixed regret and pride, she watched the new articles unloaded there, and could see Annie and her mother go in and out. She admitted to herself that when, throughout the years, she had refused to allow Will to draw on his savings to buy furniture and to put electric lights in her home, as he had wished to do, she might have had the good of some of the money she insisted that he save.

Marriage of a Son, Levinia Is Unhappy

Now she thought, Will's bank account is being cut, perhaps wiped out, so that Annie can have what she wants! But even as she thought of it in that momentary jealous light, she knew she was proud and pleased that Will could have new things in his home, that she had made it possible by being as independent as she could. She wondered if Annie would appreciate the new furniture. Her mother would, she was sure. That was part of what Albert had meant when he said Will was a good catch. Not many single men had a bank account as large as Will's.

Her pride really swelled when three days before the wedding, Will took her, his sisters and Jackie to see the home he had provided for his bride. Glad, because Annie had to be somewhere else at that time, thus she wasn't present. Levinia took everything in, the cleaned walls and ceilings throughout the house, the new furniture in each room. The girls exclaimed warmly over all they saw, and Will looked on, his face lit up with pride and pleasure. Levinia meant it when she told him it was a beautiful home and that she was glad he could manage to provide it. Then she wondered if Lillie felt let down because Will could give his wife more than Jackie could, but Lillie didn't show any reaction as she told Will she was very proud of him.

That same day the Champions received, in the mail, individual engraved invitations from the Stephens family, requesting their presence at the marriage of their daughter, Grace Ann to William John Champion, on Monday, December 26, 1892, at 8 o'clock p.m. at Mountain City, Colorado.

Levinia knew nothing of the etiquette surrounding such a formal invitation. She felt that mailing an invitation to each member of Will's family was absolutely unnecessary. She took the action as an affront, a Stephens' attempt to show the superiority of their family over that of Will.

Later, she wondered if the lateness of the mailing indicated an endeavor at the last minute, to make up for the omission of asking Will's family through this channel rather than by Will's own arrangement to have them attend. He had even seen to it that Edith knew she was to be bridesmaid, had checked to see that her dress was ready, and had hired a rig to take his family to the ceremony.

Yet, Edith also had a formal invitation at that late date. Of course, Edith, Emily and Mabel were very pleased and cited over the beautiful stiff engraved cards, with their names on the inner and outer envelopes.

But Albert was very angry. He tore his invitation across and burned it in the kitchen range. "Snobs! God damn snobs!" he raged.

Levinia was too upset to resent his language. Instead, she felt that his strong words expressed her own feelings. She brooded about the matter all evening and, when she went to bed that night, she prayed for strength to overlook what she considered a "toney" snobbish act and to refrain from talking to Will about it.

Will was nervous all the time now, anyway, she reflected. Every time he came home from the Stephens' house, he was short with them all and seemed so preoccupied and worried that he couldn't talk quietly to any of them. He bossed the younger ones unnecessarily and brought hurt into their questioning eyes.

Levinia found it hard not to interfere but, guessing that her son was going through bad times with the Stephens family, she couldn't say one word. Instead, she tried to explain to the children that Will, was nervous over his coming wedding and they mustn't think he meant all he was saying and doing.

Only Albert remained sullen, his eyes brooding as he looked at his older brother and younger sisters. Levinia felt sure she couldn't take much more from Will. She feared trouble if things didn't smooth out soon. In her anxiety she wished the wedding was over. Then Will would relax and being away from his home and responsibilities, he would be happy, a new person. She took herself to task for the very thought! How could she wish Will were married? Nevertheless, she was ready to want him to do whatever he wished. To see him happy was her greatest desire.

At peace with herself, she snuggled down in her big feather bed, which was considered a necessity in a Cornish home. She was awakened by voices in the upper kitchen. She listened. It was Will and Albert. Their tones were angry. They were discussing the wedding invitations. Albert declared the formal cards were an insult to Ma and her kids. Will answered that the sending them late in the mail, was too trivial to even talk about, much less quarrel over.

Albert accused, "You're too damn easy! You let them Stephens people walk right over you, and hurt your own mother!" Will said in anger, "Ma understands, even if you don't and won't. She's too big to let a little matter like printed invitations sent late, bother her. She didn't even mention it to me! It's just you that wants to make trouble over it! You're getting too big for your britches, little brother!"

Levinia sprang from her bed and went to the kitchen in her nightgown. Her boys were glowering at each other. She knew the minute of contact had arrived. She opened her mouth to speak, but it was too late. Will swung at Albert, hitting him in the face, knocking his pipe to the floor. Albert stepped forward a trifle and with a well-placed right staggered Will; then a wicked left drove him backward.

Realizing that Will was no match for his well-trained brother, who was a wrestler and a boxer, she threw herself between them, facing Albert as he

Marriage of a Son, Levinia Is Unhappy

came forward to set Will up for the final blow. His face was red, his eyes blazed, his lips carried a grin of triumph.

"Stop! Both of you, stop this foolishness!" she cried. From her long-implanted adherence to obedience when she spoke, came a complete stop in Albert's follow-up. He stood poised, ready, yet made no move to put her aside to get to Will. He looked right at her, regret in his eyes.

"I guess I hit him pretty hard," he admitted, and then added. "He ought to know better than to hit me." Then he waited for Will to recover his footing and his composure. Finally, he faced them, caressing his jaw where Albert had hit him.

Albert stooped to pick up his pipe. It had broken into several pieces. Levinia knew he treasured that pipe a great deal. On at least three occasions, she'd heard him mention it as his best broken-in pipe. Will realized it, too. His voice was sincere and regretful as he said, "I'm sorry about the pipe, Al and I'm sorry I hit you. I wish it hadn't happened."

She was proud when Albert grinned and, as he'd been taught in the ring after a bout, stepped forward to shake hands with the man he'd bested, or to whom he'd lost.

"You buy me a new pipe and I'll break it in," he said. Then, looking at Will's jaw, he said warmly, "I'm sure sorry you'll have a badly bruised jaw at your wedding."

"You sure do pack a wicked wallop," Will told him. "I hope it's the last one you'll ever hang on me."

"That's up to you," Albert said and looked at him pretty straight. Levinia knew he was warning Will to keep their mother out of all that might come up from the family into which he was marrying.

She spoke quickly. "You were right, Will, about the invitations. They weren't enough to bring you boys to blows. Nothing is. It's better to talk it all out between us. Let's remember that."

They nodded in the same manner she remembered throughout the years when she had reprimanded them and demanded settlement of their differences.

"And you'll be at our wedding?" Will asked anxiously.

"Sure wouldn't miss that," Albert answered quickly, and she said "Of course, Son." Then, certain the trouble was over, she went back to bed and thanked God there was no more damage than a bruise on the groom's jaw.

The next day she pressed the dresses her three girls would wear and hung her own dress at the open window to freshen. Then she finished cooking the Christmas dinner, the last one Will would eat as a single man and in his mother's home. He would be married the next day. If he came home next

Christmas, he would bring Annie, at least she hoped it would turn out that way. She wanted to be close to the bride because she was Will's wife. Her thoughts of grandchildren were in her mind when there was a knock at the door. When she opened it, she found Mrs. Stephens there. Her face showed anger; her eyes were hard.

Levinia sent the girls into the parlor and closed the door after them. Even if they heard what the angry woman said, they wouldn't be in her presence. She was glad Albert had gone down to the back yard and that Will wasn't at home. She hoped neither would come in while Mrs. Stephens was there.

From the angry words her visitor flung at her, Levinia learned that she was riled because she hadn't received an acceptance, in writing, to each invitation she'd sent the Champion family.

Levinia tried to explain that Will had taken word to her that his family would be at the wedding, but Mrs. Stephens declared that common decency required the written answer to a formal invitation. Then she intimated that Levinia didn't know any better, so she had come to find out if the family meant to attend Annie's wedding.

Levinia said it was just as wrong for the Stephens family to have sent formal invitations to the groom's family, they knew through Will, long before the cards were sent. She then tried to say there should be no trouble between the families; old friends as they were, and their children marrying. They should, forget all differences for Will's and Annie's sakes.

But Mrs. Stephens haughty and dominating, sniffed scornfully and boiling with anger, stalked out of the house leaving Levinia more disturbed than she could remember over an altercation with a friend and neighbor. In fact, Levinia hadn't had any trouble with anyone until now. She had gone through all those years as a warm friend to those near and dear and a respected neighbor to others while everyone in the community knew her as a person to be depended upon, one they could call when sickness came and when trouble closed in upon them. She was midwife and nurse, fill-in cook and housekeeper, a "child tender" and an advisor to many who came to discuss matters with her.

When Albert came in, he found her sitting in her rocker hurt and crushed. He tried to get her to tell him what had happened. She didn't want him to know. She feared he wouldn't be wise and let the matter drop, as she wanted to, and she was sure it would make trouble between her boys if Albert knew the truth. But because the girls had seen Mrs. Stephens and had heard what had gone on, she thought she'd better tell him herself.

As she had expected Albert was very angry, but he listened when she insisted it must go no farther, certainly not to Will. Finally, though he admitted she was right, he evaded giving her his promise to let the entire matter drop as she asked, which made her uneasy and troubled.

In an effort to thrust the unpleasant affair into the background, she went to the door and admitted the girls, with whom she began last minute plans for the wedding next day.

But Levinia Champion didn't attend her son's marriage. For after a sleepless night, she had the worst headache she'd ever had. She lay in her bed with a damp cloth on her forehead too ill to worry, but muttered about the wedding.

Lillie, called by Albert, assured her that she would see that the girls were ready to go to the Stephens' home, so Levinia dropped that matter from her mind. But the fear, that Albert or the girls would say something to Will about Mrs. Stephens' visit remained. So she resolved to get up and stay close to the others to avert any such possibility. She made it to her rocker, and sat there with her head back, trying to control the waves of pain that passed through it.

Around the house she could hear the preparations being made for the family's readiness. Though she listened as carefully as she could, striving to thrust the pain aside, she heard no mention of the upsetting visit of the day before. She prayed that nothing would mar Will's happiness on that very important day in his life.

Will was ready first and came to her like a boy anxious for her approval. Her heart swelled with pride. How tall and handsome he was in his dark suit! At twenty-four, light-haired, a moustache just as light, his blue eyes filled with love, he was indeed a fine specimen of a man. She thought how proud Hugh would have been of him!

"You're a fine lookin' bridegroom, my son," she said warmly, avoiding looking at the livid spot on his jaw.

"I wish you were able to go, Ma," he told her with deep concern and kissed her before he hurried away.

Albert came next, but was in his work clothes. In answer to her questioning look, he told her he was staying home with her.

"What will your brother think of that?" she demanded.

"He's glad I'm staying. You see, we agreed that someone was to stay here with you and we thought the girls would be too disappointed if they didn't get to go to the big wedding." He faltered a bit, then grinned and went on, "So I told them all I'd stay here and keep little Amy while they are away."

She smiled to herself. She knew Albert didn't want to go to the Stephens' house after what had happened the day before and that he wasn't anxious to see his brother married to Annie.

The three girls came in together just then, so she didn't need to comment on the arrangement the brothers had made. Their faces were eager and excited. In spite of her aching head, she exclaimed how sweet they looked in their white dresses.

Edith, at sixteen, was beautiful. Her fair hair was arranged in curls in front. Her dress hung in graceful folds about her slender figure. Her participation in the ceremony as bridesmaid made her feel so important that she almost danced.

Albert watched with pride and firmly said, "Now, Sis, when you are up in front of the preacher with Annie, you've just got to stand."

She dimpled and made a face at him, then moved a step or two and stood sedately. "That's the way to act," Albert said lovingly and put an arm around her. Levinia's heart ached as Emily waited, a happy smile on her lips. Emily hadn't filled out as Edith had and hadn't grown as she should have. At seventeen she was only four feet tall. She was very thin; her cheeks were almost colorless. She had pretty hair, worn in curls as fashion dictated, and her dark eyes were alight with anticipation. Unless one saw her from the side, the hump on her back wasn't quite as noticeable, for Levinia made her pretty dresses so that they concealed it as much as possible.

Levinia told herself she shouldn't feel sorry for Emily. She was happy and healthy. She never mentioned her disfigurement. She did her work well and took part in nearly everything the others did; physical activities made the only exception. She asked no quarter because of her disability. She merely smiled and took it as a small matter to be accepted, but not to be made much of. Not even when Edith, the younger sister, had been chosen over her to be Annie's bridesmaid, did Emily make any comment. Instead she was proud of Edith. The two were as close as twins, perhaps closer. In fact, through the years, they had been taken for twins. Levinia dressed them exactly alike and they were always together. Edith seemed unaware that she was always close to her crippled sister, ready to give her a hand if she needed it. Levinia thought, "I'm proud of Emily's bravery. She shows every day that nothing matters if we take trouble as it comes, to get out of life all we are entitled to."

Her eyes turned to Mabel, a plump active child, very independent and capable, with a mind of her own. She wasn't as fair as Edith or as dark as Emily. Today, Levinia saw that the little girl was brimming over with anticipation. She could hardly wait to get started for the scene of the wedding, and the fact that they were to be driven there in a rig, Will had hired from the livery, had its own great importance in the day's events.

Then Lillie and Jackie, carrying Amy, came into the room. The child, who would be two-years-old in a few days, called out to "Nan, Nan" her own contraction of grandma, and tried to get in her lap. Though her head was worse, Levinia smiled at her and said, "Sick."

The child understood but she was greatly puzzled. Levinia realized it was because this was the first time the baby had seen her indisposed. Albert took the child in his arms and carried her to the door where they watched the others get into the waiting rig and drive off. Levinia was very very glad to do as Albert said and go to bed. She sank down into the feathers and thought that she'd much rather be there, headache and all, than be at the Stephens' house.

She felt herself drift off only to be aroused when her family returned and came into her room to see how she was. Still excited, the girls talked about the cake, the candles, the flowers, interrupting each other as another item was added to the report. Lillie and Jackie, with Amy, smiled at their enthusiasm.

Mabel finally got a chance to tell what the most important part of the ceremony was to her. Giggling, she told her mother the preacher thought Edith was the bride! Then she giggled again. Emily explained that the minister was a stranger who was filling in at the church while the regular official was on vacation, so didn't know the three girls standing before him.

Edith mentioned that Annie and Lizzie wore dresses exactly alike--gray trimmed with blue.

Mabel jumped up and down in impatience, interrupting with the last bit of the outstanding event of the day, "Edith's dress was white so she must be getting married to Will. Will had to tell the preacher Annie was the bride!" Then she giggled again.

Chapter 30

Gold Mining Boom, A Daughter's Death

Beginning that year 1893, a depression known as the "Silver Panic" came. It's cause was the abrupt drop, in four days, of twenty-one cents in the price of silver down to an unsubstantial sixty-two cents an ounce! Within three days, ten Denver banks failed and such well-known silver camps as Leadville, Aspen and Creede slowed down to depression production. The situation was critical. Only gold could save it and Gilpin County had the gold!

That fact brought Gregory Gulch, with Central City as its center, to the front again. The census reports of that period said there were over eighty producing gold mines in Gilpin County at the time, and that these mines yielded one and one half million dollars! In the next ten years, though the number of operating mines dropped from eighty to seventy-seven, the yield of gold became two and one half million dollars!

Eleven of these mines were big operations and produced about as much as all the other mines put together. These eleven included Bobtail and the Gregory at Black Hawk, the Kansas-Burroughs and California at Nevadaville, and the Gunnell and Pactolus at Central City. All the mines were deep and were deepened as the ore was taken out. The California mine, in which Hugh and Jim Mitchell worked when Hugh and Levinia were married, was the deepest with a shaft of 2,250 feet.

Levinia rejoiced that Gilpin County was doing so well again after silver had crippled her production by taking the promoters' Eastern capital to the silver mining camps, instead of developing the gold mines in Gregory Gulch. Everyone now seemed prosperous and happy, her own family included.

On February 15, 1894, a second daughter, Ida, was born to Lillie and Jackie Hoskin in the bedroom of the lower part of the Champion house.

Gold Mining Boom, A Daughter's Death

This birth was an easier and shorter labor, and the baby was larger than Amy had been. Ida was as fair as her Aunt Edith and her eyes were big and blue. Her mother called her "angel," because of her beauty. Her uncles and aunts "made over" her so much that Amy, then three-years-old, was very displeased, even jealous. After being the only child in a large, adoring family, she found it hard to share her place with a sister. Her Uncle Albert observed trouble and said, "Her nose was out of joint." He tried to take her mind off the baby when he was around, and Jackie, who called her "Pet," took her in hand, and she became "Daddy's Girl."

Levinia's pride in another grandchild was very apparent, though she made no difference between the two little girls. She loved them dearly and took charge whenever she thought it wise, being very careful not to spoil either. She declared to everyone that a spoiled child wasn't as lovable and made extra problems for the parents.

She was waiting for the birth of Will and Annie's child, which would occur in a short time. She hoped and prayed that it would a boy, for she wanted the Champion name to be carried on. Into that happy situation came tragedy, blotting out all pride and anticipation.

One day in April of 1894, Emily went to school as usual with Edith. She was light-hearted and full of energy as always, eager to get to her classes where she did very good work. She wanted to see her teachers and schoolmates with whom, because of her happy nature and cooperation, she was a special favorite.

She and Edith attended classes in the big stone schoolhouse. To get there, they climbed a very long steep flight of wooden steps from the level of Lawrence Street to the street above it, or walked around the site of the grammar school on Lawrence Street, which Mabel attended. Most of the time, the older sisters went the long way around. It was easier for Emily with her restricted ability to walk rather than going up so many steps, although by holding onto Edith's arm, she could make it.

During the "recess" period that day, Emily was sitting in the open window overlooking the schoolyard when, without the least warning, the heavy raised window sash dropped with great force on her shoulder and the hump behind it. A doctor was called at once. She was given medical aid and taken home in a rig, where she was placed in her mother's feather bed instead of in her own bed upstairs. It wasn't considered a serious accident. Not even Levinia, in great worry over the child (she still thought of Emily as a child, though she was almost eighteen), thought Emily had been injured. Though there was a large, livid spot on her shoulder and the enlarged growth on her back, she hadn't been unconscious any time. She even told them she was all right and wasn't hurt a bit.

So it was thought that she was suffering from shock if anything, and would be all right soon, as the doctor said. This prediction seemed to come true, for Emily was up and around again, going upstairs to sleep, attending school and Sunday school as usual. But Levinia couldn't get her to eat as she had before, and she noticed that her color was becoming more yellow each day. In a short time, she became ill and was again put into her mother's bed. The doctor was called in and prescribed for her, but the girl didn't respond, as was hoped.

One evening, she seemed even more listless than ever and didn't try to eat, so Levinia sent for the doctor again. He came quite late in the evening and gave her medicine. He promised to be back in the morning, but insisted he be called at any hour if he were needed, which made Levinia suspect he considered Emily's condition might become worse. Fear clutched at her heart, and she prayed for her child's recovery. She placed the covers around Emily's neck tenderly before she lay down beside her.

Levinia was awake most of the night. Her mind was on the girl close to her. She bent over her time and time again and found she was sleeping quietly. But she couldn't relax enough to go to sleep herself. About four o'clock she made another examination. She couldn't hear Emily's breathing. She felt her body to see if she were warm enough. Emily's body wasn't warm as it should have been. Startled, she put her hand over Emily's heart. There was no movement there! She felt for a pulse. There was none! Sick with fear, she jumped up and lit the lamp, then bent over her child, praying she'd been wrong. There was no mistake. Emily was dead!

Albert was on night shift with Will, so she called Jackie and Lillie who ran to her at once. Jackie called the doctor. He came right away and announced that Emily had passed away quietly in her sleep. Afterwards, Levinia learned that when Will and Albert came up the grade from the mine after their night shift, they had seen a light in their mother's house and wondered what it could mean. They remembered another occasion, not long before, when they had seen light there at about the same hour and found their mother up and worried over a leak in the water line in the house.

This time, with Emily's illness in mind, they were sure the light that time of night meant that she was worse. They rushed in and found the family huddled around their mother in the upper kitchen. No one was dressed. Their faces were tear-stained, their eyes tragic. Levinia, her hands clasped tightly together in an effort to control their grief, said bluntly, "Our Emily died in her sleep."

Before they could speak, Jackie and the doctor came from the death chamber. Jackie's face was stony, the doctor's grave, even puzzled. "What happened to her?" Will demanded. The doctor shook his head, and then told them there had been a jaundice condition, and that delayed puberty had played its part, then he left them to their grief.

Will said he suspected that the old doctor had given Emily the wrong medicine, and Albert pointed out grimly that if he had, there was nothing to be done about it. "Doctors' mistakes are buried with their victims," he said bitterly.

But Levinia told them quietly that she had known from Emily's color, that she did have liver trouble. Then she went on to explain, that she had been worried for some three years over the fact that Emily hadn't come into womanhood and that there had not been the least indication that she ever would.

Albert went for the undertaker and Jackie stayed near the dead girl. Will took his mother and sisters to Lillie's kitchen, where he wrapped Levinia in a blanket and placed her in front of the cook stove oven to try to warm her chilled body. Levinia was too stunned to follow what went on around her. She had only one thought: my Emily is dead! She didn't even notice that Lillie sent the girls to get dressed or when Will left to tell Annie why he was late in getting home from work.

In the next few hours, as she came to the full realization of her loss and the stark fact that she had to face it, she found it almost too hard to bear. But gradually, knowing what was expected of her, she was able to express her wishes in the arrangements that had to be made for Emily's burial. Stoically, keeping a stern control over herself, she made her choice of the dress she wanted put on the body, the casket's color and the songs for the service. And she insisted that if he could come, her old friend, Reverend Vincent, should have charge of the burial rites. When she was told that her former pastor could and would come, she felt that he would help her as he'd done in the past when she'd lost a loved one.

The weather was nice that Sunday when Emily, in her light gray casket, was carried in the white hearse, drawn by white horses, to the church.

Levinia didn't realize until afterwards, that in order for Emily's crippled body to lie on its back, the undertaker had to remove the padding of the casket beneath the growth on Emily's back. Then he built up the rest of the casket's cushioning around it to accommodate the growth, so that the corpse could assume the prone position custom expected, but which Emily could not take in life.

Levinia thought the church service was beautiful, though she seemed to be there in a dreamlike state, so stunned her mind couldn't take it all in. Emily's schoolmates came in a body. There were honorary pallbearers from among them. There were beautiful flowers, some from treasured houseplants in the community, some from cultured growth in "hot-houses" up-town, and some ordered from Denver.

The music was very touching and reached her heart, as nothing up to the moment had been able to do. As she had expected, she received strength from the words of Reverend Vincent. She was able to ride to the cemetery to see Emily, the fifth child she had lost, placed close to her father, her two brothers and two sisters.

At the graveside, Edith seemed to realize with greater intensity that she'd lost her constant companion. Levinia did her best to help her in her grief, for she realized that Edith was now alone, in one sense. After seventeen years of giving her crippled sister help and love and supplying her with a confidence Emily had developed as her own, Edith had no one now who depended upon her.

In the days that followed Emily's death, Levinia impressed upon the family Edith's great need to fill the void Emily's passing had in her life. Their cooperation to help Edith helped them all, by comforting and understanding her, they received comfort in return. Levinia brought out the thought in her evening's daily Bible reading and family prayers.

One event that touched them all, Edith in particular, was Emily and Edith's Sunday school teacher's visit a few days after the funeral. She brought an enlarged likeness of Emily, taken out of a recent Sunday school class picture. The teacher explained that the likeness of Emily had been paid for with money the class members had brought her to buy cut flowers for Emily's service. Somehow she couldn't explain how or why the flowers she'd ordered from Denver hadn't arrived. So the enlargement of Emily had been made with the money the children had given her for the flowers.

Levinia told her she'd rather have the picture, a lasting reminder of Emily, as she had been in life. It was a very fine enlargement showing a smiling Emily, her eyes filled with amusement. Because she was in the very front row she faced the camera squarely and the disfiguring hump on her back wasn't at all apparent. Her hair and dress were as natural as if she were with them. Levinia was very very grateful. Another thing that helped her in the six months that followed was having little Amy and Baby Ida living in her house.

Chapter 31

The New Generation's Cycle of Life and Death

Jackie Hoskin received a very substantial offer from a man who believed there was a chance to open up a new lode on a certain slope in Virginia Canyon, just over the hill from Central City toward Idaho Springs. Jackie would make the preliminary efforts to prove his employer right or wrong about gold being there. He talked it over with Will and Albert, then with Lillie and Levinia. It was Levinia who without hesitation advised him to take the offer. Her resolute action grew out of her fear that if her men folks continued to work in the quartz dust, sooner or later they could all die of silicosis. That was a constant worry to her.

Having lost Hugh to the dreaded disease, and seeing other miners younger than he afflicted or taken, she was never without the gnawing knowledge that her sons and Jackie were doomed. She figured that by getting out into the sun and open air for several months, Jackie would have an advantage for that length of time. So she advised him to take the job. Her only regret was Lillie and the children would be out there with him, living in a cabin on the slope during the summer. She reasoned that if the winter were bad, Lillie and her little girls could stay with her until spring, and then go out to Virginia Canyon with Jackie again when it became warm.

"If I rent the lower rooms to someone else, there's plenty of room in the upper part of the house with us," she told them. So it was arranged. The Hoskins moved and spent the late spring and early summer in the cabin. Will and Annie moved into the rooms the Hoskins had vacated in the Champion house.

In a way, Levinia considered Will moving his wife and all their possessions into his old home very welcome. Since his marriage, there had been a gap in relationship between Levinia and her son. Annie hadn't warmed to Levinia as Levinia had hoped and prayed. She figured the rift, if there really was one, had been caused and kept open by Annie's mother who refused to allow the young people to iron out their own differences, and Levinia guessed she made light of Will's family.

So nothing Levinia had done to make her daughter-in-law mellow toward her had been received in the spirit given. Believing that she would help the new bride, she had sent Annie hand cream when she made some for her girls. It was made from mutton tallow, lemon and glycerin, which they found very effective and economical. Annie sent the lotion back at once, with the remark that she used a delicately colored, perfumed preparation from the drug store, instead of the "smelly sheep fat," as she termed it.

She also sent back the leaf lard Levinia had rendered from pork fat obtained free from the slaughterhouse. Annie said she preferred the lard sold at the grocery.

Another time when she was at Annie's, (Levinia wouldn't stay away from Will's home for fear that it would hurt him, and make them still farther apart) the girl was sweeping her carpet. Levinia suggested that instead of scattering the dust as she was doing with a dry broom, she squeeze out the left-over tea leaves from her pot and scatter them over the carpet, then sweep them off. This method, she gently explained, would clean the warp and keep the dust down.

Annie was very angry and refused to believe the tea-leaves would not ruin the carpet, so Levinia had left the house and had been very careful not to make any more suggestions or short-cuts to the hard-to-reach girl. She was careful, too, not to mention to Will any of the repulses she suffered from his wife. She thought it wiser to wait for some way to bridge the feeling between Annie and herself. At the same time, she knew from Will's elusiveness, that she had complained to him about his mother's interference. Levinia's heart was very heavy with that knowledge and she hoped that understanding would come to them. She was indeed surprised when Will proposed rather than asked that he bring Annie to live in the back rooms vacated by the Hoskins.

He merely stated that he would like to have his mother look after Annie during her confinement. Levinia didn't ask why Annie's mother wasn't going to take care of her daughter. It was enough for her to know that Will wanted her to look after his wife and child. So they moved in. Annie was quiet and subdued in her pregnancy and was willing to more or less have things taken out of her hands. Even Mrs. Stephens, who often came to visit Annie, was amiable and seemed glad Annie was there, close to a midwife, as she stated it, and near the girls, she went on pointedly. Levinia saw through that. Mrs. Stephens would thus be relieved of the work and of all the responsibility involved when the birth took place. Edith and Mabel ran errands for Annie and did much of the housework, even before the baby came. They were company for her too, Levinia knew, as she brooded at times over what was before her. She deplored the fact that Annie's mother stressed the pain a new mother would encounter at the birth, making Annie depressed and at times afraid. Levinia tried to undo that impression, but she got nowhere with Annie, who stood with her mother in that, as well as in everything else. The situation was not a pleasant one.

In the first two weeks of August, Lillie brought her little girls in for a visit. Levinia was glad. She had missed the children greatly and needed Lillie's trust and unquestioned reliance after Annie's refusal to work with, or listen to her. On August 15, the weather became very hot. The children felt the heat keenly, especially Baby Ida, who whimpered during the afternoon in the hot kitchen while her mother ironed and Levinia baked for the miners. They thought the heat was to blame for the baby's restlessness but Levinia became worried when the child developed severe diarrhea. She gave her hot milk, which had checked diarrhea in her own children.

In the evening, when Will came home from work, he took Ida out of the house and away from the heat. The baby seemed better. She smiled and she laughed when Will played with her. But within an hour, she became very ill, and vomited excessively. Nothing Levinia did seemed to help. They sent for the doctor, who stayed at her side. Albert got two horses from the near-by barn, choosing the ones he knew would cover the distance in the shortest time, and rode out to Virginia Canyon to bring Jackie. Soon after they arrived, the baby died in convulsions. The physician pronounced the cause of her death as cholera infantum, which Levinia explained in despair, was what was commonly known as "summer complaint." Little Ida Hoskin had lived exactly six months to the day and brightened the world around her. It was impossible for the grief stricken parents and the others to believe she was gone. Levinia tried to explain to them that God had but taken back his own, that he had entrusted Ida, as a delicate flower, to be loved and cared for until he needed her in His own Heavenly Garden above. Nothing alleviated their grief. At the time, as Levinia well knew, even God seemed unwelcome in their thoughts.

The little body was dressed by Levinia in its prettiest white dress and laid out like a doll, on a small table in the Champion home. Later it was placed in a white coffin and, on August 17, a service was held in that room. Then the tiny corpse in its white coffin, was taken to the cemetery on her parents' laps

The New Generations's Cycle of Life and Death

as they sat in a rented carriage, followed by the rest of the family and friends in other rigs. Ida's grave was next to her grandfather's. Levinia, holding Lillie tightly in her arms, thought bitterly, "my Lillie's troubles are just beginning."

Lillie had a lot of trouble with her breasts, for the abrupt stop in nursing her child caused her milk glands to swell until they almost burst. She experienced intense throbbing pain. She had a high fever. For a few days, she followed the advice of the doctor, but it was Levinia who had the best solution to her problem. In desperation, when Lillie's pain and fever persisted, Levinia "milked" her daughter's breasts, which brought grateful relief and reduced her fever.

On Sunday, August 19, just two days after Baby Ida was laid away, Annie's labor pains began. Levinia was called around midnight. The pains developed into an ordeal that led the struggling girl to what was in her own mind, the very verge of death.

It was a difficult and prolonged birth and made Levinia very anxious. It brought Annie's mother to such despair that Will, seeing that her mother's behavior was making his wife give up, forcibly put her out of the room. He ordered her to stay out until she heard she could come back in.

As time went on and Annie wouldn't work, Will became desperate and ordered the doctor to get on the job and bring the baby. "If anything happens to my wife and child, I'll kill you," he said grimly. The doctor shook his head helplessly. "I can't take the child by instruments at this stage," he explained. "Your wife must bring the infant down where I can reach it."

Levinia stepped to the bedside and bent down over Annie. She began to talk in earnest tones, and told the girl it was a woman's privilege to bring a child into the world. She told her, her baby would be worth all the pain and all the discomfort she had in giving life to her unborn child, the blessing God gave her a chance to bring forth. Then she explained how Annie could help herself in the task before her, and gave her her own strong hands to pull on.

Whether or not her words helped, or if Annie, rested, then went to work on her own, she never knew. But Annie gained courage and strength from some source. Following Levinia's explicit instructions, she gave birth to a daughter, whom Will named Emily, at once. The new baby, born Sunday, August 19, 1894, was a fine, strong child, with dark eyes and hair, like the first Emily.

As she cleaned the gaping child and attended to Annie, Levinia mused upon the mystery of death and life, of burial and birth in the family within two days. They had lost Ida and Emily had come to them. The fact that she had arrived on the Lord's Day seemed very significant to her, and she was pleased that there was another Emily Champion. Somehow, it seemed like a gift given to ease the pain of her recent loss of daughter and granddaughter.

Then her thoughts turned to Lillie and Jackie. They had lost their child. She understood each and every thought they were having. She prayed they would lose all bitterness and acknowledge that His will had to be carried out.

Jackie's project in Virginia Canyon fizzled out. There was no gold where he'd been hired to search. So he rented a house in Packard Gulch and went back to work in a mine as a surface boss. Seeming to sense her disappointment because he had to go back to a mine, Jackie talked to Levinia about his plan to get out of mining and into some other kind of work. She was glad, and told him she thought he was wise.

Packard Gulch was behind the Bennallack Grocery Store and was the spot where the Christmas fire had taken two lives years before. This was the Gulch from which the floods had filled the cellar of the Champion house, and from which Hugh while sick, had to be removed when the floodwaters swept through the house.

It was a narrow gulch, with houses on each side of the one street. A short distance above the house the Hoskins rented was the high trestle, which spanned the gulch to carry the trains on their way to and from Central City. The trestle was a real fete in engineering work and brought much comment in the railroad world.

The Hoskin home was a substantial building on the right side of the Gulch, as one climbed toward the trestle. Though it wasn't far from her own home, Levinia found it quite a climb when she went to visit them. But the rest of her family thought it only what they termed a "skip and a jump" from their house to Lillie's.

Amy, then four, was very dear to them all. She loved them in return and seemed to have no favorites among them. Since Ida was no longer there, she had resumed her place as the plaything of the entire family. She seemed to consider the new Emily as too little to demand a great share of the family's attention.

Amy was small of bone and very dainty. She had dark brown eyes and almost black hair, which her mother rolled on strips of rags to make long curls that were the pride of them all. Levinia conceded that though Amy's mouth was too large and too thin to make her a beautiful child, she was striking enough to draw attention wherever she went. She had a great deal of life and a wonderful personality and Lillie dressed her in cute and pretty clothes. Jackie bought her red shoes that seemed a part of her as she ran and danced in the very joy of living.

The New Generations's Cycle of Life and Death

Amy Hoskin, the author, about six years old.

Levinia said Amy was old enough to be prepared for the arrival of the child her mother was expecting. Remembering Amy's reaction to her sister Ida's birth, Levinia insisted that this time she be told of the little brother or sister she was to expect. Amy was led to plan for the new baby. She was taught that it would be partly hers and she was to love it and help take care of it. So when on July 28, 1895, seventeen months after the birth of Ida, William John Hoskin, a tiny baby was born, Amy was filled with pride and happiness.

While Levinia was there taking care of the baby and the mother, Amy eluded her and left the house. She ran to tell the rest of the family the looked-for baby had come!

"I've got a little boy-sister at my house!" she cried to Edith and Mabel, who were at home doing their housework and baking for the miners, who would come later in the day for the prepared food their mother was to have ready.

When Amy insisted they see the baby, and knowing they'd better get the excited child back home before their own mother missed her and worried, they decided to do so. The two girls reported to Annie what had happened and set out for Packard Gulch carrying Amy. They arrived there just as Levinia was coming out to hunt for the missing child.

Little Willie Hoskin was said to be a "colicky" baby. For some three months he cried almost constantly. He worried his parents, kept them from getting their rest and nearly drove them to distraction. Even the neighbors were disturbed by the child's crying. Nothing could be done to stop it. They tried everything the doctors prescribed and all that folks suggested. Nothing helped.

In time, the child seemed to outgrow his trouble, for he became the sweetest and the healthiest child possible. The hair on the top of his head was long enough to make a thick curl. His face was round and his cheeks were plump. His dark eyes twinkled at times and were inquisitive at others.

Jackie was very proud of his first son. From the very beginning, William or Billy, as Albert called him, was special with his father because he was a boy. Amy never felt her father's love or attention and always remembered it. She learned early though, that a father and his son were closer somehow and that she was to look to her mother if her "Papa" was busy with Willie. It became an established fact to all of them that Willie, being the first son, had a special place with his father. Levinia saw it and, although she might have been sorry, she accepted it as a Cornish trait. She remembered Will and Albert and Hugh, their father. She knew that at times Albert had suffered because his father considered Will first over the second son, no matter what it cost anyone. That same condition would prevail, she knew, when and if there was a second son in the Hoskin family. Cornish families, she thought somewhat bitterly, have that weakness which took toll of the boys who followed that first-born son.

Chapter 32

Mine Disaster,
A Daughter Witnesses Murder

On the morning of August 29, 1895, Levinia was down in her back yard seeing to her chickens and Jackie's Cornish roosters, left in her care when he'd gone to prospect in Virginia Canyon. Suddenly to her startled ears, came the shrill of a mine whistle on Bobtail Hill. It sent its heart-gripping warning of a mine disaster, a sound all wives, mothers and sweethearts of miners dreaded and feared.

Annie, frantic and frightened, ran out of the house with little Emily in her arms. They stood together, their eyes on the Gregory Gulch side of the hill where there were several mines. Among them was the Fiske, quite high up on the hill, the Americus to the east and lower on the slope, then the Sleepy Hollow, below the Americus. They finally decided the shrieking warning was coming from the Americus.

Levinia's mind put two and two together as she watched. Fiske, an important mine with a shaft 1,500 feet deep, wasn't in full operation at the time, so her pumps were idle. She asked herself if the water, allowed to accumulate because pumps weren't taking it out of the shaft, could have broken through, which was a fear she had had throughout the years when one mine, situated above another, became idle.

She knew the hills were cut by connecting underground drilling and that the Americus was worked on the 500-foot level and the Sleepy Hollow on the 700-foot level. If her conjectures were correct, the two lower mines were in danger and their miners doomed!

Annie broke into her thoughts with the thankful remark that Albert and Jackie worked at the Bobtail Mine down the street so weren't even close to

No Wealth for Levinia

the disaster section of the hill, and Levinia joined her in expressed relief. But her heart was with those victims in the threatened mines.

Little by little, as they watched and waited anxiously with hundreds of others, the news trickled down the hill to the streets and to those tortured by personal fear of hearing the worst.

The story was that from his position at the bucket station at the Fiske Mine that morning, the foreman noticed that on the 400-foot level the water in the shaft had gone down twelve feet in about ten minutes. He had rushed to the Americus shaft house to warn the miners there.

The Americus engineer sounded danger bells below and alerted the mines close by, especially the Sleepy Hollow, by blowing the steam whistle. Then rescue squads were formed in the mines and hurried below in search of the trapped miners.

In the Sleepy Hollow, only one man was saved. Henry J. Prisk had been working below with his young son. When Prisk saw water break through into the stope, he realized what had happened. He knew they were trapped away from the working shaft. He took the boy into an old winze (a steep passage connecting the workings of the mine) and they started to climb up the ladder to the stope above.

There were different versions of how the Prisk boy lost his life. One report was that he slipped and fell from the ladder as he climbed ahead of his father. Another was that he was tired and lost his balance on the ladder and his father couldn't hold him. A third, which received the most credence, was that the water from the Fiske brought gases and foul air ahead of it and they went up the shaft where the Prisks were climbing. The lad was overcome and fell before his father almost helpless himself could grab him. Prisk, the story went on, had kept on climbing, and came to a small ledge, where he passed out completely. The rescue squad found him there and brought him to the surface, where he fought to recover from his ordeal and the terrible shock of losing his boy.

Upon the heels of the news that Henry Prisk had been saved, came the shocking horror of the death of eleven miners other than the Prisk boy, in Cornish and Tyrolean, in the Sleepy Hollow! This staggering report was eased a bit when it was learned that only two were missing in the Americus. The rest of the miners there had been able to climb above the water level and were brought to the surface in the mine bucket, where they were greeted by relatives and friends who waited praying. In all, fourteen lives had been lost!

The thought was almost beyond Levinia's comprehension. In all the long years she'd been close to mining, this was the most lives lost at one time, and the first mining disaster she had ever known. She went at once to the homes of the miners she knew who worked in the mines affected. She stopped in to offer whatever help or comfort she could give. She met with those whose loved ones were missing but who held hope that they would be saved. She visited the homes of the known lost and of those for whom there was absolutely no hope. It seemed as though half of the homes in her community had lost a member and in some cases, more than one.

The reports of the discovery of bodies came in very slowly in the days that followed. In fact it was months before the water could be pumped out and bodies found. During that period the mourners waited, wondered and prayed. They wanted to know and to have the remains of their loved ones recovered for burial.

In her sorrow for the grieving families, Levinia was thoughtful that her own personal grief when she lost her husband and children had been easier, if that was possible, by the fact that she had been permitted to give each a decent burial and at the proper time.

Later, Henry Prisk had printed on large sheets, a long poem of twenty-five verses he wrote recounting his escape. It was entitled "My Escape out of the Sleepy Hollow Mine after the Terrible Disaster There." The poem didn't discredit any of the versions concerning the Prisk boy's death by drowning in the Sleepy Hollow, but it didn't make it any clearer, either. In fact, what Henry Prisk wrote about that particular part of his story, is given in the following lines. "We passed the pit, we reached the hole, and into this my son did fall. I heard the water splash. My son, I cried, and I called in vain. His answer I did never gain. He went down with a crash."

Levinia got a copy of the poem. She put it away with her many treasures, papers, accounts, pictures, notices, the enlargement of Emily and tintypes of Emily, Edith and Mabel.

Levinia was well aware that Edith, then eighteen, was tired of staying at home and helping with the housework and the seemingly endless baking. Levinia knew she wanted to get away from the house sometimes.

Albert advocated letting her get a job so that, as he said, she could see for herself how the rest of the world did and how others lived. "Let her work in somebody's house for wages," Albert advised. "She'll learn a lot that way."

But Levinia was loathe to let her go "into service," as her sisters had some time ago, when they gave up the sewing rooms in Cornwall and came to America. She wanted something better than that for her pretty daughter.

Her problem was solved by Abe Rachofsky, a dry goods merchant in Central City, who ran The New York Store Mercantile Company there.

Mr. Rachofsky had been a friend of Hugh and Levinia Champion many years. Levinia remembered when in about 1870, Abe, an affable young man, had come to her door as a peddler selling notions and dress material from a pack he carried on his back.

Later, as his business grew, he had a cart filled with supplies. Still later, around 1875, he rented a space uptown for a store and spread out year after year until he had an up-to-date department store in the Harris Block on Main Street.

The New York Store Mercantile Company.

For thirty years in Central City, and twenty of those years a storekeeper, Mr. Rachofsky had remained a good friend of Levinia's and often visited in her home. They had talked a great deal about their families. Abe also had a large family and admitted he had many problems in raising them.

On one of these visits, he learned of Edith's restlessness. He proposed that she work as a clerk in his department store. Levinia gave her permission, which made Edith happy beyond words.

One day, when Levinia was in the store buying dress material some of the "inhabitants" of the Pine Street sumptuous "sporting houses" made "tonier lookin" by the servants' quarters in the rear came in and asked to have Edith wait on them. They were, Levinia noticed, wearing what she surmised as the very latest in material and fashion. Their faces were "made up," their hair coiffured elaborately, they walked in studied steps that brought Levinia's disdain to the front. At that moment, she regretted that she had allowed her Edith to take the position which threw her in the company of such disgraceful and dangerous characters. She saw how very pleasant they were and how easily they were pleased, smiling at Edith in such a friendly, approving way. Levinia's blood boiled because her child was being exposed to the very worst temptation she could think of at the moment!

She went at once to Mr. Rachofsky's office and told him her great fear that Edith was receiving the wrong training and was being exposed to a danger she hadn't taken into consideration. Abe was courteous, but very frank, even blunt. He told her that he had given his girl clerks careful training in their treatment of the ladies from the "hill." They were very good customers he explained, and spent a lot of money in his store, so were as welcome in a business way, as she herself was. As for Edith's exposure to the evil she intimated in Edith's waiting on them when they came into the store, he assured her there was no danger. He said "the ladies" understood their position, and he explained that "the city dads" restricted them to the houses on Pine Street, but with a right to trade in the town stores. He assured her Edith was under his strict eye, and that he maintained a careful hold on his clerks. He sent her home with his promise to remember that Edith was the daughter of his dear friends, the Hugh Champions. Though still uneasy, Levinia said no more, but her prayers pleaded for Edith's understanding of what she tried to explain to her about the "women" on Pine Street, above and behind the Opera House.

When Albert learned of his mother's fear, he spoke out very plainly and told Edith that when she waited on them in the store, she wasn't to be any friendlier than Abe expected her to be. And he ordered, "Don't ever stop on the street, or anywhere outside the store to talk to them. To be seen with them will ruin your reputation."

To his mother he said, "They won't step over the line the 'dads' lay down for them Ma. All Edith has to do is to wait on em in the store and that's all!"

As Levinia looked back over the years, she realized that such women had been in the community from the very first, and supposed there would always be some of their kind there. She realized better than ever, that there had been "red-light districts" in the history of a mining camp and that never before had occupants been curbed and restricted as they now were. Before, such women had been thrown in with all the other occupants of the town and with what she considered "decent folks" who had to make their own segregation from what was sometimes called "a necessary evil," to protect the miners' wives and daughters from assault and rape. So she accepted Albert's explanation and his admonition to Edith and hoped he knew what he was talking about.

Edith was a valuable clerk. She was pleasant, courteous and helpful and had a natural ability in salesmanship. She learned very quickly under Abe Rachofsky's careful training and soon had a thorough knowledge of the articles that were for sale. Her own personal presentation of those articles brought her great success in selling. For she could model a hat and a suit, drape her slender figure with material to show its beauty and its grace as a garment, and developed a technique all her own in selling gloves and hosiery.

Abe told Levinia warmly that he'd done all right for himself for his store, as well as for Edith, when he'd hired her as a saleslady. Levinia was very proud and pleased and thanked him for making Edith so happy.

Edith worked for him for years. She saw the New York Store grow from one room into four large ones which sold dry goods, dress material, notions, millinery, ready-made clothes and shoes. Then the store added a separate department for Gents' Furnishings: suits, hats, caps, gloves, shirts and separate coats and trousers. At that time, there were nine employees in the New York Store.

Edith was at work in the store one day when one would have thought the "Wild and Wooly West" had come back to be reenacted. Murder, the gunning down of innocent men and the capture of their murderer, took place before her very eyes and within her hearing!

It had been from Albert, who "got around" as Levinia put it that she and Edith first heard of the man with sandy hair and mustache named Samuel Covington, whom Albert dubbed a "mysterious cuss." Covington, who had come a short time earlier to work in Nevadaville, didn't talk much, Albert mentioned. He didn't tell anything that had happened before he came, didn't drop a single word about where he'd been and didn't speak of any relatives.

Albert told them that the fellows like himself, who covered much of the towns in the Gulch, Black Hawk, Central City and Nevadaville, suspected that Covington was a fugitive or a wanted man. He knew someone was looking for him because he never entered a saloon without looking all around, examining every face with his piercing eyes, before he even called for a drink at the bar. And Albert reported, when Covington sat at a table playing cards he always sat with his back to the corner or to a wall, so that he faced the door.

"Guess he looks around that way so's nobody he can get the drop on him," Albert said, with an amused grin that told his listeners he was remembering the stranger's furtive actions.

Levinia warned him to be careful of the mysterious man and for a time she heard nothing more about him. Covington was brought to her mind forcibly on that tragic day in the spring of 1896. The grim story was told her by Edith, who saw some of the action from the store, and by other witnesses. Later The Register-Call gave the full account of that awful day as follows:

The stranger, Samuel Covington, had dropped into financial difficulties and was unable to pay his bills. He had a good job mining quartz, so one of his creditors got a judgment against him and had his wages garnished, a legal action quite usual in the community but Covington became very angry.

That April morning, he went to see Judge J. M. Seright in an office above Guildsman's Corner on Main Street, almost opposite New York Store. In a rage, he climbed the stairs to the office, entered abruptly, interrupting the conversation between the Judge and a lawyer-visitor named Hammond. Covington pointed a gun at Seright's heart and snarled that he'd come to pay his bill. Seright knocked the gun aside. The bullet went through the floor and into Goldman's gambling room. Hammond ran for help.

Seright tried to head off further trouble from the angry man by suggesting quietly that they could settle the matter in some other way. Luckily Covington replied, "Very well. Sit down and write me a receipt for the bill of $61.00 I owe, and mark it paid in full."

The judge sat down at his desk and stalled for time until Hammond could summon help to take the crazed man. He asked Covington to dictate the exact wording he wanted in the receipt. He wrote very very slowly in and put Covington's dictation on paper. They heard footsteps mount the stairs and come down the hall toward the judge's office. Covington waited until the cessation of noise indicated that someone was just outside the closed door, and then he shot a second gun, pulled from a holster under his arm.

This bullet went through the door and entered the breast of City Marshall M. F. Keleher who had been summoned by Hammond. Keleher collapsed on the floor and crawled bleeding into the office of Judge L. P. Arright near by, while Hammond ran down Main Street for more help. This time Sheriff R. B. Williams, owner of the Williams Stables and a former Mayor of Central City, answered the call. He started up the stairs to Judge Seright's office, gun in hand. Covington threw the door open. Both men fired at the same instant.

The sheriff's bullet went into the ceiling while Covington's entered William's body just above the navel. The sheriff backed down the steps he had just climbed and said to the crowd that had gathered in the street, "I've been shot!" He was helped away as Covington bounded down the stairs to Main Street, then fanning his two guns to keep the angry muttering crowd back, he ran toward Nevadaville.

Police Judge Arright quickly swore in Henry Lehman, known to be a good shot, and gave him a Winchester rifle. Then he deputized Sherman Harvey, driver of an express wagon standing in the street at the time. The two men leaped into Harvey's wagon and started after Covington. When they caught up to about forty yards of the retreating gun man, he began to shoot at them. Lehman took sure aim with the rifle and fired. Covington fell on his face and blood spurted from a wound in his body.

The crowds rushed in and took his guns from him, and Lehman gave orders to put him in the wagon. When Harvey headed for the jail, he was followed by the crowd with enraged yells of "Hang him!" The followers were so incensed that Lehman knew they would lynch his prisoner, so he called out that the man was fatally shot. Covington died just before they reached the jail, and before a doctor could be called, taking with him the secret of his past, of his mysterious behavior and of his desperate actions.

Marshall Keleher recovered after a period of time, but Sheriff Williams died a few days later and was deeply mourned by all. His funeral, the largest ever recorded in The Gulch, was held in the Opera House which was the largest building in the entire community.

It was a long time indeed before the mining camps stopped talking about the murder, and it took even longer for Edith to forget the stark horror she had experienced. The picture of Covington's retreat, as he backed away from Guildman's Corner, with his guns ready to belch out more death bullets to anyone within range, never completely left her memory.

Leah May, Will's second daughter, was born without difficulty and much more bravery on Annie's part with only Levinia on hand. Leah was strong and healthy and did very well, growing into a sweet, pretty child they all loved dearly. When she began to walk it became apparent that one little hip was a bit weaker than the other, but the doctor called in by Will at Levinia's insistence, could find no cause for anxiety. Yet, as Leah walked, she swung the one hip a little, which made Levinia remember Emily's first indication of her affliction. She prayed that same weakness wouldn't come to the precious grandchild who reminded her so much of her own Emily. Her prayer seemed answered, for Leah's childish favoring one hip, gradually disappeared, and with that assurance, the entire family rejoiced.

Chapter 33

The Hoskin Family Moves a Long Day's Journey Away, A Granddaughter's Death

Jackie Hoskin took steps to leave mining for good. He had gone on various trips to the plains both north and south of Denver in his search for land he could afford to buy. He found the areas around the Colorado capital and on all sides of it too highly valued for his meager funds. He decided that the land east of the city wasn't good farming land, so he went farther south into the "dry section" where he found good deep soil and at the price that finally settled the matter.

After a very careful search for the amount of land he wanted and could buy (he saw several places he would have liked to own but they were not for sale) he found one hundred and sixty acres for sale thirty miles south of Denver, between the towns of Sedalia and Castle Rock, at a price he figured he could handle. It had a "homestead house" on it, and was priced at $400, every cent he had in the world!

The deed, dated February 27, 1897, described the land as: *The south east quarter of the north east quarter, the north east quarter of the south east quarter, and the north half of the south east quarter of section twenty-one (21) in township seven (7) south of range sixty-seven (67) west, situated in the County of Douglas, and State of Colorado.*

Amy, then six-years-old and going to school, asked when they were to move to the "ranch," the name her father had called the place where they were to live. He explained that it would be a long time, for he had to work hard and save money for horses and wagons to move them. Then too, there would be plows and machinery to buy before they could begin to farm, and they had to have a cow. With the incentive of land in their own names, the Hoskins saved every penny they could. Jackie was then thirty-two. From then on, if he worked in the mines, the time of his life-span would be figured as settled. So he sought surface jobs only, so that he could avoid being in the dust below.

On October 14, 1897, Samuel John Hoskin became a naturalized citizen of the United States of America. Levinia counted it as a personal achievement, for she had repeatedly urged his declaration of intention since he had come into her family.

In April of 1899, the Hoskin family left Central City to live in Douglas County. Jackie and Albert each drove a wagon and team from Central City to Arvada, a town situated at the foot of mountains, and picked up the furniture shipped there by freight on the narrow-gauge railroad. There they met Lillie and the two children at the passenger train and then they all drove to the new home.

Ethelyn, Will's third daughter, was born July 24, 1899, bringing Levinia's happiness to a new height in having another grandchild, although she was greatly disappointed that it wasn't a boy to carry on the Champion name.

She was sorry that the Hoskins, who had been great workers in the church, wouldn't be present November 5, 1899, when a new pipe organ, was dedicated by her family friend, Reverend B. T. Vincent. The organ was purchased with money raised by the members of the church and a large sum donated by the heirs of Robert E. Harris. She wished they could see the beautiful new carpet and pews seating four hundred that were placed in the Sanctuary that same year. They would have been proud of the heating plant installed in their beloved old church through the united efforts of the church workers.

1899 also brought a new railroad depot to Central City. It was erected on the hill at the juncture of Spring and Nevada Streets, leaving the brick station across Spring Street to be used as a freight depot.

Gilpin County's new brick Court House was finished and turned over to the County Commissioners on February 20, 1900. It was built on the grounds of the Henry M. Teller's home, facing Eureka Street and just across Church Street from St. James Methodist Church. It was a very impressive looking building and worthy of the pride of Central City and Gilpin County.

That spring, Mabel, Levinia's youngest child, graduated from High School. She was the first and only one in the family to do so; Levinia rejoiced. At the same time, she regretted that Hugh wasn't there with her to share her pride when Mabel, who proudly stood in her beautiful white graduation dress, made by her mother, received her diploma. The impressive graduation at the Opera House, was one of the most-remembered moments of Levinia's life.

The Hoskin Family Moves a Long Day's Journey Away, A Granddaughter's Death

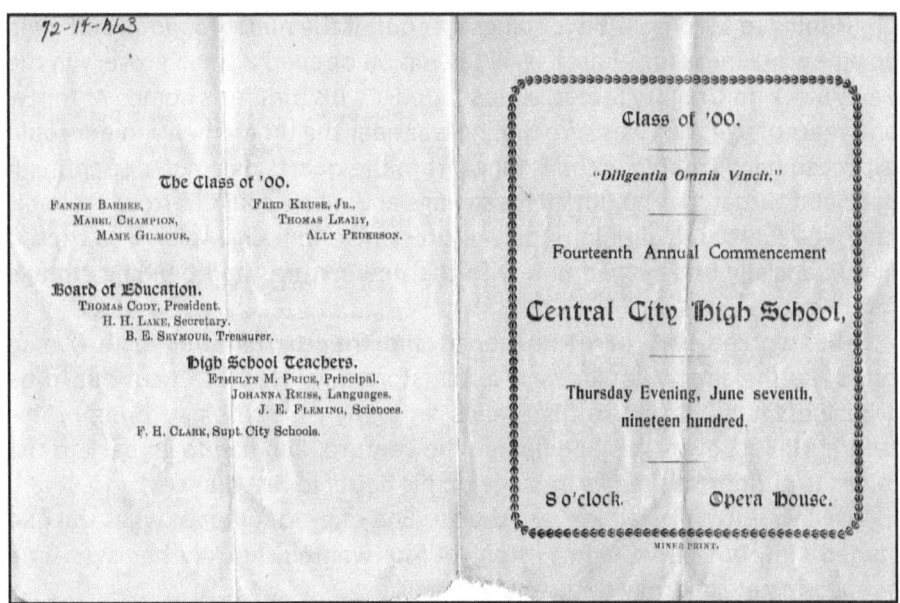

On July 23, 1900, Washington Hall, was purchased for use as a City Hall. It was perhaps the very oldest building in Central City and the one which Levinia associated with Central City history in the years she'd lived there. All that time it had been used and known as the "Court House." Now, it was the "Official Hall" and the old name of Washington Hall, as Levinia remembered it, was no longer used. She regretted this, somehow. The building seemed significant to her, as did all the associations she had built up during the thirty-seven years she'd been in Gregory Gulch, until they seemed a part of her. She could see that great progress had been made and a lot of history became part of the growth of the community and the area around it. In that significant growth, she reflected proudly, she had had a part, small though it was, and her countrymen had helped build and develop this area of the New World. She seemed to stand taller and stronger and resolved to go on, as long as God willed her, to loving the town, the county and the country. At the same time she would continue to be proud of her own people, the Cornish.

Because times were tightening in the vicinity, Albert left the mines and took a job driving a quartz wagon with the double and triple teams, thus putting his love for and his knowledge of horses to use. And most important to Levinia, the new job got him out of the mineshafts and the work that led them to the bowels of the earth. Albert enjoyed going back to driving the ore wagons and wished he had never left them and gone into the mines. At the time, it paid a few cents more a day and hadn't required any after-work time to see to the horses he drove.

No Wealth for Levinia

Hoping to accomplish two things, get out of the mines for good and build up a new business for himself, Will Champion opened a small grocery in the Davis Block on Gregory Street, almost opposite his mother's home. At thirty-one years of age, Will was sure that he was near the time when a miner could expect to have trouble with his lungs from the quartz dust, inhaled through nose and throat. So he put all his savings and all he could borrow from his mother, Albert and Edith into the venture. Uncle Tom Champion also backed him financially and helped him with the new fixtures and building storage for his goods.

Will worked very hard. He hoped and tried as faithfully as any man could. But he simply couldn't make the store pay. He wasn't cut out to be a businessman. Credit to his friends, in many cases, helped bring on his failure. He lost everything he had, in the venture, and had to go back to the mines to support his family and pay off his debts to his relatives

Levinia felt Will's failure very keenly. She offered to forget what she had loaned him, but he wouldn't listen. All he wanted, he told her, was time enough to get square with the world again.

Annie surprised everyone by trying in every way she could to help him repay that money. She even asked Levinia to show her how to save on feeding her family, so that Will could have the extra money she saved to apply to their debts. Levinia cried in the privacy of her own room, partly for her son's predicament, partly for Annie's staunch right-about-face in wanting to get by on less, and partly because Annie had asked her help.

Levinia began to show her how to economize in various ways, to substitute lesser qualities of meat instead of buying the most expensive as she'd been in the habit of doing, and to cook the cheaper cuts so they tasted almost like top quality. She showed her how to work up every scrap of leftovers into tasty dishes so that even Will, who prided himself on providing what he called "a good table," thanked her for her help.

Next she taught Annie to make garments for herself and her girls, instead of buying ready-made clothes or having them made by a dressmaker.

Annie accepted all of Levinia's suggestions gratefully and together they worked out ways to relieve Will's straits. Annie grew into her place with an efficiency that pleased Levinia very much and made Will proud of his wife, all of which drew them all more closely together.

But the Will Champion struggles were complicated further when little Leah May came down with diphtheria. No one even knew where she got the contagious germ. There had been no other case of the fatal disease in the vicinity, and no one else came down with it, not even in her immediate family.

The Hoskin Family Moves a Long Day's Journey Away, A Granddaughter's Death

The child became ill very suddenly. Levinia, with her constantly in the last few hours she lived, knew from the very first that no medical help could check the disease, but they tried to do so. They had doctors who held consultations in order to do all they could to check the possible spread of the dreaded diphtheria. They could do nothing for Leah. Death was inevitable.

Levinia and Leah's parents would never forget the struggle the child made to get her breath as the fatal membrane cut off her life. When death came on April 1, circa 1905, Levinia thanked God the child was at last released from her hopeless battle. Even Will and Annie couldn't wish her back.

Because of the contagion, there could be no church services for the little girl, a fact that hurt Levinia very much. A service was held in Levinia's parlor where the little body lay in a white casket that was narrower at the foot than at the head, which Leah's grandfather Elisha Stephens, had chosen and purchased. Then the child's body was laid away as close to her cousin Ida Hoskin as possible, but over the fence in another cemetery, The City Cemetery, where Will had purchased a family lot.

Soon after that, Will and Annie decided they'd better move out of their mother's house and to save money, rent a smaller cheaper place. Levinia tried to tell them they could stay with her for less than they'd been paying her, or could stay for nothing, until they were free of debt. But Will told her he wanted his family to himself until they could face life without Leah May. Levinia understood that they found it hard to live in the rooms where they'd lost leah May, so said no more about their staying.

The house Will rented was on lawrence Street between Levinia's home and Black Hawk, so she had but a short distance to go to visit them, which she did often.

She rented the vacant rooms to bachelor miners and locked the doors between the lower and the upper parts of the house where Albert, Edith, Mabel and she lived. Albert and Edith contributed to the family pool, which Levinia strengthened by selling baked foods.

Chapter 34

A Daughter Marries and Divorces, More Grandchildren

Through Albert, Levinia learned that Edith was seeing a great deal of a handsome young barber named Ed Bates, who worked in a barbershop across the street from the New York Store. The intimation that Edith was interested in a man was news to her, but to hear that that man was only a barber shocked her beyond words. And when Albert reported that the young couple was in love and intended to marry, she was completely stunned.

She questioned Edith and learned that the report was true. The girl explained that, because she realized her mother and family would be against Ed and her marriage to him, she had not told them of their plans. She said they had been meeting in places Albert seldom went. But he had tracked them down. She was tearfully explanatory but declared that she loved Ed and would marry him in spite of everything they said and did.

Levinia was surprised at Edith's vehemence. She had always been so obedient and so willing to do everything she had wanted to do, that she was quick to blame the stranger for Edith's sudden stubborn stand. Albert tried to tell Edith that Bates wasn't the man for her and that she wouldn't be happy with him. Edith was still determined, so he came right out with the derogatory stories he'd heard about the man she was defending. Edith accused Albert of holding a measuring stick on others when he, himself, "was no angel," and did the very things he was stating against Ed, showing a spirit they didn't know Edith had and making Albert grin in admiration of her "spunk."

Will said she should marry a Cornishman and mentioned a few he would consider as a brother-in-law. He said he'd never welcome Bates into the family.

Finally, Levinia consented to Edith's plea that she bring Ed Bates to see

A Daughter Marries and Divorces, More Grandchildren

her. When he came, Levinia was surprised to find that he was well-built, well-dressed and had such perfect manners she suspected he was an actor, or was trying to impress her, which she was absolutely positive he couldn't do.

But she had to admit that he was a handsome young fellow, dark haired and blue-eyed, and really was in love with Edith. Indeed, he declared that he was and, with what she thought a very glib tongue, told her he was from Golden, Colorado and came from a large and well-known family of business and professional people. He added that he was one of several children whose parents still lived in Golden where his father was in business.

In spite of herself Levinia was impressed, for she did regard family as a first recommendation. But she wouldn't give in and sent the young man away, leaving Edith in tears but staunch in determination to marry Ed Bates without her mother's permission and consent.

Levinia checked on the young barber's story of his family. It was all true. So she had to fall back on the belief backed by Albert that Ed was from a highly respected family, but was what was termed its "black sheep" and mustn't marry their innocent, inexperienced Edith.

But they had to give in. For Levinia realized that if she didn't give her consent, Edith would run away. So, in order to be sure she was actually married, she gave her reluctant permission with great misgiving. Even her prayers for help in deciding didn't seem to get the result she sought and expected.

Edith, wearing Mabel's graduation dress, was a beautiful bride. In spite of the strong current of disapproval that her family held, she was married on the evening of February 25, 1901, in Levinia's parlor, becoming Mrs. Ed Bates.

The groom, well-dressed, well-pleased and well-mannered was the picture of accomplishment. Levinia thought he smiled at her in what she believed was a sly realization that he'd put over what he set out to do, to take Edith away from under her very nose. But he didn't take Edith away from her house, for the newlyweds stayed in her home in the downstairs bedroom which Levinia gave them and she slept upstairs.

Afterwards, Levinia realized that if the young people had gone away, where she wouldn't have to see Ed at every meal and have Edith home all day with her in addition to sharing her home with him in the evenings, it would have been better for all concerned. Edith quit her job, and Mr. Rachofsky hired Mabel in her place, while Edith helped her mother with the food she sold the miners.

Though Edith never lost her pleasant manner or her loving care, Levinia found it hard to refrain from mentioning her disapproval of what the girl had done. So she didn't speak of Ed at all, and didn't try to advise Edith. Her child had chosen, so Levinia figured the matter was out of her hands.

No Wealth for Levinia

It was Ed who made the next move. Levinia saw the strain he was under in the house where only Edith paid any attention to him. She wasn't surprised when he told that her he had taken employment in his hometown of Golden, and was taking Edith there at once.

They moved in with Ed's father and mother who, Edith wrote, were wonderful people and treated her with love and pride and understanding. Levinia knew this part of the letter was a reprimand to her and to her entire family, but told herself it was easy for anyone, even Ed's family, to love Edith and to be proud of her was a foregone conclusion. But she went so far as to admit that in her home Ed hadn't been treated as his own parents treated him.

In the back of her mind, there lay self-criticism of her past actions toward Ed and Edith, and she hoped that she could make amends in some way, sometime, to them both. A part of that chance came before she realized it, for Ed Bates moved to Denver where he and Edith rented an apartment and invited her to visit. Levinia decided not to go, for she was sure Ed would not appreciate having her there. She resolved to wait and see what developed before she made the trip.

Finally, she went to see them. She found the apartment comfortable and Ed a very attentive young husband. Edith seemed happy and contented. Levinia returned home with a far different opinion of her son-in-law. In fact, she was ready to accept him into her family circle.

But suddenly that revised opinion was shattered, for after two years of marriage Edith came home bringing all her personal belongings. She simply said she'd left Ed for good. She didn't explain what had happened between them. She didn't tell her family what had driven her to take that decisive step. But one day she admitted to her mother that, to her great sorrow, she had learned that her family had been right about Ed Bates.

No one said, "I told you so," as she seemed to expect. They merely opened their arms to her, welcomed her home, did all they could to make her happy and asked no questions.

Edith went to work for a lawyer up town and on the surface she was the same charming girl, but Levinia knew her child was torn inside, and her heart ached for her. But Edith didn't talk about her troubles.

Ed Bates came to the house several times and tried to talk to Edith, who refused to listen and ordered him to go away and leave her alone. He tried to get her to hear his side of the unexplained problem, but Edith was adamant. He then came to Levinia and asked her to explain to Edith that he loved her very much and was very sorry she misunderstood him. He begged Levinia to try to get Edith to listen to him, to give him another chance to prove that loved her.

A Daughter Marries and Divorces, More Grandchildren

Levinia found herself listening to his plea and actually tried to get Edith to at least see him. But Edith wouldn't even discuss the matter. Suddenly, she filed for a divorce from Ed! In those days, divorce was a public disgrace. At first, Levinia found it very hard to keep a stiff upper lip against some of the openly slighted remarks about Edith in that shameful situation, which was one of the very first among their friends and acquaintances. When she heard the words infidelity and adultery given in court as Edith's plea for separation, she saw that divorce was the only solution. Then she stood behind Edith and helped her face the serious matter squarely, defying the criticism of her and of her action, both before and after the legal separation. Things fell back into place. Edith was at home, worked and to all appearances, the two years of marriage hadn't happened. Though Edith never mentioned it, Levinia knew that no woman could forget the deep hurt she had received.

Two grandsons were born in 1902 and Levinia officiated at the births. Will Champion's son, William Hugh, was born in May at the house down the street toward Black Hawk. Lillie Hoskin's Hugh was born in June at Levinia's home. Lillie came from the ranch at Sedalia for her confinement, bringing Amy 11, and Billy, 7, whose presence Levinia enjoyed. She had missed them so very much in the years they'd been on the ranch. She had only occasionally seen them when their parents brought them on the train or when, on very rare occasions, she had gone to the ranch for short visits.

Levinia had different thoughts about the new little boys. First, Will's son, whom they called "little Willie," really was little. At birth he weighed less than six pounds. His frame was short and thin and his hands when out-stretched, were the exact size of the face of is father's watch. But he was strong and wiry, and did well from the very first. Will was so proud that he had a son he could hardly act normally, making Levinia remember her former thoughts about a first son in a Cornish family.

Hugh Hoskin on the other hand, was large, weighing almost eleven pounds and his extra long hair and finger and toenails made Levinia suspect that he had been carried in his mother's womb more than the usual nine months. And, because this boy was the second son born to the Hoskins, Levinia knew the new boy was to occupy just that place in the family. She thought about the fact that William John Hoskin, the first son, would always be considered more important in his father's eyes, the example set by Cornish custom for the first-born son. She wasn't sure this particular Cornish custom was right or just. Remembering Albert, her own second son, she felt this matter keenly. But she concluded somewhat bitterly, that was just another circumstance that had to be endured.

While Edith had been away, a new brick school, named Clark School after the superintendent of the Central City Schools, F. H. Clark, had been built on the grounds where the old Congregational Church had been used for about twenty years for the lower grades. The new school building was first occupied on September 3, 1901, and the next year the old church, its purpose served, was torn down.

Another change was that Levinia's eyesight had failed so badly that she was unable to see to read the papers she had always gone through so carefully to keep up with what happened far and near. And reading her Bible became a hard task, making her depend more and more upon her memory of its contents. She was thankful she could quote page after page of the verses she relied upon so much.

When an "eye doctor" came to Central City on his periodical visits, Edith took Levinia to have her eyes tested, and saw that she got glasses. Those "specs," as she called them, opened up a new vista for her. With them, she could see much better than she had for many years, so she widened the scope of her reading to books.

Chapter 35

A Daughter Marries and Moves to California, A Son's Death

Mabel abruptly announced that she was having a young man call at the house one evening to meet her. Levinia realized that after Edith's experience of not letting the family know of the man she was seeing, Mabel was plunging right into the matter before any harm was done in that direction.

Though Levinia was jolted severely by the realization that her baby was twenty-years-old and "grown up," she was glad she had taken that way of breaking the news of her interest in a particular man. It also confirmed the spirit and independence Mabel had always shown.

The man, a young handsome mustached Cornish miner named Herbert Tredinnick, had an assurance about him. It told Levinia that he had a mind of his own and wasn't likely to back down before anyone or anything, certainly not the family and especially the mother, of the girl in whom he was interested. Young Tredinnick fell right into their hearts. There was no objection to him or to his marriage to Mabel.

On May 25, 1903, Mabel, wearing her graduation dress, was married in her mother's parlor by the Methodist minister. Levinia thought the bride dignified, as well as beautiful, in her great happiness. Her only qualm at the moment was her realization, that because both Mabel and Herbert had strong minds and independent natures, each was apt to speak out without considering their words or their effect upon the other. She reflected that it wasn't easy to get along with a Cornish husband. She told herself that his wife is supposed to listen and allow her husband to do her thinking. "Like Lillie does," she added to herself. Lillie, she felt, was an ideal Cornish wife. She remembered her own rebellion at times when she'd wanted to share plans with Hugh. She hoped Mabel would work out some plan as she had so as to get along with her husband and not seem to lessen his importance in his own eyes and in the eyes of others.

Perhaps, she thought, she should talk to Mabel and try to give her the benefit of her own experience as a Cornish wife. She made up her mind to do her best to help her daughter, by telling of her own taut situation during her marriage.

But she didn't have the chance for Herbert told her he was taking his bride to California where he planned to settle! Levinia couldn't believe it, but it happened. After a very brief honeymoon at the Hoskin ranch, they came back to Central City, packed and left for the western border state. She never saw either of them again. She had that premonition when she kissed Mabel goodbye and gave her youngest her most prized possession, the beautiful Paisley shawl Will had brought her from Denver years before.

For the first few days after Mabel's departure Levinia really suffered. Her family had been broken up again, this time by a greater distance than when Lillie had moved. But letters and books from far-off California helped her get over the void left by her youngest child. Mabel wrote that everything was fine with her and Herbert. They were very happy and Herbert had a good job as a miner in a community called the Mother Lode. And there was a chance for him to carpenter, an added accomplishment of the young Cornishman she had married. But each letter seemed to emphasize the great distance Mabel was from her old home.

Levinia reminded herself that she still had Edith and Albert with her and Will was close by. She prayed for all of them.

Yes, Will was close by but he wasn't well. She first realized it at the Fourth of July celebration when, as usual, he'd taken part in a rock-drilling contest and had almost fainted from the exertion. She was sure the extreme activity did much harm to her son's lungs. Next, Will had to give up blowing his beloved tuba in the City Band, which he had been a part of for years, and had made many trips with its members to Denver and other cities on exhibitions and celebrations. Now, he didn't have the breath to play.

Her heart ached with the knowledge that Will's days were numbered, and there wasn't a thing anyone could do to prevent his lungs from filling up completely. Her thoughts were bitter ones. Will's family was so young. Emily, his oldest child, was only ten and his youngest was two years old.

Rebellion rose in her heart. It was hard to take the inevitable quietly but she knew she had to do it. She couldn't even mention his condition to anyone. She had to be brave for Will and Annie and their children. She had to watch her beloved son grow worse, day by day. For two years, she saw he did less and less exercise, cut out all extra activity, stopped to rest along the way when

A Daughter Marries and Moves to California, A Son's Death

he went to work and then the failure to work at all. Finally, the inability to lie down and the straight chair that came into use as he tried to rest sitting up.

Again, as with Hugh, she went through the torture of watching a silicosis victim die. She prayed for strength to endure and questioned if death by accident wasn't easier and more merciful to both the victim and the remaining loved ones. At least, she reasoned bitterly, the shock in an accident came all at once; it wasn't drawn into tortured days and weeks and months, even years. But again she had to bow to circumstances, she had to accept His will, as hard as it proved to be.

In an effort to ease Will's breathing, Albert took him to the Hoskin ranch by train, and left him there. The fresh air and the lower altitude did help him, but Will became so homesick he had to return. Levinia realized that he wanted to be with his family every minute he had left.

In order to be close to her own father and mother while Will was out of work, Annie rented a very small house on Bates Hill, not far from them. Levinia went along in the rig Albert rented to take Will to the house. When she went home, she knew her son would never get down the hill again, wouldn't get out of that house until he was carried out for the last time. She would need every ounce of strength she possessed to compose herself before Will and his family. Inner sorrow, she admitted grimly to Albert, as they rode down Bates Hill, is the hardest to bear. Silently, Albert put his arm around her and held her tightly, while she shed tears that somehow eased her tension.

During Will's last days, Albert, Edith and Levinia took turns with Annie's parents, so that Annie could get some rest. While Levinia spent as many hours there during the day as she could and still keep up with her baking, Albert and Edith took turns at night. Annie's parents were in and out at all hours, always on hand and on call, Annie's mainstay in her trouble.

Levinia got together as much money as she could, for now that Will wasn't earning anything, she felt that she had to help out with the family. Besides, she realized bitterly, there would soon be even more expense. Her throat filled up as she repeated, "soon." No one knew when the crisis would come.

On the morning of January 20, 1906, Levinia was in her kitchen getting breakfast for Albert, when Edith, who had spent the night sitting with Will, came in. With her was a neighbor, Mrs. Parsons. From that fact and from their sober faces, Levinia knew what had happened. Now that the end had come, all her fortitude left her. She went all to pieces, failing on her knees, calling for help from Above.

Albert rushed at once to Will's house to take charge and help Annie. Mrs.

Parsons stayed with Levinia and Edith until Levinia could pull herself together and talk to Edith, who was shaken by the experience of seeing death come to her brother. Then Mrs. Parsons left and, as was the custom among neighbors, went to see that food was provided for the bereaved family.

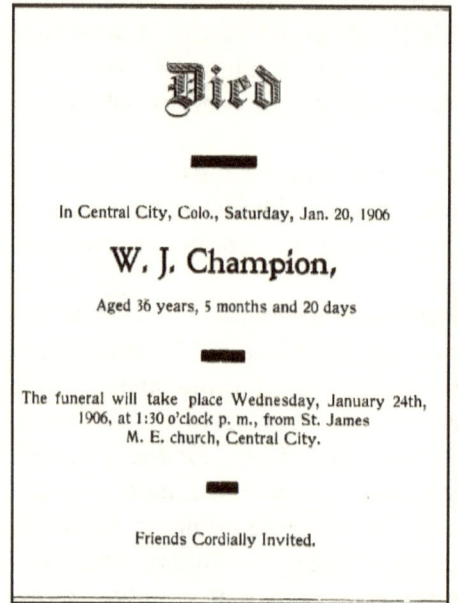

Two days later, for the ninth time, Levinia left a loved one at the cemetery. Her husband, five children and two grandchildren lay there. Now Will was laid there close to his little daughter Leah May. Will was only thirty-six.

Levinia thought, he leaves three children: Emily twelve, Ethelyn nine, and Willie four. I know what hardships Annie has before her. I'll help her all I can.

In spite of all outward calmness and her resolute determination to carry on and help her dead son's family, it was a long time before Levinia could face her lot bravely. She just couldn't feel reconciled to the loss of Will. Finally, she took herself to task over the fact. She admitted that the sorrow of Annie and her little ones and of Albert and Edith must not be intensified by her tears or her attitude. "If I am strong, I can help them all," she told herself.

So, with Annie and the little ones, she made special efforts to speak calmly of Will. To Annie, she spoke as a mother, as well as a friend, and was sure both Annie and herself were helped. For Annie told her, gratefully, that she knew she'd gone through the same sorrow, so she realized how she felt and what had to be done.

Levinia tried to show Will's children that God had taken their papa home to Heaven. Small comfort to them she concluded, and quailed inwardly as she wondered if she, herself, really believed what she said.

It was quite some time and after many prayers for understanding before Levinia could answer yes to the questions in her own heart, and much longer before she could take up her old life with her own children.

Chapter 36

Levinia Shares Keepsakes with Granddaughter Amy, The Champion Name Is Hopefully Preserved

Another daughter, Elsie Louise, was born to Jack and Lillie Hoskin on August 23, 1907. The baby was fat and dark, active and strong. She was the only grandchild in all eight, Levinia hadn't brought into the world, a fact that brought her a great deal of regret.

But, she knew it was better this way, for the folks on the ranch were very, very busy with chores and crops that time of year. So it would be better if Lillie stayed at home for this birth, instead of coming to Central City to be with her mother.

When approached with this statement, Levinia agreed and then turned down the Hoskin proposal to come to the ranch for the birth. She didn't want to be away from home for those several days, perhaps for two weeks, or more. She had her own work to do, preparation of food for the miners and keeping house for Albert and Edith, who worked each day except Sunday, at their jobs.

But the main reason, understood by all concerned, was that she felt she ought not to lose any chance to make as much money as she could baking. She was helping Annie with money and working with her in a project of keeping boarders to support her fatherless family. So she didn't go to the ranch to help with the new grandchild.

At the ranch, it had been planned that Amy, then sixteen, would cook the meals and keep house, as well as do her share with chores. A neighbor, who was a nurse, would come every day to look after the new mother and baby. The family doctor at Castle Rock, the County Seat eight miles to the south, would be called by telephone to the Hoskin ranch when the birth was at hand.

But the baby came too suddenly. She arrived one night so rapidly that Jack had to make the delivery, which was complicated because the cord was wrapped twice around the child's neck, almost strangling her as she came into the world. But Jack, carrying Lillie's instructions and using his own good judgment, saved the life of his baby daughter, while Amy called the doctor and nurse.

Lillie wrote her mother that she thought the wrapping of the cord had been brought about the day before Elsie's birth. At that time she had been pumping water with a hand pump to water the cows. All at once as she pumped regular and even strokes the pump lost its "priming" and the handle, thus released and made useless, dropped abruptly, throwing her heavy body forward with violence and brought her to her knees.

There were no other complications. Elsie grew and thrived on her mother's milk, a question that had worried Lillie and Levinia no end for although all three of the older Hoskin children had been breast-fed, Hugh, for no apparent reason, had refused to take the breast. After a great deal of worry and trying out foods to find that which would agree with the baby, he had been started on steel-cut oatmeal, cooked into a very thin gruel and fed from a nursing bottle.

In addition to the news about little Elsie, Levinia was thrilled by the plans the Hoskins were making for a new brick house. It was to be built, close to the old "homestead house" they'd lived in while they were getting started on their ranch venture.

Another bit of news was the report that Amy was doing very well in her high school work at Douglas County High School in Castle Rock. Levinia knew she drove a horse and spring wagon those eight miles, taking Willie with her to the grade school he attended there.

Levinia felt that she knew Amy best of all her grandchildren. First, because she was the oldest and had been around her more, and second, the child had been curiously interested in what Levinia told her about Cornwall and in what she had done when she was a little girl. Levinia remembered when, as a small child, Amy had been hurt and frightened when her playmates in the street called her a "Cousin Jenny" and ran away without explanation. Amy had come to her grandmother in tears. Levinia comforted and explained what "Cousin Jenny" meant and told her she should be proud of the fact that her people had come from Cornwall. She had then showed the child the small country of Cornwall, colored pink on the map, and pointed out the big ocean she crossed in a ship to come to America.

From that moment, Amy had been intensely interested in the past and asked many questions and remembered what she heard about her grandmother's experiences in the new land, America, and gold camps in which she'd lived. Amy had gone with Levinia to see the buildings she mentioned and the streets she pointed out as she told the history of the town in which they lived, Mountain City, and its sister camps: Black Hawk, Central City, and Nevadaville. As Amy grew older, she looked at all the pictures, clippings, papers, books and an article Levinia had accumulated throughout the years. She was fascinated by each bit of information about the past and the family members. As Levinia showed the child those mementos, the past became much more vivid in her own mind because the girl's interest brought memories of what she'd seen and lived and what had been a part of her innermost experiences.

Another reason she felt so close to Amy was because, around the age of ten, Amy had expressed her wish that she could see what Levinia and the people of that period wore and owned at the time of the events her grandmother related. Instantly, Levinia's thoughts flew to the personal articles she put away out of sight for sentimental reasons, some things belonging to the dear ones she'd lost. For a long time, those belongings had made her uneasy and conscious of some weakness in her "make-up," some failing in her strong nature. Most of her secret locked away possessions were from a past filled with sorrow and grief. Every time she saw them, she relived every minute of each loss. Every article revived her dead, emphasized her great sorrow, and shook her for hours as memories flooded over her. Many times, throughout the years, she had wished she hadn't kept them. More and more she had come to realize that a clean break would have been easier at the time she'd lost each one, rather than hanging on to some of their personal belongings. Though she was sure she'd be better off in mind, even now, if things were removed from all possibility of her getting them out to look at and shed tears over, she just couldn't bring herself to do it, for they seemed so much a part of her.

Then, with Amy's wish to really see the very things she had put away, not to have them recall sad memories but to visualize, in this way, the history that was so fascinating to her, Levinia saw how she could use those treasures as family history. Those very articles would give Amy a much better understanding of Cornish clothing and of Mountain City, and the town of Central City, which had absorbed the oldest mining camp in Gregory Gulch.

Thankfully, she resolved to use her collection of hidden stored-away articles as part of history. This new use would give them a new value and would release her from what she'd considered her personal weakness in giving way to renewed grief at the sight of them.

So she showed Amy the contents of the locked bureau drawers upstairs, and told her about each article. There was the dress she had worn when she had arrived in Mountain City and her wedding dress, made in Cornwall, which Maude Whitesley had silently criticized so long ago. There was the big hat with plumes she'd worn in the early days of the gold camp, and a purple dress worn by Cornish women at that time on "dress-up" occasions. There were shoes she had liked, but could not wear when she had to walk so many miles raising her children and cooking and baking for bachelor miners.

She had saved Hugh's square-toed shoes, that he hadn't lived to wear out, his favorite necktie and his "Sunday" hat. There were baby dresses, bonnets, and shoes. Each ownership was clear in her mind. There was the first doll Edith had cherished, and a purse Emily had loved to carry. There was something there of each dear one from the first William John through the life of the last William John, and an old band cap he had worn at many celebrations.

In addition, she had put away some token of each child still alive, cramming the drawers to the brim. There were cards Lillie saved as girlish mementos of her school days, and three black fans which Will had brought to Lillie, Edith and Mabel, from one of his trips with the City Band.

Afterwards, when Amy helped her add these articles to the pictures, papers and so on, as historical items, dating each and naming its Champion family owner, Levinia felt great pride in the new value placed upon them. Silently, she thanked the child for her part in dispelling the "weakness" in character she'd felt for many years. She continued to keep the tokens that spoke of a place in the history of Central City and the Champion family, donating another drawer and another, for the storage needed.

Albert Champion, then thirty-two, barrel-chested, wiry and strong, much like his father in looks and build, was the apple of Levinia's eye. She was proud of his ability as a boxer and as a wrestler, but mostly because for years, he had been a regular faithful member of the Mountain City Alert Fire Team, whose house was at the juncture of Miner and Lawrence Streets, not far from Levinia's house.

Although she called him Albert, Edith and his friends called him Al, or Tug. Levinia maintained that the name Tug had been given him because he was one of the men who tugged the fire cart and was one of the "wheel horses," so to speak, working next to the cart, itself.

But some folks said Albert was dubbed Tug because he'd won over a reputed tough boxer in a bout in the town's ring. At any rate, Tug Champion was quite well known in the vicinity and in the mining areas around the country for his athletic ability and his staying qualities.

Levinia had a picture of the Alert Fire Team and knew the men personally: Robert Johnson, Dick Davies, Harry Peters, "Deadman" Williams, Leroy Mills, Will Bates, Ben Wilson and Albert.

This picture has been reproduced in books, shown in museums and is in the State Historical Society at Denver and in Central City. It was included recently, in the "Cornet" of May 1960, (pages 128 and 129), in Mark Twain's "America" and was on TV on the anniversary of Twain's death, depicting his travels about the country.

Levinia had kept a ribbon won by Central City Alert Hose Team No. 2 at Silver Plume, Colorado, July 3, 4, 5th, with the names of the men on the team: Richard Davies, Capt., Albert Champion, John McCallister, Jos. Datson, George Launder, Harry Warren, George Williams, William Ralph, William Peters, William Lamont, Hank Hepburn and Harry Peters, Manager.

Though his family knew he drank, kept questionable company at times, and gambled on any and every occasion, they never found him wanting in care and devotion, and he helped his dead brother's family as much as he could.

He declared that if he married, it wouldn't be while he had a home and two women to look after, that he'd stay single while he had his mother, but both Levinia and Edith doubted that he'd ever marry. They were right, he didn't. Levinia wished he would marry, for there was only little Willie Champion, Will's son, to carry on the Champion name. She would have liked to have had several other Champion grandsons for Hugh's sake.

At home, in addition to the Cornish cocks Jack Hoskin had started him out with, and which Albert still used for fighting, he became interested in the greyhound, known as the Cornish "narrow faced dog," and "Cousin Jack Race Horse." He took these swift dogs very seriously and went into their "coursing" very thoroughly, concentrating on breeding for speed, for which they were noted.

After raising several greyhounds and trying out many, he selected a brindle female he named "Missile" because of her excessive speed, as his best bet in coursing for money. He went into Missile's training and racing all the way, sparing neither time, nor money. He took her to places selected by coursing officials. He traveled with her over the state, even into other states where such events were scheduled. He bet every cent he had, and all he could raise from every source, on his beloved bitch. He lost in every instance, for Missile never once won first-place money. She always came in second best, with all the rest of the pack running behind her.

He gave her more training but it was of no use. She never did any better than hanging just behind the lead dog, though Albert was positive she had more speed than the winner in every case.

Finally, after heart-breaking disappointment and financial set-backs, he realized that Missile simply wouldn't pass the dog in the lead. If it happened that the leader was really a fast dog, Missile would stretch her speed to keep up. If the leader was a slower runner than she, Missile cut her speed so as to come in just a nose behind whichever dog was leading, but she never allowed any of the others to pass her. In fact, she managed to push the lead dog in order to keep the other dogs behind her.

With the realization of what Missile was deliberately doing, Albert made more money, for he no longer bet on her to place first. He bet on her to "show," or, in most cases, he bet she would make second in each race. Now he had a sure thing and he made the most of it, encouraging his friends to back her in her new role. This paid off well and Albert felt that he could now afford to have his mother ease up on the hard work she was doing.

His first move was to suggest to her that, because he needed access to the back yard for his cocks and dogs, she should stop renting the back rooms. He pointed out that she received only a small sum for the rent anyway and he promised to make up the difference if she would tell the miners she wasn't renting any longer. So she did.

After what he seemed to consider a wise wait, Albert told her she need not do outside baking. It was time he said firmly, that she had some time to herself. It was enough for her to keep house for Edith and for him. Edith, who worried about her mother's hard work in her advancing years, fell in with Albert's plans. She pointed out that now that she had gone back to work for Mr. Rachofsky when Mabel married, she was making more money than she'd made in the lawyer's office, so she could help more with the household expenses. Levinia promised to do what they wanted her to do.

After that, he three made out very well. Each child contributed and Levinia found out that she didn't need to work as hard and had much more time to help Annie meet the obligations of raising her family alone.

But gradually, Levinia began to find time growing heavy on hands. She had but little sewing to do. She had enough rugs and "tidies" and aprons. She wasn't a "visiting woman," as she termed going from house to house to simply call and chat. She went only when she knew she was needed or when someone called her in to help in some way. So she planned to use the time for her own interests, which she'd put aside through lack of time: helping with the work in and for the church. And to herself she expressed hope that she could wander about the mining camps as she'd done years before, an activity she had missed and greatly regretted, the years when work had kept her so close to home.

When she mentioned leaving home to "gad about" as Albert put it, he reminded her gently that she couldn't walk and climb as she had once done. He promised to rent a rig and drive her around some day when he had the time. And Edith told her it might not be wise for her to try to make the effort to retrace the old trails she had once followed, even if Albert took her part way, because she wasn't able to stand up and do what she wanted to do.

Levinia thought about that for some time. Her feet were sore, were calloused in spots and hardening in other places. But the urge to go forth and see for herself what changes had been made, became more and more driving. Remembering Amy's intense interest in the vicinity and in all that pertained to it, she wrote and asked the girl to go with her on what she called her "Check-up" on the changes she'd find in the country she'd been too busy to follow as she'd wanted to. She pointed out to Amy that she knew she could drive the horse Levinia would hire from the livery and that they could take all the time they wanted to look around.

Amy, who taught school in Douglas County, promised to come the next summer when she had her vacation. So Levinia waited and planned. She made notes of what she wanted to see and checked and jotted down what seemed very important to her, and she was sure, to her granddaughter.

Realizing that Will's widow was having a hard time keeping her children, Levinia asked her to come in as often as she could to eat with her, Albert and Edith. Annie seemed to welcome the break in keeping boarders and ran in as often as she could. Sometimes, the three children came to stay with Levinia. They called her Nan, as Amy had first named her when she was trying to say Grandma. All the years since that time, the family, even the neighbors, had adopted that name for her. In fact, many thought her name was Nan Champion, for Levinia had almost dropped into disuse.

Levinia loved those visits with Will's children and was very thankful they lived close enough to come and see her as often as did. They were very, very dear to her and she showed her great love for them by "making over" them far more than she had her own children. In fact, she enjoyed her grandchildren more and explained to herself that this was because she didn't have full responsibility for them and wasn't quite as careful not to spoil them.

She wished Lillie's children lived as close, though she was thankful the move to the ranch had been so beneficial to Jack who, at forty-three showed no signs whatsoever of the dreaded silicosis.

He worked very hard at his ranch work, but was out in the air and sunshine all the long days.

Samuel John "Jackie" Hoskin.

At times, to get some ready cash for some implements he needed for his ranch work or to spend on weekly groceries for his family, he came to Mountain City, got a job as surface man, and stayed with her for the time he was there.

Levinia longed to see Mabel's children, Edith and James, who from pictures, were quite large for their ages and looked like both their parents. She had thought so seriously about their births, for Mabel had written that Edith weighed twelve pounds at birth and James thirteen. Levinia could hardly believe that her "baby" had such large babies.

Mabel wrote, too, that Herbert was working very hard at mining and at carpentering and admitted that times were very hard but they were getting along all right. Levinia sighed and thought, "California is so far away from Central City that I'll never get to see my Tredinnick grandchildren." She was right.

One evening when she had invited Annie and her children to eat at her house, a man came with them. He was a stranger to Levinia and to Edith, a kind-looking, somewhat shy man, who seemed to fit well into Annie's family circle. Albert knew him and called him by name, Bill Fowler, but scowled at the inference he seemed to draw from the man's presence with Will's widow and children.

Levinia also realized the possible significance and began to boil inside. Annie's nerve in bringing a man, any man into Will's home and with Will's children, made her so hurt and angry she could hardly be courteous to Fowler while they ate. She was glad that Annie took them all away soon after the meal, leaving Will's mother, brother, and sister to discuss Annie's thoughtlessness and open defiance in presenting Bill Fowler in such a way.

Annie and he were married soon afterwards without a word to Levinia, although Bill Fowler came to Albert and told him he was marrying Annie. Albert wasn't at all agreeable, but that didn't seem to bother Bill Fowler one bit. After the marriage, he took his wife and family to Nederland where he worked in the tungsten mines, and later to Russell Gulch, where he held down a good job, Albert reported.

Levinia didn't see Will's children often after that, only on short visits when their step-father came to Central City on business or when Annie came to see her own parents. On such occasions, she allowed the children to come to their Grandmother Champion's house. But Annie wasn't as friendly as she had been before, and Levinia knew her own attitude when Annie had brought Bill Fowler to see her had a great deal to do with that. She was sorry, but she just never got over being disturbed by Annie's marriage so soon after Will's death. It didn't seem decent to her.

Wisely, and a bit slightingly, Albert declared that Annie had seen an easy way to have her children taken care of and provided for without working to raise them alone. But Levinia, knew from experience what a widow with children was up against, took Annie's part against Albert. She told him that Annie had been worse off than she herself had been under the same circumstances. Annie had no sons of seventeen and twelve to help her. After all, she pointed out, Emily, Will's oldest, was only twelve, and a girl. She reminded him that Lillie had been fifteen, quite old enough to help her with the boarders and roomers.

Finally, Albert seemed to see her point, and relented somewhat, while Edith accepted the situation and made special efforts to keep in touch with Annie and the children. She stated that she was sure Bill Fowler was kind to them and was a good provider for his newly acquired household.

So they all welcomed Annie whenever she came and tried to be as friendly as she would let them be. But it was an uneasy period, a period during which Levinia's greatest fear was that Bill Fowler would adopt Will's children. That arrangement would give Willie the name of Fowler. She wanted Willie to grow up a Champion and have his own sons named Champion, not Fowler.

One day she dared to call Bill Fowler aside and express that wish to him, ending with the plea, "You see, Willie is my only hope for the name William John Champion to be carried on." Bill Fowler studied the matter before he told her he hoped to have a son, or sons, of his own, so he wouldn't adopt his wife's children by another man. Then he put his hand on her shoulder and waited for her next move.

Levinia, humbled and thankful, found it easy to tell him that he had proved that he was very understanding, and she wished him well. After that, there was a new feeling between them and she wished he would come more often so that she could know him better.

Over and over she repeated the name: "William John Champion," "Will Champion," "Willie Champion," and knew the boy would carry it as long as he lived. She hoped for the continuation of the American Champions, who had begun with Hugh.

Chapter 37

Levinia Leads Granddaughter Amy on Nostalgic Tour of Central City

In the summer of 1910, Amy came as planned, and Albert made arrangements at the Livery Stable for a rig she was to take out to drive Levinia, over what she called a "check-up" on Gregory Gulch. As they drove along, Levinia answered the many questions Amy asked and made comments on the past and the present. Other times, Levinia pointed out what she remembered and exclaimed over the new businesses and residences erected since she'd been in the vicinity.

They began their explorations at the spot where the stage route came over Dory Hill from Denver City into Black Hawk at the Toll Gate. Levinia said Black Hawk was still the milling town of The Gulch and had a population of around 1,000. She pointed out the Toll Gate Saloon, the "Lace House," which was a very fine specimen of "gingerbread" trimming, and the old church on the hill. They looked at the new railroad depot that had taken the place of the old stone mill building used as a depot until 1878. They saw great activity in the many operating mills and mines on the surrounding hills.

They drove up the grade along Lawrence Street from Black Hawk and passed the still open mountainside where John Gregory discovered lode-gold fifty-one years before and where the Bobtail mine that that had figured so strongly in mining history for Hugh and sons, was located. Levinia pointed out the house along the street to the left where Will and his family had once lived, the Stephens house on the hill across from her own home, the smaller house to which Will had taken his bride, and the house in which he had died.

Next, they turned off to the left again, went from Lawrence Street into short Miner Street on which the Parsons, Edwards, and Andrews' houses were situated, then came to her own home. Levinia commented out loud upon the growth of Mountain City since she'd come there. She pointed out the old Post Office that had once served the entire Gulch, and the Rule Barn where Albert started to work as a young boy, tending the horses that led he heavily loaded ore wagons. She drew Amy's attention to the quite new brick Davis Block across Miner Street, almost opposite her own house, the Bennallack Grocery, the Hill Barber Shop, Parsons' Saloon and the spot where the first Masonic Meetings had been held in the new gold camp.

Then they turned left again and entered Packard Gulch where some 200 persons lived on its one street. Levinia mentioned the floods that had rampaged down Packard Gulch and dwelt at great length upon the particular flood so very important in her memory of the Champion family.

At the head of and over Packard Gulch there was a railroad trestle, which the trains going to Central City crossed. Levinia reported that at the time that trestle was built, it had been considered an outstanding feat in the railroad and engineering fields. She said the trestle had helped build up Central City, carrying freight over it by rail instead of hauling supplies from the depot in Black Hawk by teams and wagons. She went on to say that though passengers to Central City could ride the passenger car over the trestle most of them chose to come by local "hack" from the depot in Black Hawk, rather than take what was considered a "perilous ride," as the train crept slowly and cautiously over the trestle.

She pointed out the house where the Hoskins had lived at the time of Billy Hoskin's birth and named several other families who had been their neighbors. Amy remembered the names Carter and Rug, whom she mentioned because their children were her playmates when she was very young and her schoolmates when they started to school in Central City. Levinia added that the father of the Carters worked in the mines with Amy's father and that the Rugs had become truck farmers on land back from Central City and brought vegetables into the towns of Gregory Gulch to sell.

They left Packard Gulch and returned to Mountain City. They turned left to follow Miner Street a short distance to the surface installation of The Gregory-Buell Consolidated Gold and Milling Company. This extensive Buell addition almost blocked the area, but the buildings that housed both mining and milling operations were now under one roof, the structure extended over the street itself, leaving ample space for all vehicles and pedestrians beneath the overhead runway.

Levinia explained that the Buell Mine had once consisted of some 600 feet of ground, which crossed the road above Mountain City, with modest buildings for the hoist and allied machinery and a stone stamp mill. These, she pointed out, had been enlarged until the structure on each side of the street covered a large surface with a mill 50 x 35 feet and a large series of offices needed to manage the large and profitable operation into which it had grown.

From under the over-head Buell Mine structure they came to the Alert Fire Station just beyond. The building and its bell were very important to Levinia. First, because they meant protection from fire and second, because Albert was and had been a part of that efficient organization.

Just beyond the firehouse, they crossed a plank bridge over Gregory Creek into Lawrence Street and turned left up the grade. At their left between Lawrence Street and the creek, there was a quite narrow pedestrian sidewalk. At intervals, a narrow footbridge led from the sidewalk over the creek to Gregory Street on the other side, running parallel to Lawrence Street into Central City. There were a few buildings along the wooden sidewalk. One of these was the Tea and Coffee Store, owned by a blind or near-blind man named Lidinger. The store was a favorite place for the children, for Mr. Lidinger sold candy and gum as well. Amy said she remembered the store and its owner for she had gone into it often as a child.

At the outskirts of Central City, they passed the Anderson Furniture Store on the left and saw the much wider wooden sidewalk on the other side of Lawrence Street. Along that sidewalk a row of houses had been built above the street, on yards on top of stonewalls, that retained the hillside. Levinia pointed out one of these houses and explained that, when Amy was quite small, her parents Jack and Lillie Hoskin, had lived there. She went on to say that one day Amy had tumbled, head over heels, down the dozen stone steps from the yard into the traffic below. Luckily, she hadn't been touched by the ore wagons or the other rigs.

From their position on Lawrence Street, Levinia pointed out the many homes built on the steep mountains above them. The entire mountainside had been cut out at intervals to make space for the series of walled-up streets. She named them aloud: High Street, Second, Third, Fourth, Fifth and Sixth. "Every space has been filled," she announced proudly and Amy agreed.

On their way into Central City, which Levinia explained had about 4,000 people, they passed the Raynolds Powder Building and residence where Kate Raynolds had helped stop the two fires that had threatened the city. They entered town at the corner of Main and Eureka Streets. They went along the right side of Eureka first, and Levinia pointed out the buildings she knew: The Pharmacy, Couch's Candy Store, The Golden Eagle Dry Goods, The Register-Call-Masonic Building, and then the building she had known as Washington Hall. Next was the St. James Methodist Church and across Church Street, the Court House, The Teller House and the Bank on the corner of Eureka and Main.

They then turned right along Main. Levinia was very proud of that Street. From the Bank there was a row of successful businesses. The Harris Block, built of brick, housed the New York Store, the Sauer Me Shane, The Hawley Mercantile, and the Post Office. On the other side of Main were Rule's Bakery and several businesses and on the corner, the Chain O' Mines Hotel which had been built on the site of Guildman's Corner, where Covington had committed murder.

It was decided that Levinia had done enough for that first day, so they went home. After supper, Levinia said she guessed she had better rest for a day before she went on checking the growth of The Gulch. She felt contented and satisfied as she discussed what they had seen and Amy asked questions concerning the history laid out before her on that one day. Then she mentioned that they hadn't gone into a single building. They made notes of those buildings and laid out a sort of plan of the trips ahead of them. Levinia was very eager to go back over the area she loved, so set the pace for each bit of "wanderings."

One day, they drove up Eureka Street above Central City. This area was filled with memories which Levinia relived. There she saw the Brewery, the Reservoir and the Slaughter House. How vividly she remembered the picnics at the Brewery Gardens and thoughtfully recalled the many times the butchers at the Slaughter House had sent her (or had her boys pick up) the parts of the animals they had left on their hands or couldn't sell: hearts, livers, kidneys, sweetbreads, brains, tripe, hogs' heads, pigs' feet, suet, leaf lard, mutton fat and soup bones. All these led to her meager store of supplies and actually helped feed her family and boarders. She admitted to Amy that she simply couldn't have done without those extra supplies and added that she'd been glad she had known how to work them into the food she made out of them.

The reservoir made her express the wonderful relief she had experienced when water had come through pipes to the hydrant in the house instead of getting it from the various tank wagons through a hose and storing it in the cellar under the house.

One day they went up on the mesa above Eureka Gulch and visited the several old cemeteries there. Levinia's heart saddened as she led the way over the stile, at the side of the wide gate, to the Knights of Pythias Cemetery and covered the few steps to the Champion family plot. With Amy she stood at the spot where Hugh, three daughters, two sons, and her granddaughter, Ida Hoskin, slept.

Her eyes went to the adjoining Cemetery, where just inside the dividing fence, laid her son William John and his little daughter, Leah May.

Levinia stood there a long, long time and Amy waited in silence with her

Levinia Leads Granddaughter Amy on Nostalgic Tour of Central City

arm around her. Levinia looked at the space at Hugh's side, the space left for her own body. Realizing that she was seventy-three years of age, she knew she would be there before long. But there was no reluctance and no regret in her heart or in her mind. She was ready when His call came for her to join Hugh and the departed members of their family. As they left the cemetery and went home for the night, she felt calm expectation.

Levinia rested the next day, and then they went back to Main Street and noted again the fine buildings and the bustle of business in and around them. "That's real evidence that our city is thriving," Levinia said complacently.

They stopped at the New York Store and Edith took them through the ladies' department, then the men's section of the store. Levinia smiled to herself as she remembered Abe Rachofsky's humble beginning as a foot peddler in The Gulch some years before. His rise in success, she told herself, shows what America offers to a person who has the "pluck," "know-how" and the never-give-up determination it takes.

They did a walking tour through the businesses on Main nd Eureka Streets, and Levinia visited a bit with the merchants she knew. Next they went through the Methodist Church, the Teller House and the Opera House. By that time, Levinia was ready to ride back home and rest in her bed for a while.

The next day they drove around the corner of Main Street, passed the old stone Stage Stop, the Express Office, the Concert Hall, the Amory Hall and the Theatre on its second floor, and looked to the right. There they saw the Railroad Depot on Spring Street and the great pile of Chain O' Mine tailings that covered the old depot and the baseball field completely!

They headed up Nevada Street to their left and went about half way up the street toward Nevadaville where Levinia pointed out the long loading trestle that led from a mine to a dumping device that dumped the ore from cars into ore wagons below to be hauled to the mill. Close by was the house the Hoskins had lived in when they left Central City to live on the Sedalia dry ranch. Then she mentioned families that had been neighbors. Amy remembered names of playmates and schoolmates from the Augers and Oakes families.

At Nevadaville, Levinia pointed out the California Mine in which Hugh, Jim Mitchell and Jackie Hoskin had worked, the cabin she'd lived in as Hugh's bride and the house in which Amy's parents had spent their honeymoon.

The California was in full operation. The cabin where she'd lived on her own honeymoon was gone! On the spot where it had stood there was a new growth of aspens. But she needed a visible sign to help her remember the happiness she'd shared there with Hugh. Her thoughts flew back to the explanation an embarrassed Hugh had made about the key he had to Maude Whitesley's cabin. He said Maude had given him the key when she and he made preparations for Levinia's arrival and planned the wedding. After he had opened Maude's door, he had thoughtlessly put the key back into his pocket and had forgotten to give it to her later.

"Ee was just a helpin' me as I asked 'er t'," Hugh insisted and kissed his bride with a fervor that set aside all her questions about the key and its owner.

As she looked at the aspens that covered the cabin site, she was glad there wasn't even a trace of the building left. She was glad that there was only the beauty of Nature there.

The Hoskin house was old and dilapidated. It was hard for her to explain to Amy the very nice and comfortable home it had been.

On another drive, they went up Spring Street, climbed the steep slope to the top of Virginia Canyon, and went down the "Shelf Road" to the prospect hole where Amy's father had been working when Ida died. The cabin the Hoskins had lived in still stood beside the tunnel Jackie had driven into the mountain in search of lode-gold. Levinia saw the girl shudder as she stood in the cabin's doorway and looked in. She knew she was trying to imagine living in that small space with the scant furnishings Levinia described as ordinary surroundings of pioneer miner-prospectors. She explained that her father planned to send his family to live with the Champions when cold weather set in and the hot summer came.

Amy turned and looked with awe, down into the steep, rugged canyon below the "road" which Levinia told her had been the stage route and over which the many quartz wagons served the numerous mines on the hillsides. She explained Albert had been one of the men who drove strung-out teams down the perilous grade and around those dangerous and sometimes hidden curves. She told her it took great driving skill to keep the wagon upright on such a narrow trail-road and that the stagecoach drivers took great chances to take passengers over the Shelf Road of Virginia Canyon into Idaho Springs. Later in the month, they went to Caribou, where silver mines were still in operation, but Levinia could see the decline taking place there. The house, in which Albert was born thirty-years years before, was still standing, but its deterioration was pitiful, which made it hard for Levinia to make Amy see it as it had been at that time.

One day they called on Annie and her family in Russell Gulch, another mining camp included in the "Richest Square Mile on Earth." They found them all happy and doing well. Bill Fowler solemnly told them that the mines "were producing less and less each month."

Levinia looked at Will's children lovingly. They had grown more than seemed possible since she had last seen them. Willie was tall and looked so much like Will that she found herself reliving her son's youth.

Amy went home later in the summer to begin classes at Greeley State Teachers College, for the second half of the summer session. Thus leaving Levinia happy that she had been able to go over the old ground once more and to see for herself what changes had taken place since she'd been there.

She meditated over these changes, comparing them with the past she remembered from the years that had gone by. One thing that stayed with her was the fact that nature had been so kind in restoring the mutilated hillsides, bared by the miners' great need of wood by sending up new growth of yellow pine, spruce and fir. These now hid some of the gaping prospect holes and openings that had disfigured the landscape when she'd first seen the mining camps and their surroundings. Time, she noted with satisfaction, had healed that desolation. There was serenity and peace hanging over the hillsides now.

She thought of the wild strawberries, in the sheltered spots on those hillsides, the beauty of the wild flowers: columbine, Indian paint brush, yellow sweet peas, crocuses, and the native pink roses, with their single row of petals that grew in great clusters on the slopes.

She summarized that it was a beautiful country! The mine dumps, with their variegated soft colors of green, purple, blue, copper, rose and subdued reds, dug from its depths, gave an outstanding beauty to the view. Even the plumes of smoke from the mines and the mills added certain softness as it drifted peacefully over the vicinity to fade away eventually in the distance.

No Wealth for Levinia

As she considered everything, Levinia felt contented and happy with the country of her choice, and wouldn't have skipped any of her many experiences, sad as many of them had been, for she was sure that she had been broadened and strengthened by them.

Chapter 38

Levinia Sees Herself Through a Photograph

At the insistence of Edith and Albert in person, and by letters from Lillie and Mabel, Levinia had her picture taken that fall. In one, she wore her small black bonnet of crepe, ribbon and beads, and simulated black flowers that stood up some three inches from its base. In the second picture, she was bareheaded.

Levinia's criticism of her likeness was that the camera had seen far too much. Or, she amended to herself, "It has revealed a woman I didn't realize I am." She knew she was large, and what she termed "stout," weighing about a hundred and sixty-five, and was above the average in height for a woman. But she hadn't known she was so stern-faced and straight-lipped, nor that she had such a firm chin, large nose and heavy eyebrows.

In the picture with her bonnet, she wore the headgear quite close to the front of her head, revealing only a small portion of her straight, tightly drawn back hair. The bonnet was kept in place by wide and long ties of double-faced black ribbon fastened at its back and drawn behind her ears to her throat, where a graceful bow was tied a little to the left of her chin. The ends hung over the front of her dress, flaring as they fell.

No Wealth for Levinia

In her bare-headed picture, she sat straight and determined with her thin gray hair parted in the middle and combed down behind her ears, then back into a tight knot at the back of her head. Her dress was of black watered silk and plain satin, pleated in front to the waist, and decorated by rows of the same material covered buttons that fastened the bodice. The sleeves of satin were full at the shoulders and tapered to the wrists and were finished by wide cuffs of the watered silk. The neck was set off by deep black ruching that stood out stiffly around her face and a pretty brooch was fastened at her throat.

The more Levinia studied the pictures of herself, the more she thought they were much like her after all. Finally, she admitted to herself that she was the woman pictured there: stern, firm, determined, large of features and of body, and that her age and experiences had left their marks on her face. Whimsically, she thought of further marks of experience that were not recorded, the many calluses on her feet.

At the same time, she maintained secretly what had been in her heart wasn't and couldn't have been portrayed, that her love of God and for all mankind didn't show in the camera's revelation. Somehow, she was very glad her inner feelings weren't shown for she wouldn't want folks to know, or even guess, the indecisions, the weaknesses, the wavering she had gone through at times throughout her life. And she wondered if it weren't better to have folks think of her as the unrelenting woman in the pictures rather than the one she knew she was. It was enough that her loved ones and friends knew she was the person they could depend upon for love and help, and backing, and that she was willing to do what she could, in her simple way, and would pray for them always, hoping and trusting, knowing that He would hear!

She kept busy with her house and the church, filling her leisure time with reading and answering questions Amy asked her in letters about the past. Almost two years went by quickly, and Easter of 1912, was almost upon them.

Chapter 39

Levinia's Death on Easter Sunday, 1912

Easter was a very important event to Levinia. It was the season of love, of hope and redemption. It meant the resurrection of the Christ she served so diligently, and the observance of His ascension into Heaven to join the Father, who had given His only Son because He so loved the world.

In her church, there were special services, solemn, yet joyous ceremonies in keeping with the day. She made plans to attend the morning service, building everything else around that hour. She had many personal plans for Easter. She always made a certain kind of bread, known as Hot Cross Buns, from a Cornish recipe she had brought from her home country and used only at the Holy Easter Season. And she always had roasted leg of lamb, accompanied by baked potatoes and mint-flavored, green tinted apple jelly she made herself, for just that occasion.

In preparation for the coming of the day itself, she cleaned the entire house, got the washing and the ironing out of the way, and was ready to undertake the Easter baking and cooking. But that cooking didn't come about for Levinia, nor for her family. On Tuesday before Easter Sunday, she didn't get up to prepare breakfast for Albert and Edith, nor to pack Albert's lunch to carry to the Williams Livery Stable, where he took care the horses.

When her children came to her room to see why she hadn't appeared she told them quietly that she'd felt too tired to get up early that morning. She said she'd lie in bed for a while and then she'd get up and do the breakfast dishes she instructed them to leave. Then she turned over in her feather bed and went to sleep. When she awoke, she found that the children had called a neighbor in to stay with her until Edith came home at noon. Levinia smiled at the concern her unusual action of staying in bed had caused and told them she'd still felt tired, so hadn't left her bed.

215

No Wealth for Levinia

The neighbor stayed through that afternoon and got her to drink tea and eat a piece of toasted bread. Levinia made light of her delicate appetite, after eating so heartily all her life. And she didn't dwell upon the weary feeling that had come over her so suddenly.

"I guess I'm a bit old to tear about cleanin' and scrubbin' the entire house in such a short time. Next time I'll take longer and save myself a bit," she mused.

She slept well that night. Edith, who had thought it best to share her mother's bed, reported to Albert next morning in her hearing, that Levinia was ready for breakfast. But when food was brought to her bedside, she said it was silly to spoil good "vitals" when she wasn't one bit hungry. She did drink the strong tea, however, and smiled cheerfully as she did so.

When Albert, in great anxiety, asked her to tell him exactly how she felt, she answered quickly, unconcerned, "I'm just tired, sort of worn out, like I need rest before I get up and do my work."

She declared stoutly to the doctor they called in distress, that it was a "bother" for nothing when he examined her.

She heard his report to her worried children: she was right in her own diagnosis. She was tired and worn out. He added something she didn't understand fully, but heard him say something about our human machinery. She wasn't curious about it. She simply closed her eyes and took a nap.

On Wednesday, she awoke to find Lillie there with her. Lillie explained quietly and soothingly that Edith had telephoned the ranch and it had been decided that Lillie had better come and stay with her instead of having a neighbor come in and keep her company, as Lillie put it.

Lillie was with her from then on, even at night, which was much against Levinia's strongly expressed wishes. For she scoffed at the idea that someone, anyone, should stay with her. And she declared vehemently, that all such attention was against principles of independence. Yet, deep down in her heart, she found it pleasant after all, to be cared for so tenderly and was thankful. But she still maintained that it was silly for them to wait upon her when she wasn't sick, not even one-bit sick.

At times she realized that her mind wandered and that she talked out loud as she rambled back into the past with Hugh and their babies. She talked of the deaths of Emily and Will. Then remembered the preparations she had to make for Easter. She insisted upon getting up and going to work on the planned Easter dinner. She said she had to set the yeast for her Hot Cross Buns, and that she had to order the leg of lamb brought to the house from the meat market as usual. It was with real distress that she remembered that she had not made the mint jelly to go with the lamb. But it didn't matter to her, for she talked to Mabel whom she saw there with Lillie, Albert and Edith. She smiled happily and said, "You are all such good children." Then she rested.

Through Friday and Saturday she didn't speak. She slept quietly and peacefully. When Albert questioned the doctor at her bedside, he said, "Her heart is strong," but he shook his head.

Early on Easter morning, April 7, 1912, she roused suddenly and in a strong, happy voice spoke to Hugh as though she were greeting him. Then, seeming to see others with him, she repeated the names of their children who had gone from her: William John, Lillie, Edith, Emily, John Sherman and Will. An instant later she died without a struggle, a happy smile on her lips.

Chapter 40

Levinia's Burial Next to Hugh Twenty-six Years After His Death

Lillie washed her mother's body, combed her hair and helped the undertaker dress her in the dress she had called "my best." Then she was placed in the dark colored casket the family had chosen. After a discussion among the three children, the black bonnet she'd worn on "special dress-up occasions," was placed beside her in the coffin. She was "laid out" in the parlor for the interval before burial.

Neighbors took turns sitting in the upper kitchen "waiting up" as custom demanded. They made trips to the parlor at intervals to see that all was well there, especially to see that no cat had gained entrance to the room. For the Cornish believed that cats would molest bodies.

On the day of the funeral, Levinia was carried out of the home she loved and, surrounded by the flowers brought by her family and friends, was placed in the black hearse drawn by black horses and taken to St. James Methodist Church. The service was as though Levinia herself had planned it. The family and friends sat in front of her open casket. The beautiful pipe organ music, accompanied by blended Cornish voices rose in her favorite hymns. The pastor spoke warmly of her as "Nan" instead of her formal name. He told of her work in and for the Church and for her friends and community. He mentioned her great pride in her family and in America, her adopted country. He closed with a warm tribute to the pioneer life Hugh and Levinia Champion had lived when mining was developed in that area. He then asked God's blessing on their descendants.

The long procession of carriages followed the tasseled hearse up the long climb to the Champion burial plot on Cemetery Hill. Levinia's body was placed beside Hugh, who was placed there twenty-six years before and close to their children.

That evening, relatives and friends from Sedalia, Denver, Russell Gulch and Central City joined Lillie, Albert and Edith in a supper brought to the house by neighbors. Then Albert and Edith were left alone in the old home.

The Weekly Register-Call of April 12, 1912 contained the following article.

DIED in Central City, Colorado Sunday, April 7, 1912, Mrs. Levinia Champion, aged 75 years. Deceased came to Gilpin County 49 years ago, was married in Central City on September 26, 1863 to Hugh Champion who came from Cornwall 2 years before her. They had 10 children. She is survived by one son, Albert and a daughter, Edith, who resided with her, and by 2 other daughters: Mrs. Lillie Hoskin of Sedalia, Colorado, and Mrs. Mabel Tredinnick who resides in California. Mrs. Champion lived in Mountain City. The residence in which she died had been her home for 46 years. Her family is one of the oldest in the County where they have a large circle of friends who extend their sympathy in their bereavement. Funeral services were held from the Methodist Church in this city on Wednesday afternoon at 1:30 o'clock. Interment in the Knights of Pythias Cemetery.

Epilogue

By Amy Hoskin Hill circa 1970

In July 1912, the year of Levinia's death, only four of her ten children were living; my mother Lillie, Albert, Edith and Mabel. Lillie had married and moved to Sedalia, Colorado and Mabel had moved to Sacramento, California.

For a while after their mother's death in 1912, Edith and Albert lived in the Champion home in Mountain City, then known as the lower part of Central City. Edith continued to work in the New York Store for Abe Rachofsky until he suddenly closed his well established department store on Main Street and shipped all the Dry Goods to Burlington, Colorado where he opened a store, hired a manager and semi-retired.

Edith was stunned by his move. She didn't know what to do, for there was no future for her in Central City. Fortunately, Mr. Rachofsky obtained a position for her as clerk in the May Company, one of the larger Department Stores in Denver. If she accepted that offer, she was to report for duty there at an early date, which gave little time for her and Albert to decide what to do with the house, its furnishings and the personal possessions in it.

Albert, who was employed at the Williams Livery Stable, stayed in Central City for a period of time and then moved to California.

During that summer, I spent part of my vacation with them and shortly after I left to get ready to resume my teaching.

Albert and Edith had a real problem, as there was no market for the property. Times were so hard that real estate was at a complete standstill. Many residents of the area had moved out. Some took their furniture and left their homes standing vacant. Others simply walked out and left their possessions in their abandoned homes.

To make matters worse, Albert broke a leg and had to stay in a rented room uptown to be near a doctor and Edith had to go there to consult him about their mutual problems.

Their uncle, Tom Champion, helped them decide what to do. He also bought some of the furniture, and stored the dishes and pans in his own cellar, and sold them whenever he could find buyers.

After hurried conferences, Edith packed some of her mother's things and shipped them to my mother Lillie, Mabel and me. Lillie received her mother Levinia's large feather bed and I the smaller one. Lillie got the family striking clock that had been in her family so long no one could remember when or from where it had come into their home. Edith stipulated that the oldest girl in the family was to have the old clock. So when Lillie and her family moved to California, I received the clock and it is now in my home at Stinson Beach, California. Some day it will belong to my oldest daughter, Dorothy, and then it will pass into the possession of the oldest girl in each generation.

I also was given Levinia's big "day pillows" and the beautifully embroidered "shams," the long strips of linen placed over these pillows when Levinia made her bed each morning, to give it what she called a "finished appearance" or a "company look."

Edith kept some of the personal things her mother loved: the big Family Bible with its dates and special observations, and her significant and important papers, notes, cards and clippings she had put between its pages and inside the back cover. She also kept the long gold chain Levinia had brought from Cornwall and had worn in her formal photograph, and the quite valuable coin collection she had built up during her life in the gold camp. Edith packed some of her mother's handwork that showed her beautiful kinds of stitchery. She intended to divide these originals with Lillie and Mabel for their daughters and she meant to see that Will's daughters, Emily and Ethelyn, got their share.

There was no ready money on hand to keep up the house or pay the taxes due, so with deep regret, they had to leave the entire property. Edith shed bitter tears as she walked out of the treasured old home, and closed the door behind her for the last time.

Edith moved and began her job in Denver. Albert lived a short time in Central City, and then moved.

Later, the house was torn down for its lumber and much later, a placer mining company paid the back taxes on the lot and every inch of ground was worked over in search of gold. Albert remarked that the area under the house and in the yard with their flood deposited dirt from Packard Gulch must have yielded a good bit of the bright metal. In a short time, the placer mining made such a complete change in the property that it was hard to locate the exact spot on which the Champion house had stood. When I visited The Gulch in 1934, I found only the hydrant that had stood between the upper and the lower parts of the house, still standing. So I knew exactly where the old house had been. Its location was made more positive by the fact that two houses still stood on the street: the Parsons and the Edwards homes. I could estimate the distance between them and the Andrews house which had stood between them and the Champion home. Above that spot there were no buildings remaining.

The hydrant is the only indicator of the Champion homesite in this 1932 photo.

Here I will tell what I know about Hugh and Levinia's four children that were living at the time of her death and of their families.

Hugh and Levinia's fifth child, Lillie (my mother) married Samuel John Hoskin (Jackie) in Central City on April 19, 1890. I was born in Central City, as were three of my four siblings. My parents' last child was born in Sedalia, just south of Denver, where my parents had moved.

Lillie and Jackie Hoskin sold their ranch near Sedalia in 1916, and moved to California where they purchased ten acres of raw land near Sacramento. Lillie and Jackie developed their acres into a very valuable piece of property and were doing very well until, in the Crash of 1929, they lost every cent they had put into the bank and and had to begin all over again, with only 15 pennies in cash to do so.

To make matters even worse, Jackie Hoskin lost his voice completely when he heard their savings had been wiped out. From then on, he spoke in

Epilogue by Amy Hoskin Hill

a forced whisper. He refused, however, to sell any of the ten acres to obtain cash. He maintained that some day those acres would be worth so much his family would be well-off.

So the couple actually did start all over. They raised chickens and rabbits which they dressed for market, sold eggs and baby chicks they hatched in incubators they had in operation at the time, and raised and sold vegetables.

They were able to make ends meet and were able to realize how lucky they had been, for just two days before the banks closed, they had turned down a very good cash offer for their entire ten acres. If they had accepted that tempting offer, they would have put every cent into the bank and been entirely destitute. As it was, they had those acres upon which to make a new start.

Lillie Champion Hoskin and Samuel John Hoskin.

OBITUARY

Lillie Hoskin, long-time resident of Douglas County, died at Sacramento, California, July 14, 1960, at the age of 89 years and four days.

Lillie Champion, the fifth of ten children, was born July 10, 1871, at Central City, Gilpin County, Territory of Colorado, to Hugh and Levinia Champion, who came to the two-year-old gold camp in 1861, from Penpall, Hayle, Cornwall, England. She was married April 19, 1890 to a hard-rock miner, Samuel John Hoskin, of Perranporth, Cornwall. To this union, five children were born: Amy, Ida, William John, Hugh, and Elsie Louise. Ida and Hugh preceded her in death. The surviving children are: Mrs. Amy Hill and Mrs. Elsie Watts, of Stinson

Jackie Hoskin died quite suddenly September 15, 1934, at the age of 68, of pneumonia and was buried in a plot in Sacramento.

Lillie found it necessary to sell two and a half acres of her land to pay expenses and begin a new life for herself in the home of her second son, Hugh. As time went on, she had to sell five more acres. These acres were bought by her son William John (Billy) Hoskin and his wife Fay.

Lillie Hoskin lived to be 89. She died July 14, 1960, and was buried beside her husband in Sacramento.

223

I was Lillie and Jackie's first child. I married "Harry" (Thomas Harrison) Hill. We eloped and were married in the County Court House in Littleton, Colorado. We lived at Louviers, Colorado where Harry was employed by the Dupont Powder Company.

T.H. "Harry" Hill.

Amy Hoskin Hill.

We had three children. Dorothy was born in Louviers, Nina Aida was born in Waterville, (near Cheyenne Wells), and Harry Garth was born in Arapahoe.

Dorothy Hill

Our first child, Dorothy, married Ernest Mayfield. They had two children. She has four grand-children.

Epilogue by Amy Hoskin Hill

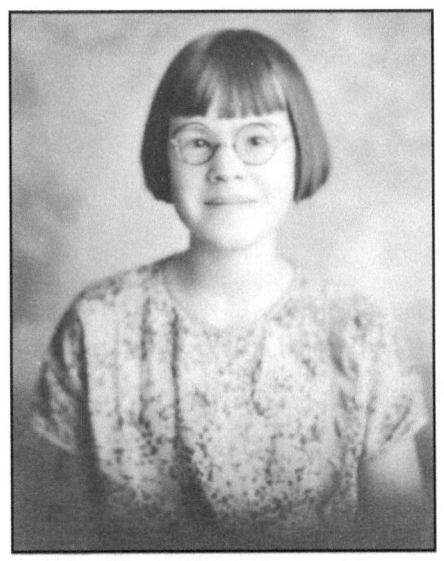

Nina Hill

Our second child, Nina Aida, married Thomas Lawrence Wold. They had three children. She has four grandchildren.

Garth Hill

Our third child, Harry Garth, was killed, at an early age, by a passing car while crossing a street in front of our house.

No Wealth for Levinia

Lillie and Jack's second child, Ida, died in infancy.

Lillie and Jackie's third child, William John (Billy) Hoskin, married Alta Fay Taylor. They did not have children.

William Hoskin.

Lillie and Jackie's forth child, Hugh Hoskin, married Marion Smith. They had one son.

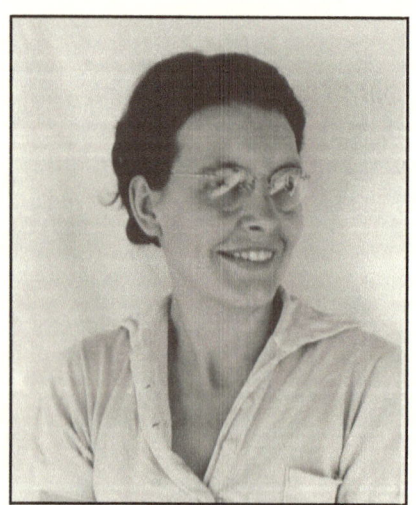

Lillie and Jackie's fifth child, Elsie Hoskin, married Vilas Watts. They did not have children.

Elsie Hoskin.

Epilogue by Amy Hoskin Hill

Hugh and Levinia's sixth child, Albert Champion, moved to California and became a rice farmer. He died unmarried on July 6, 1926, of asthma at the age of 52.

Edith Champion.

Hugh and Levinia's eight child, Edith Champion, left her job in Denver and moved to California where she was employed in a large department store in Sacramento. There she met and married Albert (Bert) Turner. When Bert died of a heart attack, Edith moved from their home in northern California to Mill Valley, California, some nine miles from me. Edith Champion Turner died December 18, 1961, at the age of 85 and lies beside her husband in Sacramento. She had no children.

Mabel Champion.

Hugh and Levinia's tenth child, Mabel Champion, married William H. Tredinnick and moved to Sacramento, California. She was the last of Hugh and Levinia Champion's ten children. She died November 28, 1973, at the age of 91 and was buried in the family lot near her husband in Sacramento. She had two children.

Mabel and William's first child, Edith Tredinnick, married Frank Webb. They did not have children.

Mabel and William's second child, James Tredinnick, married Ernestine. I do not know her maiden name. They had four children.

No Wealth for Levinia

No complete history can be given here of the Champion's family because I know very little about Hugh and Levinia's second child, William John. I know that he married Grace Ann Stephens in Central City and that they had four children. I know that he died January 27, 1896 of silicosis at 38 years of age, and that his wife, Grace Ann, later married William Fowler.

William John and Grace Ann's first child, Emily Champion, married Bill Kemp. They had two children.

William and Grace Ann's third child, Ethelyn Grace Champion, married a man named Tipton. I don't know whether or not she had children, nor if she is still living.

William John and Grace Ann's forth child, William Hugh (Little Willie) married, had children, and died in his 60s. I do not know if he had a son to carry on the Champion name. I do know that an attempted adoption by his mother Grace Ann's new husband, William Fowler, was blocked by Levinia, hopefully allowing him to retain the Champion name.

Afterword

By Dennis Mayfield

If the author, Amy Hoskin Hill, was able to look forward following her death in 1984, she would be aware of the following:

The family striking clock was passed to her daughter, Dorothy Hill Mayfield. In the later years of Dorothy's life, she passed it to her daughter, Meda Kay Mayfield Patskoski. The clock sits on a shelf in her living room. It will continue to be passed to female descendants, as requested.

Levinia's big "day pillows" have disappeared.

The Champion family Bible which was originally in posession of Levinia's daughter Edith, following her death had disappeared.

The gold chain that Levinia brought from Cornwall, England and wore for her family photograph has disappeared.

The coins from Levinia's collection were passed to her daughter, Dorothy Hill Mayfield. I have the coins, but do not know for sure if these are the coins noted.

Her daughter, Dorothy Hill Mayfield, died at age 97, in Florida. By the time she died, her family consisted of four grandchildren and seven great grandchildren. Her descendants live in California, Florida, Oklahoma, North Carolina and Mexico.

Her daughter, Nina Aida Hill Wold, died at age 91, in California. By the time she died, her family consisted of five grandchildren and seven great grandchildren. All her descendants live in California.

The children of Hugh and Levinia's son, William John Champion, moved to the Pacific Northwest with their mother, following his death, in Central City. While Levinia was aware that William John's wife, Grace Ann Stephens, remarried, she had lost contact with his children, Emily, Ethelyn Grace and William Hugh.

I learned of this family when a great granddaughter of William Hugh posted a query on the Internet that led her to my Champion family information, also on the Internet. I then traveled to the Pacific Northwest to meet her and her father. I was told that William Hugh had two children,

No Wealth for Levinia

six grandchildren, and eleven great grandchildren. I was also told that five of William Hugh's eleven great grandchildren were born with the Champion name. It is impossible to express how happy I was to learn that the promise made to Levinia, by William Fowler, Grace Ann's second husband, to not change the last name of William John's son, William Hugh, from Champion to Fowler, was kept. Thus Levinia's dream that the Champion name go on, was fulfilled.

Grace Ann is buried next to her second husband, William Fowler, in Idaho.

William John Champion's daughter, Emily Champion Kemp, is probably buried in Washington State and at least one of her children lived there.

William John Champion's daughter, Ethelyn Grace Champion, who she thought married a man named Tipton, really married a man named Turpin. They were probably married in Colorado, about 1919.

I learned of this family after being contacted by a great granddaughter of that marriage. The granddaughter was interested in genealogy and also found my Champion family information on the Internet. We corresponded and exchanged family information. I was told that Ethelyn had three children, two grandchildren, and nine great grandchildren. Ethelyn Grace is buried in Idaho. Most of her descendants are in the Pacific Northwest.

Through these two contacts, I was to be able to help link these descendants of Hugh and Levinia's son, William John Champion, to their past.

I also learned where, in the City and the Knights Of Pythias Cemeteries, in Central City, five of Hugh and Levinia's children and two of their grandchildren are buried. However, absent a plot map, I don't know exactly which child is buried in which plot.

Levinia Champion was buried next to her husband, Hugh, on April, 7, 1912. At that time, the graves of six of their children Lillie (I), William John (I), Edith (I), John Sherman (I), William John, Emily and two grandchildren, Ida Hoskin and Leah May Champion, were marked by simple wooden markers. William John and his daughter, Leah May, were buried in the City Cemetery while the others were buried across the fence in the Knights Of Pythies Cemetery, but in the same row.

I found a draft letter the author (Levinia's granddaughter, Amy Hoskin Hill) wrote to the Central City Newspaper Weekly Register-Call dated April 1980. She wished to explain why a cemetery survey taken by historian, Leola Blanchard, in 1953 only included the large Champion stone, the smaller Mother, Father and daughter, Emily, stones and some form of marker for granddaughter, Ida Hoskin.

The letter indicated that Hugh and Levinia's son, Albert Champion, Levinia's only living son at the time of her death, placed the large Champion stone, plus the Mother, Father and daughter, Emily stones. It was her assumption that Albert also placed the William John and granddaughter Leah May, stones. I took a photo of those stones in the 1960's proving that they were the same stone and design. However, it is possible that a descendant of William John placed them to match the stones Albert Champion placed. The stones are not there now. I assume they were stolen.

The letter said that Albert intended to have the names, Hugh and Levinia, and their dates carved on the large Champion stone, and to replace wooden markers of the children and grandchildren.

Unfortunately, his leg was broken and shattered and the money he had identified to make stone grave markers had gone for treatment to save his leg. By the time he was able to move about, Central City had dwindled to what was thought to be on its way to oblivion. Even his sister, Edith, had moved from Central City to Denver, as the dry goods store where she was employed, had closed. Albert then moved to California and the wooden markers deteriorated leaving the burial locations unidentified.

To further try to determine when those markers might have disappeared, in 1980, I spoke with Nina Hill Wold, Hugh and Levinia's great granddaughter. She told me she recalled visiting the cemeteries with her mother (the author, Amy Hoskin Hill) in circa 1942, and remembered her pointing out the burial sites with flat wood markers adjacent to the large Champion stone. She indicated that that was where the Champion children were buried. That indicated to me that the grave site markers for all but the author's sister, Ida Hoskin, disappeared after 1942 and before the survey in 1953, and that the marker for their granddaughter, Ida Hoskin, disappeared sometime after 1953.

In 1999, I arranged for a plaque to be placed in front of the Champion stone containing Levinia and Hugh's names and dates. I will see to it that the row of graves of the five children and two grandchildren are appropriately marked.

No Wealth for Levinia

Finally, I learned where, in Mexico, Hugh and Levinia were planning to move following the gold and sliver bust in the Central City area, in April, 1864.

From a newspaper article in the Guadalajara, Mexico Colonial Reporter, by David Agren, I learned that a Cornish village called Real del Monte, located 100 kilometers northeast of Mexico, City, still exists. It noted that the city's Cornish influence, imported nearly a century ago, survives. Apparently, in the 1800s, there were as many as 350 Cornish there, exploiting a silver vein in an English-owned mine. Recall that Hugh had been listening to a promoter, who had mining interests in Mexico, and was soliciting workers to move there for work.

The following provides a summary of Hugh and Levinia Champion and their children.

There were ten children; all except Albert were born in Mountain City, an area that later became Central City, Colorado.

HUGH CHAMPION was born at Pen Pal, Hayle, Cornwall, England on September 7, 1838. He immigrated to Gregory Gulch, Colorado Territory in 1861 to do hard-rock mining. He died of silicosis in Central City on January 1, 1886, at the age of 48. He was buried in the family lot in the Knights of Pythias Cemetery in Central City. His burial site is in front of the large Champion stone and is marked Father.

LEVINIA PERRY CHAMPION was born at Pen Pal, Hayle Cornwall, England June 26, 1837. She immigrated to America in 1863, to join Hugh Champion. They were married at Central City, Colorado on September 26, 1863. She died at the age of 75 at Central City on April 7, 1912. Her body was placed in

Afterword

the family lot in the Knights of Pythias Cemetery in Central City, beside that of her husband, Hugh, and six of their ten children. Her burial site is in front of the large Champion stone and is marked Mother.

WILLIAM JOHN CHAMPION (I) was born on September 23, 1864. He died August 11, 1865, at less than one year old. He was first buried in a churchyard, but when his sister Lillie (I), died and was buried in the family lot in the Knights of Pythias Cemetery, he was moved to be next to his sister. The gravesite is no longer marked.

LILLIE CHAMPION (I) was born January 31, 1866. She died September 7, 1866, less than eight months old. She was buried in the family lot in the Knights of Pythias Cemetery. The gravesite is no longer marked.

EDITH CHAMPION (I) was born November 24, 1867. She died July 17, 1877, less than ten years old. She was buried in the family lot next to her brother William John (I) and sister Lillie (I) in the Knights of Pythias Cemetery. The gravesite is no longer marked.

WILLIAM JOHN CHAMPION II (known as Will and Willie) was born July 27, 1869. He died of silicosis January 20, 1906, at 38 years of age. He was buried in the family lot in the City Cemetery. The gravesite is no longer marked.

LILLIE CHAMPION II was born July 10, 1871. She died July 14, 1960, at the age of 89 at Sacramento, California. She was buried next to her husband, Samuel John (Jackie) Hoskin. Jackie was buried in the Masonic Cemetery, plot 105-182, in Sacramento, California.

ALBERT CHAMPION was born at Caribou, Colorado March 5, 1874. He died July 8, 1926, of asthma at the age of 52 at Sacramento, California. He was buried in Sacramento, California.

EMILY CHAMPION was born June 2, 1876. She died April 5, 1894, at age 18. She was buried in the family lot in the Knights of Pythias Cemetery. Her burial site is in front of the large Champion stone and is marked Emily.

EDITH CHAMPION II was born November 25, 1877. She died at the age of 85 in Mill Valley, California. She was buried next to her husband, Albert, in Sacramento, California.

JOHN SHERMAN CHAMPION, born February 11, 1880. He died April

23, 1880, at less than three months old. He was buried next to his brother, William John, and his sisters, Edith (I) and Lillie (I), in the Knights of Pythias Cemetery. The gravesite is no longer marked.

MABEL CHAMPION was born January 5, 1882. She died November 28, 1973, at the age of 91. She was buried near her husband, William, and granddaughter, Joannie, in Sacramento, California.

Here are two of my favorite family photos.

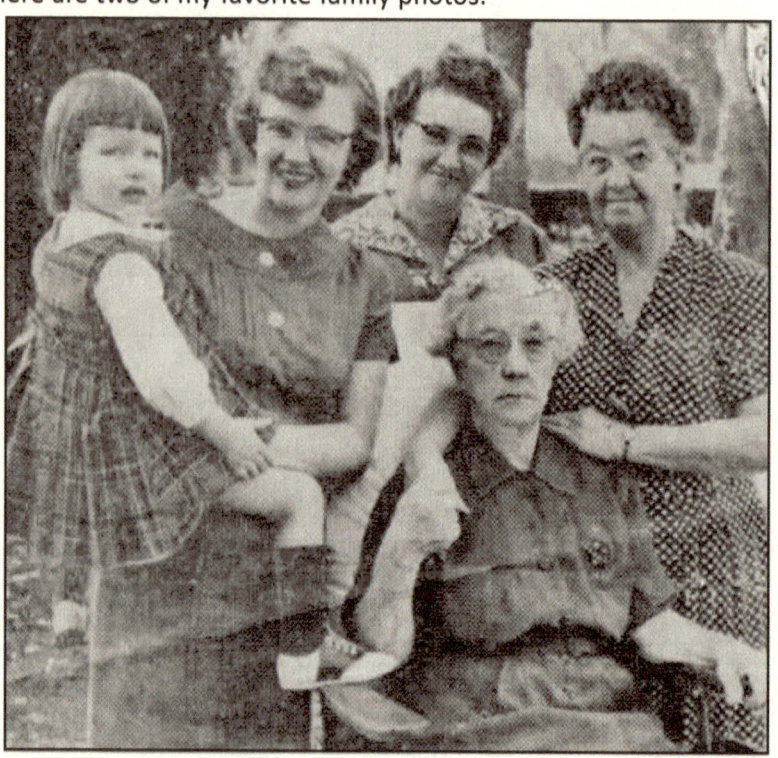

FIVE GENERATIONS: (above) Levinia's daughter Lillie Champion Hoskin is seated. Standing (right to left) is Amy Hoskin Hill, the author. Next to her is Lillie's granddaughter Dorothy Hill Mayfield, then Lillie's great granddaughter and great great granddaughter. The photo was taken October 27, 1958 and appeared in the *Sacramento California Bee* newspaper.

Afterword

Amy Hoskin Hill (above) the author at age 31. Photo was taken ten years after her grandmother Levinia Perry Champion died.

Finally, is a photo of the gravestone for my grandmother, Amy Hoskin Hill, the author. It is special because of the "Buried in California" note below her name. She and my grandfather had purchased a plot in Bear Canyon Cemetery in Sedalia, Colorado to be near their son Garth and other family members. When she and my grandfather died in California, it wasn't practical to bury them there. The family however wanted each to be recognized as being with their family.

Dennis Mayfield,
September 2010

Addendum

The Champion Family Bible, which was in possession of one of Hugh and Levinia's children following her death, had disappeared.

To my utter amazement, I received an e-mail from a wonderful lady telling me she had found it as part of an estate sale many years ago. She told me she vowed to someday try to find a descendant, as it contained many family photos as well as an envelope of dried flowers.

Her search led to my genealogy web site. There she found a perfect name and date match of all Hugh and Levinia's children. She returned the Bible to me stating in part, "What a moving story you told me about Levinia and Hugh and their family. I am ecstatic that I found the Bible's home. I am moved to be a small part of that story."

The Bible is now in a family home just thirty miles from where it began. It is a family treasure beyond words.

Dennis Mayfield
November 2012

Bibliography
Books and Pamphlets

* "Central City, Colorado's Salzburg"- Caroline Bancroft.
* "Colorado" - Hafen and Hafen.
* "Colorado" - American Guide Series 1941.
* "Colorado's Little Kingdom" - Donald C. Kemp.
* "Cornish Miners" - A. K. Hamilton-Jenkins.
* "Cornwall and the Cornish" - A. K. Hamilton-Jenkins.
* "Cornish Seafarers" - A. K. Hamilton - Jenkins.
* "Everyday Memories of Central City" - Frank Bedford.
* "From Candles to Footlights" - Melvin Schoberlin.
* "Ghost Towns of Colorado" - American Guide Series.
* "Guide to Central City" - Caroline Bancroft.
* "Gulch of Gold" - Caroline Bancroft.
* "Where They Dug the Gold" - George P. Willison.
* "Historical Souvenir of Central City" - Minnie Morgan.
* "Little Kingdom" - Lynn Perrigo.
* "Mines in Central City" - Register-Call 1937.
* "Mining Camps" - Charles Howard Shinn.
* "Murder a Mile High" - Elizabeth Dean.
* "New and Selected Poems" - Thomas H. Ferril.
* "The Bonanza Trail" - Muriel Sibell Wolle.
* "Theatre Arts Monthly" - The Opera House in Central City, Colorado.
* "Turning Back the Pages" - H. H. Lake.
* "Eureka Street,Central City, Colorado" - Teller House Publication.
* "Murder on the Mountain" - Amy Hoskin Hill.
* "Gilpin County Gold" - H. Wm. Axford.
* "The Little Kingdom of Gilpin" - George Dewey Harris.
  California Folklore Quarterlies:
* Volumes I and II - 1942-1943 - "The Cousin Jack."
* Volume V - 1946 "Butte Miner- Cornish" - Wayland D. Head.
* Volume IV - 1945 "Folklore of Central City, Colorado"- Caroline Bancroft

Colorado Magazines

* Volume 14, May 1937 - "The Cornish Miners of Gilpin County" - Lynn Perrigo.
* Volume 14, March 1937 - "Susan B. Ashley's Recollections."
* Volumes 14 and 17,1937 - 40 - "George Pullman."
* Volume 17 - March 1940 - "Keith's and Mrs. Keith's Letters."
* Volume 14-17 - 1937-1940 - "The Family of Gregory"• - W. A. Gaydon.
* Volume 14-17 - 1937- 1940- "Boyhood Recollections of Central City,Colorado" - C. H. Hanington.
* Volume 14-17 - Central City, "The Concord Coach" - C. H. Hanington."
* Volume 18-21, 1941-1944 - "The Catholic Church in Central City, Colorado" and "My Recollections of Pioneer Life in Colorado"- James R. Harvey.
* Volume 19. No. I- Jan. 1942 - "Early Days of Central City, Colorado" - C. H. Hanington.
* Volume 19 - "Author's Letters."
* Volume 20, No.4. July - 1943 - "The Elusive Life of John H. Gregory" - Caroline Bancroft.
* Volume 20,1944 - "Cousin Jack Stories from Central City" Caroline Bancroft.
* Volume 21. No.6, Nov. 1944 - "History of a Ghost" Town-Caribou" - John W. Buchanan.
* Volumes 22 and 23, 1945-1946 - "William Zane Cozens,Sheriff" and "Food Facts" from Rocky Mountain News, Denver, Colorado and "Hotel De Paris, Georgetown, Colorado" from The Mountain News, Denver,Colorado.

About Dennis Mayfield

Dennis Mayfield, influenced by his grandmother and author, Amy Hoskin Hill, has chronicled his later life in journals.

The first titled "Thoughts Above 30,000 Feet" was, and still is, written only from a seat in a commercial airliner. The views from the window and the views of his life, cover a span of nearly 16 years of constant corporate travel, and now less frequent personal travel.

He and his wife, Gay, write a monthly "Personal Journal" that began in 1996. Those words outline their personal and travel experiences that led to their home in San Miguel de Allende, Mexico.